Screening Nostalgia

Screening Nostalgia

Populuxe Props and Technicolor Aesthetics in Contemporary American Film

Christine Sprengler

Berghahn Books
New York • Oxford

Published in 2009 by

Berghahn Books

www.berghahnbooks.com

©2009, 2011 Christine Sprengler

First paperback edition published in 2011

All rights reserved. Except for the quotation of short passages for the purposes of criticism and review, no part of this book may be reproduced in any form or by any means, electronic or mechanical, including photocopying, recording, or any information storage and retrieval system now known or to be invented, without written permission of the publisher.

Library of Congress Cataloging-in-Publication Data

Sprengler, Christine.

Screening nostalgia : populuxe props and technicolor aesthetics in contemporary American film / Christine Sprengler.

p. cm.

Includes bibliographical references and index.

ISBN 978-1-84545-559-0 (hbk) -- ISBN 978-0-85745-161-3 (pbk)

1. Nostalgia in motion pictures. 2. Motion pictures--Aesthetics. 3. Motion pictures--United States--History--20th century. I. Title.

PN1995.9.N67S67 2009

791.43'653--dc22

2008047740

British Library Cataloguing in Publication Data

A catalogue record for this book is available from the British Library

Printed in the United States on acid-free paper.

ISBN 978-1-84545-559-0 (hardback)

ISBN 978-0-85745-161-3 (paperback)

Contents

List of Illustrations	vii
Acknowledgements	ix
Introduction	1
1. Setting the Stage: The History of Nostalgia	11
2. The Fifties: Nostalgia's Privileged Object and the Origins of its Dominant American Strain	39
3. The Nostalgia Film in Practice and Theory	67
4. *Sin City*: Reading the Tails of a Populuxe Prop	93
5. *Far From Heaven*: Creative Agency, Social History and the Expressive Potential of Costume	117
6. *The Aviator*: Deliberate Archaism, Technicolor Aesthetics and Style as Substance	139
Conclusion. *The Good German* and the Good of Nostalgia	163
Filmography	175
References	181
Index	191

List of Illustrations

1.1 Rita Hayworth and James Cagney in *The Strawberry Blonde* (1941) — 26

2.1 'The 50s', Cover of *Life*, 1972 — 44

2.2 David, Ricky and Harriet Nelson with the Hotpoint Stove, *The Adventures of Ozzie & Harriet* (1952–1966) — 53

2.3 The 'Living Garage' as featured in *Home and Garden*, 1958 — 55

3.1 Mary Astor and Humphrey Bogart in *The Maltese Falcon* (1941) — 70

3.2 Robert Downey Jr., Patricia Clarkson, George Clooney, David Strathairn and Matt Ross in *Good Night and Good Luck* (2005) — 82

4.1 Ant Farm's 'Cadillac Ranch', 1974 — 93

4.2 Charles Martin Smith as Terry the Toad driving Steve's tail-finned car in *American Graffiti* (1973) — 101

4.3 The 1957 Plymouth Fury on the assembly line in *Christine* (1983) — 103

5.1 Julianne Moore and Viola Davis unload groceries in *Far From Heaven* (2002) — 120

5.2 Olivia Birkelund, Barbara Garrick, Patricia Clarkson and Julianne Moore in *Far From Heaven* (2002) — 125

5.3 Dennis Quaid and Julianne Moore photographed for the Hartford gossip magazine in *Far From Heaven* (2002) — 127

5.4 Julianne Moore, Dennis Haysbert and Jordan Puryear at the Modern Art show in *Far From Heaven* (2002) — 133

6.1 Leonardo DiCaprio in *The Aviator* (2004) — 143

6.2 Howard Hughes in the New York tickertape parade,
July 15, 1938 — 151

6.3 Leonardo DiCaprio and Matt Ross watch Jane Russell
on the screen in *The Aviator* (2004) — 155

7.1 George Clooney and Cate Blanchett in *The Good German*
(2006) — 164

Acknowledgements

My fascination with nostalgia began in the mid 1990s and, as such, many individuals deserve my sincerest gratitude. First and foremost, I want to acknowledge Bridget Elliott, who generously volunteered to read the entire manuscript for this book, providing detailed and insightful comments. As a brilliant scholar, she is an inspiration. As a colleague, she has been a dedicated mentor and role model. And, as one of my dearest friends, she has been unfailingly supportive, working tirelessly to help me every step of the way. I simply could not have done this without her.

I am also deeply indebted to Laura Mulvey who encouraged me to pursue my interest in nostalgia and investigate its uses in British film and television serials of the 1980s and 1990s and, specifically, in relation to the work of Dennis Potter and Terence Davies. Doing so helped me to recognize nostalgia's complexities, appreciate its critical potential and enabled me to look at its American variants anew for this project. Her enduring kindness, patience and encouragement over the years have been truly invaluable.

While a doctoral student at Birkbeck College I was extremely fortunate to receive support from Mike Allen, Francis Ames-Lewis, Ian Christie, Pam Cook, Annie Coombes, Peter Draper, Charlie Gere, Mark Glancy, Lynda Nead, Amy Sargeant, Simon Shaw-Miller, Ken Trodd and especially Tag Gronberg. During my time in London I also had the pleasure and privilege to lecture at the University of East London and to benefit from the guidance of many dedicated and wonderful colleagues including Paul Dave, David Butler, Jessica Edwards, Paul Gormley, Jill Nelmes, Michael O'Pray and Andrew Stephenson.

My colleagues, students and friends at the University of Western Ontario deserve my sincerest thanks for various forms of intellectual stimulation, research assistance and cheerleading: Wayne Barco, Sarah Bassnett, Kathy Brush, Leanne Carroll, Margaret DeRosia, Susan Edelstein, Andrew Gugan, John Hatch, Jennifer Kennedy, Madeline Lennon, Patrick Mahon, David Merritt, Kim Moodie, Debra Nousek, Kirsty Robertson, Donna Sasges, Susan Schuppli, Jennifer Slauenwhite, Sandy Smeltzer, Daniela Sneppova and Kelly Wood. I also want to single out Tony Purdy and Veronica Schild for their inspiring commitment to research and incisive wit. I am also grateful to the University of Western Ontario for the pre-tenure term off that allowed me to begin work on this book and for granting me an SSHRC Internal Research grant to assist with the preparation of the manuscript.

Mark Stanton at Berghahn deserves my heartfelt thanks for helping me every step of the way and for making what I expected to be a terrifying experience remarkably pleasant and enjoyable. I also want to acknowledge the thoroughness with which the two anonymous readers engaged with my manuscript and thank them for their many perceptive, insightful and thought-provoking comments. Jamie Vuignier at The Picture Desk and Pete Berenc at Getty Images were also indispensable in helping me track down images.

The friendship and encouragement warmly offered by Pippette Eibel, Sylvia Carlyle, Jennifer Cottrill, Daniel Morgan and Kim Wahl has helped through the years and for this I am grateful. I also want thank my mother, Ursula Sprengler, for her unwavering support and instilling in me the value of perseverance and hard work. Finally, I need to acknowledge my partner, Devin Henry, for his heroic editorial efforts, uncompromising dedication to academic pursuits, unconditional understanding of my need to spend the better part of nine months confined to a concrete cell in Weldon Library and willingness to assume all dog-walking duties during that time. It is for these—and many other—reasons that I dedicate this book to you.

Introduction

I want to open this book by making what may seem like an obvious claim: nostalgia remains a vital part of contemporary life. The nostalgia thought to have been activated by fin-de-millénnium anxieties certainly has not subsided as we head towards the end of the first decade of the twenty-first century. Any number of wholly unscientific experiments confirms this. As I write this sentence, 'nostalgia' yields over thirty-two million hits on Google's search engine, even when limited to the past year. It also yields over sixteen million hits on Google's *image* search engine. Academic studies continue to appear that examine the phenomenon (or emotion, type of memory, attitude toward the past, etc.) through a variety of disciplinary lenses. This diversity of approaches to nostalgia has spawned the articulation of countless types and conceptions of the term and has made it nearly impossible to define in any concrete way. To simply say that nostalgia involves a longing for the past cannot accommodate its expressions that have no basis in feeling or emotion. There are too many variables at work that inform different understandings and variants of the term, ones that extend beyond disciplinary or methodological parameters and include the contextualizing forces of temporal periods, geographical regions and even smaller cultural constituencies. What nostalgia means in Japanese culture may be quite different than what it means in American culture. Indeed what it means to Hollywood executives in 2007 may be at odds with its meaning for those living in rural Idaho in the same year. What is more, these differences may have nothing at all to do with assumptions about what one could or should feel nostalgia for, in other words, which objects are worthy of the sentiment.

Predictably, nostalgia's protean nature has led many to claim that 'nostalgia isn't what it used to be'. But while its original definition as a kind of homesickness experienced by Swiss mercenaries bears little resemblance to its current function of describing the resurrection of past media aesthetics, there is one significant way in which nostalgia is precisely what it used to be. Nostalgia is, and has always been, a concept shaped by the cultural and political contexts in which it circulates, by its uses and theorizations as well as by prevailing views on history and memory. Other terms, too, necessarily bear traces of their age, shifting to accommodate the concerns and values with which they are most closely aligned. However, rarely do such concepts manage to attract the attention of highly divergent discourses, each of which produces highly divergent understandings of the term.

Despite the wealth of research on the subject, the continuing proliferation of new types of—and uses for—nostalgia means that gaps still exist in the literature. This book seeks to fill one such gap by excavating the origins of one of these types of nostalgia and exploring its significance. It also argues for the critical recuperation of this nostalgia's cinematic expressions. More specifically, I am interested in the type of nostalgia that relies primarily on the creation of *visual* pastness: the nostalgia at work in American popular culture, which is most often maligned for commodifying history, falsifying history and replacing history proper with the history of aesthetic styles. It is the kind famously criticized by Fredric Jameson (1991) for effacing history, for turning the 1950s into Fiftiesness and the 1930s into Thirtiesness.

What I propose to do here is sketch some loose parameters around what constitutes this kind of nostalgia and consider how and why it emerged on the American visual cultural landscape of the twentieth century. I want to consider whether its cinematic expressions do more than simply sever our connection to history. More specifically, I want to ask whether critical potential can be located in this most vilified form. I will explore if and how the visual aspects deemed responsible for a film's identification as a 'nostalgia film' can fuel, rather than impede, engagements with history, initiate critical or oppositional readings, generate multiple layers of meaning that enrich the filmic text and the cinematic experience and produce analytical pleasure for the invested spectator. In short, I want to rethink nostalgia's value, rescue it from its strictly conservative uses and identify critical potential in its most derided expressions.

In order to recuperate this nostalgia and show that it is not inevitably regressive or reactionary, we must consider the relationship between the nostalgic experience (e.g., the longing for an irretrievable ideal) and the nostalgic object (i.e., what one is nostalgic for). To accomplish this we must first explore its history, including the ways in which it has been shaped and reshaped by discourse and use, the factors that determined its current dominant strain as well as those that gave rise to its privileged objects in American popular culture.

We also need to acknowledge its malleability and its fracturing into both a mood and an aesthetic mode, as Paul Grainge (2002) eloquently argues.[1]

Nostalgia is something *worth* recuperating because it represents a way of engaging with the past, offering us insight into the relationship between the past and the present. It tells us something about our own historical consciousness, about the myths we construct and circulate and about our desire to make history meaningful on a personal and collective level. Given the prevalence of nostalgia across contemporary visual and popular culture and the ease and frequency with which the term is used in both academic and popular discourse, we need to investigate precisely what nostalgia can and does accomplish including, for example, how it brings to light aspects of our past neglected by historians' more traditional methodologies.

The focus of this study is on American popular film. However, the Hollywood 'nostalgia film' is something that must be situated within the broader context of contemporary cultural nostalgia. One cannot come to grips with cinematic nostalgia without first understanding nostalgia's more general social significance and manifestations across visual (and political) culture. As such the first three chapters are devoted to tracing its history, defining its dominant American strain and articulating its cinematic uses and expressions. In the remainder of the book I offer three case studies of films released since the turn of the twenty-first century including *Sin City* (2005), *Far From Heaven* (2002) and *The Aviator* (2004), concluding with some thoughts on *The Good German* (2006). Each of these films was selected for its use of the features and strategies that attract the 'nostalgia film' label. They mobilize props, costume and 'deliberate archaism' (i.e., visual pastness) in ways that suggest the source of a film's engagement with nostalgia might also be the source of its critical consciousness. Separating my discussion into these components of mise en scène or cinematography may seem artificial, for they naturally work in tandem with one another and with other aspects of the film to produce meaning. However, this separation is necessary if we are to identify the font of the nostalgia film's critical potential and recognize precisely how it delves into rather than effaces history.

Sin City, *Far From Heaven* and *The Aviator* were also selected from a number of candidates for other reasons. They engage, to different degrees and in different ways, with nostalgia itself as well as nostalgia's privileged objects. Whereas *Far From Heaven* sets out to deconstruct the mythic image of bourgeois bliss in postwar America,

Sin City indulges in the visual seductiveness of an array of past media forms with little concern for the harmful stereotypes it revives. *The Aviator* falls somewhere in between with its fascinating application of Technicolor but somewhat sanitized portrait of Howard Hughes. This disparity in the critical intent of the works selected provides us with an opportunity to see how, say, props might initiate oppositional and critical readings regardless of the film's ostensible narrative purposes. Furthermore, given my eventual argument for the dominance of the Fifties in contemporary expressions of nostalgia, *Sin City* and *Far From Heaven* were ideal candidates because they mobilize, to varying extents, this particular nostalgic construct. *The Aviator* sets its sights on an earlier period of American history; however, it is included because it represents the kind of film that models its engagement with the past and visual pastness on that seen in the Fifties nostalgia film.

My approach to these films is one inspired by the close semiotic, visual analyses produced in art history, design history and material culture studies, and the detailed textual analyses that remain an important part of film studies.[2] There is a deep and underlying concern here with the politics of representation. I am interested in how objects and visual constructions bring their own histories into a film and work to generate meaning in the context of specific scenes or narrative moments. The props, costumes and visual styles at work in my case studies are ones which have a rather busy life outside the cinema, circulating in advertising, television, print, music videos, video games and other facets of popular culture and the nostalgia economy. As such their cultural, social and historical significance must necessarily come into play and inform how we make sense of their place in a film.

In the past this type of close visual analysis has been met with suspicion. One might object that it is rather unrealistic to expect audiences to think carefully about what a particular car or dress might contribute to a scene. But this objection is becoming increasingly unwarranted, especially with regard to the nostalgia film. On the one hand, as Vivian Sobchack (1996) has argued, our age is one marked by a growing historical consciousness. History is everywhere, existing in multiple representational and tangible forms to be consumed and explored. We have become adept at reading into visual styles and objects their history and period, in recognizing the source of tropes and conventions enlisted in the service of intertextual practices. On the other hand, our consumption of films extends well beyond the filmic text itself. Promotional ventures, discussion boards, fan sites and product tie-ins encourage investment in the particulars of any given work. Fan sites can be extremely obsessive in the detail with which they analyze a film, from the significance of the time on a clock to the specific make and model of the clock used. DVDs encourage this kind of invested spectatorship through the multitude of featurettes and the hours of extra (typically documentary-style) footage that accompany a film to show how it was made. Director's commentaries have also become a staple on DVD releases. Although they seem to have done much to resurrect the author from a premature death, these commentaries can also arm viewers with additional information that encourages a more analytical and perhaps even critical kind of spectatorship.[3]

Whether or not the details of a film's production are spelled out for us, by failing to embrace opportunities to probe our cultural artefacts we risk losing access to a number of things. We might fail to appreciate how even the smallest (visual) detail contributes to the ways in which a film is implicated in broader political and social currents, how it both reflects and shapes our desires and anxieties and how it perpetuates or deconstructs well-entrenched ideological constructs. We might end up denying ourselves the benefits of such insight, including the analytical pleasures (motivated by epistemophilia) that even films ostensibly catering to escapism and spectacle can offer.[4]

But what does this kind of insight ultimately accomplish? And is it enough simply to recognize how a trope, for example, might reinforce a particular construct? While Roland Barthes' (1972) seminal and still highly compelling study of myth made a strong case for the positive political consequences of demystification, of exposing as cultural and constructed that which ideological forces attempt to pass off as natural and thus justifiable, I think we can go further. Specifically, we need to do more than be satisfied with recognizing the constructed nature of the Fifties or a particular brand of femininity. Such moments may brim with the potential to negotiate meaning, to question the authority of certain voices, to challenge the legitimacy of apparent truths and current conventions. Postmodern intertextual devices need not be dismissed as vacuous winks to a series of familiar, widely-circulating representations. There is much more to be gleaned from these devices if we are willing to pursue their significance and meaning-generating potential to their logical ends. For example, we can explore how the self-reflexive and intertextual strategies at work in *Far From Heaven* do more than simply demystify a set of ideological constructs. We can examine how these strategies also speak to the origins of these constructs, reveal how they operate, expose what sustains them and recognize the actual and potential consequences of their proliferation and acceptance.

These are some of the issues that inform this study and ones that I plan to pursue in the pages that follow. The first chapter begins by tracing the history of nostalgia from its origins as a medical condition affecting Swiss soldiers to a term used to describe contemporary American popular culture invested in recreating the aesthetics of past media expressions. My aim here is to show how the concept of nostalgia has been shaped by both discourse and circumstance as well as the ways in which it shed and accrued meaning as it travelled through geographical, cultural and temporal contexts. In addition, by charting nostalgia's development in the United States during the first half of the twentieth century, I show how it entered popular speech much earlier than is commonly thought and was mobilized in ways that prefigure its uses decades later. While nostalgia is a term often adopted to describe the literary and artistic culture of the United States between 1900 and 1950, its iterations in the popular press (and popular film) during this time played a key role in establishing understandings of its current dominant strain and especially its meaning in contemporary cultural criticism.

In the second chapter I flesh out just what constitutes nostalgia's current dominant strain in American popular culture and explain what facilitated the emergence of its privileged object—the Fifties. I consider how the Fifties, as a nostalgic object, was shaped by both the self-mythologizing efforts of the 1950s and the social and political realities that rendered the 1970s prone to a specifically Fifties nostalgia. I also explore the complexities of the relationship between nostalgic and consumerist desire and the relationship between nostalgia's object and the nostalgic experience. Conflating object and experience has been a common practice in the critical literature and one responsible for nostalgia's virulent derision throughout the 1980s and 1990s. In this chapter I outline the benefits and limitations of engaging in the kind of philosophical operation that separates object and experience, what this means for Fifties nostalgia specifically and the value of nostalgia generally. Charting the history and applications of Fifties nostalgia is a necessary first step to gaining insight into the workings and significance of the contemporary nostalgia film.

Chapter 3 examines the nostalgia film as a product of both the uses of nostalgia in the cinema and theorizations of nostalgia in film and cultural theory. I start by elaborating on the points of intersection between nostalgia and film—those lying outside the filmic text (e.g., fan practices) as well as those put to use within the filmic text (e.g., strategies employed to generate or otherwise engage nostalgia that involve narrative, music, opening montage sequences and period casting). My aim in the first half of this chapter is to provide a brief survey of strategies that are not specifically visual and (though necessarily acknowledged at certain points throughout this book) will not be the focus of the case studies that follow. The second half of this chapter evaluates the foundational debate between Fredric Jameson (1991) and Linda Hutcheon (1989) that informs most theorizations of nostalgia in the cinema, including recent attempts by Paul Grainge (2002) and Vera Dika (2003) to recuperate the concept and its association with visual pastness for critical ends. I also draw on a neglected article by Marc LeSueur (1977) whose terms 'surface realism' and 'deliberate archaism' are highly relevant and ripe for appropriation in light of the visual practices central to recent nostalgia films.

Chapters 4–6 provide detailed analyses of films that show why the facets responsible for *visually* articulating a film's pastness are not always, necessarily or exclusively indulgences in surface, style and spectacle. Chapter 4 investigates the tail-finned car as a 'Populuxe' prop—to borrow Thomas Hine's term for describing the 'popular luxury' manifested through ostentatious design in postwar consumer goods.[5] The aim here is to reveal how one of the objects at the heart of the contemporary nostalgia economy (and, more specifically, what might be called the 'Populuxe Fifties') can source critical engagements with both the history of and myths about postwar America. I start with a brief review of prop scholarship to acknowledge how key objects generate meaning throughout the course of a film and then consider how design history might help carve out a space for thinking about the contributions of props selected in the first place because of their cultural significance. I discuss some of the tail-finned car's early cinematic uses in the nostalgia film in order to explore how such an object might function as a conduit to history and meaning, before turning to its role in *Sin City*. In this film the tail-finned car helps to bring existing nostalgic constructs into collision in a way that challenges representations of postwar consumer capitalism as benign. In the process, it enables an oppositional reading of *Sin City*, one with the capacity to yield analytical pleasures.

Chapter 5 deals exclusively with *Far From Heaven* and specifically with how costume—another kind of prop often charged with indulging in visual spectacle and commodity fetishism—has the capacity to generate additional layers of complex meanings that deal directly with postwar social and political realities and provide an outlet for characters' creative agency. In other words, costumes say what characters cannot. They express socially prohibited desires, speak to social inclusion and exclusion, articulate characters' experiences of social spaces and supplement the film's narrative critique of postwar America's racism, sexism and homophobia. Costume does not always accomplish this independent of other production design strategies. As part of a carefully planned colour scheme that echoes Douglas Sirk's postwar palette, it is central to both the film's engagement with history and its generation of affect. *Far From Heaven* may be deeply nostalgic on many levels, but what is responsible for activating an emotional response is also at the heart of its stinging critique of postwar *and* present-day bourgeois America.

The final case study focuses on *The Aviator* and its digitally manufactured 'deliberate archaism' (a concept that will be explored later). It recreates the look of two-strip and three-strip Technicolor to tell the story of Howard Hughes' contributions to aviation and filmmaking from the 1920s to the 1940s. In doing so, it not only provides a kind of access to film history and specifically the uses and debates about colour in the cinema, but also, in its approximation (rather than exact replication) of Technicolor processes and aesthetics, the film offers contemporary viewers the chance to inhabit the position of Slavoj Žižek's 'mythic naïve spectator' (1991: 112) and thus experience what Robert Burgoyne describes as the 'affective truth' of (film) history (1999). *The Aviator's* deliberate archaism (or, more specifically, what I shall call its 'Technicolor aesthetic') is also juxtaposed at critical points with archival footage in a way that suggests how 'official' history is no less a mediation of the past and no less effective in granting access to the past than non-representational aesthetic codes.

Through these analyses, I hope to make a contribution to scholarship on nostalgia (and its specifically cinematic forms) that, only recently, has started to question the once seemingly obvious and readily accepted criticisms of nostalgia. I hope to show not just how nostalgia remains a vital part of contemporary life, but also the kinds of pleasure and knowledge that it has the capacity to yield.

Notes

1. I also hope that this study extends into new terrain—to encompass the realms of material objects and cinematic aesthetics—the kind of investigation offered by Grainge on the black-and-white image.
2. More specifically, I have been inspired by the approaches of Dick Hebdige's *Hiding in the Light* (1988), Anne Massey's *Hollywood Beyond the Screen* (2000), Raphael Samuel's *Theatres of Memory* (1994), C.S. Tashiro's *Pretty Pictures* (1998) and Richard Dyer's *Pastiche* (2007).
3. *Sin City, Far From Heaven* and *The Aviator* all offer featurettes explaining nearly every aspect of their production design while *The Good German* lays out its cinematographic strategies on a website.
4. I use 'epistemophilia' in the way Laura Mulvey (1996) does to signal a desire to know, one motivated by intellectual curiosity and which yields intellectual pleasures.
5. A fuller definition and discussion of the origins of Populuxe will be offered in chapter 2.

Chapter 1

Setting the Stage: The History of Nostalgia

Although a basic sense of longing for something lost in time or space remains a central component of the nostalgic experience, the meaning of nostalgia has evolved over the last three centuries. Migration of the term into new social contexts and discourses have added further dimensions. According to Edward Casey, there are three distinct stages in nostalgia's evolution. The first involved its exteriorization and the missing of specific physical sites. Whereas pathological symptoms affecting the body defined the phenomenon during this initial medical phase, in its second phase nostalgia became a disease of the mind. This involved the deliteralization of place and the emergence of a 'cerebral longing for reunion with metaphysical origins' (Casey 1987: 370). In its third phase, nostalgia became increasingly personal, a private psychological phenomenon affecting potentially every human subject.

To unpack these three stages I will chart nostalgia's European development from the seventeenth through to the end of the nineteenth century. This will help us conceptualize and contextualize nostalgia's emergence in its fourth and current phase and specifically its dominant form in twentieth and twenty-first century American popular culture. In doing so, this chapter will trace its uncharted American history through the first half of the twentieth century as well as address how popular and academic discourse since the 1950s have shaped its meaning and determined its value.

Conceptual and Geographical Expansions: Nostalgia in Europe, 1688–c.1900

Nostalgia was first coined by the Swiss physician Johannes Hofer in his 1688 dissertation, using the Greek words *nostos* (a return home) and *algos* (denoting a painful condition) to name the disease he observed in young Swiss soldiers serving abroad (1934: 381). For Hofer, the sound of the word called to mind 'the sad mood originating from the desire to return to one's native land' (1934: 381). Though rooted in place and an 'afflicted imagination', it caused serious physical symptoms including 'disturbed sleep either wakeful or continuous, decrease of strength, hunger, thirst senses diminished, and cares or even palpitations of the heart, frequent sighs, also stupidity of the mind' (1934: 386). If those found suffering were left untreated (i.e., not sent home), death could result.

Since its publication, Hofer's dissertation has been cited and celebrated as the inaugural text in virtually every history of nostalgia across the disciplines of medicine, psychiatry, psychology, sociology, literature, philosophy, marketing and visual culture. But it is not his discovery and description of the nostalgic condition that deserves acclaim. Rather it is his foresight to name a term that seemed to offer insight into the anxieties, preoccupations and desires of both his own and subsequent eras. After all, by his own admission, Hofer was not the first physician to research this particular battlefield ailment. He felt that 'certain new phases' of the disease required elaboration in the medical literature and made it his task to build upon what was 'up to now ... explained by many of the doctors' (1934: 380). He synthesized their research and foregrounded those aspects that enabled the concept to be adapted to different geographical, cultural and temporal circumstances. In fact, the role afforded the imagination in mediating 'small external objects' and 'images' of the 'Fatherland' remains central to much current scholarship on nostalgia (1934: 381). Drawing on the increasing authority of medicine, Hofer diagnosed a condition rooted in antiquity with the potential to explain both personal and collective responses to the wars, political upheavals, social transformations and mass migrations of the eighteenth through to the twenty-first century.

Nostalgia's capacity to be invoked to explain everything from Homer's *Odyssey* to Homer Simpson[1] has provoked debate about its protean nature. Is it universal and eternal or culturally and historically specific? A few commentators, working primarily in the sciences and social sciences, regard nostalgia as a biological feature of life itself, a consequence of the 'homing instinct' (Martin 1954: 103), a 'species of remembrance' (Kaplan 1987: 469) and a 'psycho-physiological condition' that is 'more fundamental than any particular culture' (Ruml 1946: 7). Calls to limit its scope have been issued on the grounds that nostalgia is not equivalent to, but instead a type of, homesickness, written into existence in the pages of Hofer's dissertation. Svetlana Boym and Lynne Huffer reject the claim that the journey writing of classical antiquity could be described as nostalgic because nostalgia, according to them, surfaces only when return home becomes impossible (Huffer 1998: 14; Boym 2001: 7). Implicit in this position—and stated explicitly in the work of Felski (1995) and Tester (1993)—is the belief that Hofer's efforts were premature, for nostalgia belongs specifically and exclusively to Western modernity. In this formulation, the Swiss doctor's term finds its best application not in military medicine, but as a concept to explain the social effects of industrialization and modernization in nineteenth-century Europe.

However, to claim that a kind of 'nostalgia proper' first emerged in response to modernity is to obscure the role played by the highly politicized medical discourses of the eighteenth century. Advancements in medicine at the turn of the eighteenth century, including the development of extensive nosological schemes, helped to legitimate nostalgia as a distinct and common disease. Françoise Boisseir de Sauvages divided nostalgia into simple, complicated and simulated varieties while Thomas Arnold classed it as one of sixteen different types of insanity (see Jackson 1986: 376–77). Such official recognition prompted interest in this new condition, launching efforts to identify specific symptoms, likely causes and a whole host of potential cures. Given the political implications of Hofer's dissertation, it is hardly surprising that some students of nostalgia, especially those invested in particular ideas about Swiss nationhood, should attempt to refine his science to accord with the patriotic ideology of the day. J.J. Scheuchzer, a contemporary of Hofer, found rather distasteful the insinuation that the homesickness experienced by Swiss soldiers revealed a deficit of character. Appealing to the study of 'iatromechanics', he shifted the blame to the physiological effects experienced from the loss of Alpine air pressure on individuals forced beyond the borders of their homeland (see Starobinski 1966: 89). And yet, however palatable this revised diagnosis may have seemed or however much it protected soldiers from charges of cowardice, it did not compensate for the costs incurred by outbreaks of nostalgia on the battlefield. Low troop morale, malingering and desertion, incapacitating illnesses and suicide all threatened the success of military campaigns and, in turn, national wealth and prestige (Davis 1979: 3, n6).[2]

Scheuchzer's iatromechanic account lent credence to the initial claim that nostalgia and its attendant military costs were a specifically Swiss phenomenon. But Switzerland was not alone in waging wars of expansion and aggression, and as word of this new disease reached other regions so too did the incidence of its suffering. Nostalgia's geographical expansion throughout the eighteenth century brought about its conceptual expansion. Increasingly entwined with the developing consciousness of nation states, the term came to manifest cultural and political anxieties specific to the affairs of the various countries in whose armies it surfaced. In post-revolutionary France, nostalgia was seen as a sign of patriotism, evidence of the strong attachment and sense of duty that French soldiers felt toward their homeland (Roth 1991: 15). Loyalty to the Republic and Napoleonic Empire was no doubt particularly beneficial at such a crucial moment in France's history. Nostalgia's political potential was embraced and quickly spread under the influence of Romanticism with nearly every European nation coining a term to encapsulate what they insisted was unique to them and untranslatable into any other language. By articulating a feeling of longing for the homeland, nostalgia—or *heimweh, mal de corazon* or *maladie du pays*—served well, in many instances, 'the *homogenizing* requirements of the modern nation state in the face of ethnic and cultural diversity' (Robertson 1990: 49).

Nostalgia's political usefulness was instrumental in triggering several key perceptual shifts. Ideology, not geography, now determined its force, which in turn precipitated a shift from viewing nostalgia as a pathology to thinking about nostalgia as an appropriate response to protracted absences from an idyllic and esteemed homeland. New discoveries in medicine also helped to distance the concept from earlier physically based complaints. Progress in the fields of pathological anatomy and bacteriology attributed nostalgia's original symptoms to tuberculosis while the ineffectiveness of listed cures raised questions about its precise nature. Military reforms introducing better treatment, higher pay and less severe punishment seemed more effective in reducing the number of soldiers purportedly suffering from nostalgia than medically sanctioned remedies such as sending them home (Starobinski 1966: 99).

Nostalgia's demise as a medical condition can also be explained by a growing interest in mental afflictions in the late eighteenth century which in turn gave rise to the increasing popularity of 'respectable' ailments. A pronounced affinity with the then quite fashionable melancholia made nostalgia itself seem more acceptable. Through this connection it lost its associations as a disease of the common soldier and entered the middle classes where it acquired a more philosophical profile. The bifurcation of nostalgia into a scientific and a social phenomenon further diminished its medical salience, a rupture consistent with the rise of Cartesian dualism. Boym explains that nostalgia appeared before art and science 'severed their umbilical ties and when the mind and body—internal and external well being—were treated together' (Boym 2001: 8). This split confirmed what the architects of eighteenth-century European nation states suspected: nostalgia had greater viability as a sociopolitical phenomenon than as a physical disease.

During the nineteenth century, the key social transformations of industrial capitalism caused a shift in cultural emphasis from space to time as concepts of progress and history changed. Time itself became subject to fundamental reconceptualizations that affected how it was perceived, experienced and visualized in everyday and economic life. These changes impacted understandings of nostalgia in several important ways, not least of which was the need to accommodate the loss of an historical as well as a personal past. It now had to account for the perception that modern ideas of progress rendered this collective historical past irretrievable. Progress, no longer exclusively a concern of the arts and sciences, had become part of the ideology of industrial capitalism, a force which left little socially, economically or culturally unchanged (Boym 2001: 9). In these circumstances, nostalgia became a necessary coping mechanism with the capacity to make modernity inhabitable (Tester 1993: 70). It relieved the anxieties generated by progress, the swift loss of a way of life and traditional ways of interacting with the world.

Despite the ascendancy of time and mind in the experience of nostalgia, space and body continued to play a role. Urbanization, the movement of people from the country and close-knit community (*Gemeinschaft*) to the city's impersonal ties (*Gesellschaft*), was a potent trigger for nostalgia. How life was lived in the past was defined by where it was lived; time and space could not be separated. Thus, whether in response to anxieties caused by change or a deep dissatisfaction with places occupied in the present, nostalgia retained its spatial dimension. It also retained its bodily dimension, but with a difference. Changed perceptions of time and the effects of progress had a significant impact on the idea of history, transforming it from something *studied* in the eighteenth century to something *felt* in the nineteenth century (Brandt 1978: 60). The loss of a collective past, something experienced by all inhabitants of modernity, provoked an affective response. In other words, the irretrievability of the past, while not causing acute physical illness, nevertheless generated deep feelings of loss and longing that could not be classified as purely cerebral.

Other changes happening within modernity *because* of industrialization, technological modernization and urbanization would also have a lasting impact on the concept of nostalgia, including the privatization of the family. In the late nineteenth century when the family assumed the 'educational and particularizing function' of the village, the village became interiorized (Starobinski 1966: 102). This development signalled the start of the 'underground' stage of nostalgia, its retreat 'inward and downward into the human subject' and the shift in responsibility from the community to the family as the source of longing and sentiment (Casey 1987: 370). With these seismic transformations in social and psychological organization came the replacement of the childhood home with childhood itself as the privileged object of nostalgia. As this happened, two new emerging features moved to the centre of the experience: the irretrievability of nostalgia's object (something already suggested by the Romantic emphasis on the past) and the attachment of nostalgia to a specific stage of human psychological development. With the loss of the past, time displaced space. Whereas nostalgia qua homesickness posited an actual physical home which the sufferer could conceivably revisit, nostalgia for a specific time denies the possibility of return.

The second feature, owing much to the work of Freud, represents a remarkable development in nostalgia's history, mainly because he did not, as such, name this nostalgia for childhood.[3] Freud chose not to deal with nostalgia because, according to him, nostalgia had nothing to do with the unconscious or the return of the repressed. And yet, from a contemporary perspective, many key psychoanalytic concepts have a nostalgic structure. 'Fixation' and 'regression' share with nostalgia the attempt to return to a place of origin and the inability of recollection alone to facilitate this return.[4] In the Oedipal trajectory, the male child's longing for unity with its mother and to return to its first home (the womb) is a desire for an ideal and irretrievable past stage of childhood. Like nostalgia, this desire in the male for a prelapsarian state motivates behaviour in the present to regain what is lost; it prompts a search for a female other who is like the mother. This desire for an earlier stage of psychological development also reflects another key feature of the nostalgic experience: a desire to return to the time that immediately preceded significant change. Nostalgia has been theorized as a sentiment that attaches itself to periods on the verge of transformation and to the moments marked by the availability of choice (Wood 1974: 345). Although early stages of psychosexual development such as the Oedipal moment do not contain such options, they are, in retrospect, identifiable (from the perspective of the adult self) as distinct phases marked by significant changes in the way the subject relates to others and to his or her environment.

Freudian psychoanalysis was not the only discourse borne out of late-nineteenth-century modernity to be structured by a nostalgic logic. Sociology too enjoyed this distinction. As a discipline, sociology 'crystallized' between 1880 and the 1920s, a period characterized by 'modern wilful nostalgia' (Robertson 1990: 46). According to Shaw and Chase, sociological thought did not employ a process of 'painstaking investigation of historical record' when defining the past, but instead 'posit[ed] a series of absences or negatives'. They explain: 'If we now have Gemeinschaft, there must have been Gesellschaft; if our consciousness is fragmented, there must have been a time when it was integrated; if society is now bureaucratised and impersonal, it must previously have been personal and particular' (Shaw and Chase 1989: 8). In short, the changes effected by modernization, industrialization and urbanization evoked a desire to reclaim the perceived opposite to what typified the present.

While nostalgia's European history and its popularity in post-1970s mass media have received scholarly attention, a distinct gap remains in its history in the United States from the turn of the twentieth century to the 1950s. This is not to suggest that the presence of nostalgia in American public and private life has gone unremarked, nor that this period failed to manifest impulses that we would rightly want to label nostalgic. Scholars often use nostalgia as a theoretical framework through which to explore the cultural products and political rhetoric of this era. Unavoidably and necessarily, these studies mobilize understandings of nostalgia that are refracted through the presents (e.g., 1980s, 1990s, etc.) and disciplines inhabited by their authors. I certainly have no issue with this and freely admit to doing the same in the chapters that follow. What remains to be examined is how the uses of the word 'nostalgia' in academic and especially popular discourses of the first half of the twentieth century have shaped its meaning and, in the process, laid the foundation for its current dominant cultural form. Thus what follows is a cursory sketch of where and how nostalgia was used during this sixty-year period. I offer this in the service of my argument that this was an important transitional time for nostalgia in the United States, one during which it led a rich double life. In one incarnation, it persisted as a medical condition suffered by soldiers and exiles. In the other, it appeared increasingly in cultural criticism and everyday language and, quite crucially, in a way that prefigures its use decades later.

Death and Dancing at the Beer Garden: Nostalgia in America, c. 1900–1950

Though the following will focus on this neglected period in nostalgia's history, it is worth noting that signs of its double life predate the era in question. Throughout the American Civil War (1861 to 1865) nostalgia was blamed for incapacitating countless soldiers on the battlefield. According to the official *Medical and Surgical History of the War of Rebellion*, 5,213 cases were reported among Caucasian troops of the North in 1861, translating into an incidence rate of 2.34 per 1000. During the second year of battle this number increased to 3.3 per 1000 (Zwingmann 1959: 85). T. Calhoun, the Surgeon-in-Chief of the Second U.S. Division, believed that soldiers of the Civil War were particularly prone to the disease because of the rapid deployment of troops, the long duration of the war and what he saw as the distinctly American penchant for letter writing. Taking their cue from research out of Europe, Calhoun and W.A. Hammond, the Surgeon General of the Army, classed nostalgia as a type of insanity, a mental affliction that could develop into typhoid fever and other serious ailments affecting the gastrointestinal tract.[5] Prescribed treatments included sympathy, kindness, bathing, exercise and, in extreme cases, returning the patient home. Even ridicule and, failing that, reason, were recommended antidotes for incapacitating bouts of homesickness (Zwingmann 1959: 81–83). Thus, in the context of the Civil War, nostalgia was understood as a medico-military condition, one remarkably similar to Hofer's initial conception of the disease.

But, in 1863—a year commonly regarded as critical to this conflict—the term also appeared in the 'Gossip From Paris' column in the *New York Times*. Here it was used to describe the emotional response of the nouveau riche who returned to their old, poor neighbourhoods in the Faubourg St Antoine and were 'seized with a fit of nostalgia for poverty' (10 May 1863: 4). This is one of the first appearances of the term in the popular American press that does not treat it as a disease nor as something tied exclusively to a loss of place. Although place—the old neighbourhood—triggers the sentiment, the implied object of nostalgia is a state of being, namely, poverty. Nostalgia, however, appeared only sporadically in the popular press during the second half of the nineteenth century. A decade after this 'Gossip From Paris' column, exciting discoveries about the 'disease' by French Medical Academy scientists were reported. Exactly a decade after that a review of the seventeenth volume of the *Encyclopaedia Britannica* attributed to nostalgia the 'silly' habit of placing the prefix 'New' in front of British city names to create monikers for American towns and settlements. The reviewer cites this practice as the reason for a laudable increase in American content in this publication (*New York Times*, 28 September 1884: 5). Hence, this 'silly' and, significantly, 'harmless' nostalgia yielded a tangible benefit.

Despite these intermittent and highly divergent uses, as well as the impact of significant medical advancements on nostalgia, the concept managed to retain something of Hofer's original definition in the academic discourse of the twentieth century. Studies published in the 1940s and early 1950s continued to situate nostalgia in the clinical landscape of psychiatry and military medicine (McCann 1943; Ruml 1946; Fodor 1950). Many of these, including a series of statements printed in 1943 and 1944 in *The Naval Medical Bulletin* and *War Medicine* predictably coincide with America's involvement in the Second World War. Whereas these examined contemporary incidents of suffering, others, like *The Minds and Nerves of Soldiers* (Hanes 1941), looked to the First World War to gain insight into the potential consequences of nostalgia. Although this spike in activity may have also had something to do with Carolyn Kiser Anspach's English translation of Hofer's dissertation in the 1934 issue of the *Bulletin of the History of Medicine*, wars seemed particularly effective at generating these sorts of analyses.

A medico-military understanding of nostalgia as potentially fatal also circulated in the popular press, spreading both knowledge and incidence of the disease. It was described as a 'great foe to health and happiness', a condition for which the 'the Government makes the greatest allowances' (*New York Times*, 22 May 1903: SM4). Several deaths, among men and women, the young and the old, the famous and the anonymous as well as civilians and military personnel were announced in the *New York Times* from the turn of the century up to the 1930s: 'A Death from Nostalgia. The Case of Private Atkins, Who Died of Homesickness, Regarded as Remarkable—One of the Rarest Diseases' (29 July 1898: 12); 'Fatal Nostalgia. Woman Died Because She Could Not Live Away from New York' (7 August 1899: 7); 'Wolkow Suicide Laid to Nostalgia. Ban on Her Return to Russia Said to Have Preyed on Mind of Trotsky's Daughter' (12 January 1933: 4); 'Death Laid to Nostalgia. Stamford Boy Scout was Homesick, Doctors Assert' (16 July 1933: N4). Some were lucky and survived because officials had the foresight to send them home. This prescription may have saved a Civilian Conservation Corps member from succumbing to 'acute nostalgia', but it failed to prevent his mother from filing suit for damages (13 July 1935: 15).

Even the death and actions of animals were attributed to nostalgia, suggesting a belief in the universal scope of the disease. The *New York Times* reported that Mlle Ninjo, America's only living gorilla, was 'ailed' by nostalgia because she 'could not endure our civilization' (6 October 1911: 1). More remarkable is the story of Max, a dog which, in 1937, walked 750 miles from Des Moines, Iowa to Denver, Colorado after his family relocated. He gave Denver a week and then abandoned his family to embark on a 47-day journey back to his old home. Former neighbours discovered Max sleeping on their lawn and shipped him back to Denver (19 January 1937: 25).

Public officials were also thought to suffer from nostalgia, a diagnosis which prompted debates about treatment, fitness for duty and patriotism. In 1914 Sergeant-at-Arms Robert B. Gordon was charged with deciding whether or not nostalgia actually 'incapacitates a member of Congress from attending to his official duties' (*New York Times*, 30 August 1914: 15). After speaking with the stricken congressman and upon learning that the German Army recognizes homesickness as a disease, Gordon was 'inclined to believe that nostalgia was sufficient as an excuse'. If relocating to Washington in the above instance was enough to induce nostalgia, then surely Ambassador Fletcher had a solid case in 1929 when he pleaded to return from Italy. The author of the column agreed, arguing that Fletcher's desire was evidence of his devotion to his country and therefore proved his 'fitness' for diplomatic service (*New York Times*, 27 June 1929: 17). A later article seemed to flip conventional (European) wisdom on its head by suggesting that patriotism was a form of nostalgia, and not the other way around. In his address to the American Psychological Association, Beardsley Ruml elaborated on this idea, insisting that nostalgic sentiments 'are the foundation of patriotism and nationality' (Laurence 1933: 15).

On the eve of and throughout the United States' involvement in the Second World War, reports surfaced detailing the causes and even the potential sinister uses of nostalgia. Concern was expressed on several occasions that family members attempting to 'pamper' soldiers might inadvertently induce nostalgia (*New York Times*, 24 August 1941: 57). Letters asking 'when can you get home?' and radio programs that 'frequently carry the same note of nostalgic sentimentality' threatened morale (*New York Times*, 15 February 1944: 19). Afflicted soldiers serving in Britain were prone to 'bragging' about the United States in a way that often offended their hosts. A four page pamphlet targeted at British women working in canteens urged them to not interpret this talk as an attempt to decry Britain nor to allow it to 'drive a wedge between the nations', for this would only be 'a round in the battle for Hitler' (Long 1942). The Germans too seemed fully aware of the effect of nostalgia on American troops and used this as part of their propaganda campaign. Pamphlets dropped near Rome and the Cassino front 'recall to the Americans that juicy steaks, swing bands and thrilling movies are fun' (*New York Times*, 13 April 1944: 5).

These reports from the *New York Times* show that nostalgia maintained its military associations throughout the first half of the twentieth century. However, it also appeared on the pages of this and other national publications, including the *Wall Street Journal*, *Life* and *Time*, in very different contexts. In some cases, use of the term bore traces of its medical history. Three months to the day after reporting one 'indignant' mother's plan to sue the Civilian Conservation Corps for giving her son nostalgia, Supreme Court Justices themselves were said to be suffering from their move into a new building (Wood 1935). In other cases, it began to show signs of a stronger influence by European Romanticism, including the sense that a time rather than a place had been lost and that cultural forms such as art and literature might generate a longing for the past. In short, it came to be used in more general and popular terms and, crucially, much earlier than has been previously thought. Fred Davis' oft-quoted claim that nostalgia did not enter popular speech until the 1950s is refuted by the over four thousand instances of its use *outside* the realm of military medicine in the *New York Times* alone from the 1890s to 1950.[6] In fact, by the late 1920s nostalgia is used colloquially and in the service of literary, music, art, theatre, and film criticism. And by the early 1930s we even see evidence of a self-conscious 'decade nostalgia', one with its sights turned to the styles of the past.

Even in the context of discussions about war, nostalgia in this sense appeared divorced from the fatal homesickness with which it also continued to be associated during the 1930s. A 'bittersweet' quality, an attachment to a past time as opposed to place, and the belief that nostalgia emerges on the brink of significant change inform Allan Nevins' use of the term as he prepares the American reader for the outbreak of the Second World War: 'To turn back to the years just before the Great War is to revert to a phase of history so much calmer and sunnier that the experience awakens a deep nostalgia, a regret half bitter and half sweet' (Nevins 1939). This signals a shift in attitude from only a few years previously when the spoils of war were looked upon through rose-tinted glasses: 'A nostalgia for full employment, for high wages, high salaries and high profits, for consumption which expands as fast as production can take care of it; a picture of the war years as seen down the street of time, in short, tends to have an especial allure in these thin days' (*New York Times*, 9 July 1936: 4). Here, the deficiencies of the present have given rise to a desire to locate in the past that which is perceived to be missing.

The political uses and potential value of nostalgia, the latter of which has seemingly only recently come to light, were points of discussion during the 1940s. Charges of obfuscation and regressive conservatism proclaimed in response to nostalgia's political uses were already issued in a *Wall Street Journal* 'Letter to the Editor' in 1944. An anonymous political official lambastes the 'Capitalists, Tories, Economic Royalists, etc.' for 'keeping alive a feeling of affection for the evil days of the past'. The author charges these individuals for trying 'to arouse in the unthinking a nostalgia for days when people were so backward' (7 December 1944: 6). In marked contrast, Anne O'Hare McCormick describes nostalgia as 'wholly admirable' for it calls to mind a past, utopian time to which the present should aspire and which it should make efforts to recreate (O'Hare McCormick 1947). More wistful are a series of articles whose titles alone betray a longing for the 'good old days' and for realities independent of specific times and places; for example, 'Prices Fifty Years Ago. Nostalgic Look is Taken at Low Cost of Living Then' and 'Nickel Nostalgia. Lament for the common five-cent piece, which soon won't buy even a New York subway ride'. In the case of the latter, a tangible object is invested with the potential to evoke the sentiment: 'The nickel, once a symbol of small equalitarian luxuries, is falling so low it is virtually a national insult to Thomas Jefferson ... [T]he five cent transaction is fast becoming a memory of the "good old days"'(Schumach 1948).

The increasingly colloquial uses of nostalgia aided its proliferation as a common adjective in, and subject of, cultural criticism. Literary reviews used nostalgia to describe the experience and motivations of protagonists in fictional novels and historical biographies. When homesickness does inform select uses of the term, it is not necessarily figured as a negative experience, disease or illness. For example, in her review of Cornelius Weygandt's *A Passing America. Consideration of Things of Yesterday Fast Fading From Our World*, Florence Finch Kelly writes: 'An appealing flavor of wistfulness runs all through this new book ... Now and then it deepens into a real nostalgia that is keen enough in the author's mind to enable him to put a touch of homesickness for the old America that is no more into the feeling of his reader' (Finch Kelly 1932). This acknowledgement of the capacity for literature—for textual descriptions of a past time—to induce lament and longing is a rather significant development in the conceptualization of nostalgia. It is a point that today still elicits debate.[7] Moreover, it is not necessarily a personal past evoked in the pages of the book reviewed, but a collective, national past. The same can be said about how Stanley Walker's *The Night Club Era* promises to evoke in its readers nostalgia for the experience of one kind of public space (the Speakeasy) as determined by the culture of a specific time (Prohibition). The reviewer also notes how the author managed to achieve a 'curious' mix of nostalgia and satire, something seemingly more suited to postmodern representations of the past (Van Gelder 1933).

In art criticism as in literary criticism, nostalgia's link with homesickness starts to dissolve early in the twentieth century. It is displaced by the belief that the experience of yearning for lost idyllic times constitutes nostalgia. Whereas in the *New York Times* of 1903 the pose assumed by an Italian girl in a William Bouguereau painting suggests 'fatigue, the expression that of an exile suffering from nostalgia' (3 July 1903: 5), in the same newspaper in 1926 'colorful places' (3 October 1926: X9) and in 1930 'what had had its day' (Jewell 1930) become viable objects of nostalgia in visual representations. In her review of an art show, Ruth Green Harris suggests that while '[o]ne single artist would have been discarded ... the group becomes a nameless master'. This 'master' facilitates 'a kind of nostalgia for a time we never should have known without his help' (Green Harris 1938). This past, according to Green Harris, is one that has been invented and constructed through its representation. As a composite image or impression, it may be mythic but no less capable of invoking nostalgia as a result. It even retains enough force to induce the sentiment in viewers who have not personally experienced the past or place depicted.

In the theatre, the ability to evoke nostalgia in the audience through performance, music and mise en scène was considered laudable. The use of setting and costume to 'call out the graces, the sentimentalities ... of middle nineteenth century Paris' was celebrated in reviews in the *Wall Street Journal* of Constance Collier's production of *Camille*. For it to be 'tinged with nostalgia' was clearly an asset (3 February 1931: 4), one shared by the 'pleasantly nostalgic' musical comedy *Sally* (*Wall Street Journal*, 10 May 1948: 8). Even the sequel was said to have its nostalgic charms. George M. Cohen's *The Return of the Vagabond* is a look 'back at the olden days of the Drama with nostalgic eyes' (*Wall Street Journal*, 15 May 1940: 11). Musical scores and the performance of songs were often singled out for their role in evoking nostalgia. For some reviewers, even the sound of a particular instrument, like the tin horn, was imbued with this potential (Hodges 1944).

The capacity for sound to elicit in audiences a nostalgic response was also the topic of film reviews.[8] Arguing for the importance of the score in the 'modern motion picture', one critic explains how in *To Mary, With Love* (1936), 'the note of poignant nostalgia was successfully projected by a musical score which had as its motif Irving Berlin's haunting "Remember"' (*New York Times*, 12 March 1939: 53). While music was often credited with evoking nostalgia, a vast array of disparate objects also held this potential. *Lost Horizon* (1937) promoted 'nostalgia for a better life to large audiences of movie goers' (*Wall Street Journal*, 4 March 1937: 17) while Charlie Chaplin advances an 'obscure nostalgia … for liberty, simplicity, poetry, leisureliness, dreams' among American, French, German and Chinese audiences alike (*New York Times*, 1 April 1931: 23). In *Silk Hat Kid* (1935), actors absent from the screen for a number of years brought a 'nice nostalgia' to the film (Sennwald 1935), something the stars of the silent screen also manage to elicit from 'keen-eyed movie patrons' (Brady 1941). In *How Green Was My Valley* (1941), the combination of John Ford's 'directing, beautiful photographic effects, a well chosen, competent cast, and harmonious singing' permitted the audience to experience nostalgia for 'the years spent, long ago, in that little Welsh mining district' (*Wall Street Journal*, 30 October 1941: 11). In these and countless other reviews, visual and aural effects are identified and emphasized (over and above narrative strategies) as triggers of longing for the past. Here the sentiment is celebrated rather than derided.

However, not all agreed. In a report on Will Hays' presidential address to the motion picture industry, Bosley Crowther foregrounded Hays' belief in the therapeutic value of the cinema and his warning about the 'nostalgic impulse' in recent films. Crowther selected the following passage to bring to the attention of the *New York Times* readership:

> It has, incidentally, been interesting to note that a tendency toward nostalgic retrospection has been pronounced in recent months, what with 'Back Street,' 'Strawberry Blonde,' 'Cheers For Miss Bishop' and 'Adam Had Four Sons.' Now, we have no bone to pick with nostalgia and honest sentiment; they can make for strong dramatic effects. But there has been an apparent inclination to overdo the hearts-and-flowers, to revert to the old-fashioned tricks of deliberate, unrestrained tear-jerking. That strikes us as being a distinct and deplorable retrogression in films. (Crowther 1941a)

For Hays, a little nostalgia is fine. But too much overwrought emotion has no place in film. The four titles he offers as examples, all of which were released in 1941, provide insight into his understanding of nostalgia. *The Strawberry Blonde* is a romantic comedy set during the 1890s. *Back Street*, a drama, opens in 1900 and follows its protagonist, Rae Smith (Margaret Sullivan) across three decades. *Cheers for Miss Bishop* begins in the 1890s and traces the eponymous heroine's 50-year teaching career. And *Adam Had Four Sons*, a romance drama, recounts a decade in the life of the Stoddard family from 1907 to the end of the First World War. With the exception of *Cheers for Miss Bishop*, these films are not concerned with representing the nostalgia experienced by its characters nor with the actions stemming from their nostalgic impulses. The nostalgia represented is not a personal one. It is not enabled by identifying with characters who wistfully long for past times, childhood or home. Instead, it lies in the recreation of an era and typically the two decades flanking the turn of the twentieth century. As such, this nostalgia relies not on narrative but on aesthetics—visual and aural strategies used to reconstruct the past. And because none of these films are musicals, it is arguable that the real force of nostalgia stems almost entirely from the film's visual dimensions, most notably its costumes, sets and props. Only *Adam Had Four Sons* enlists the political and social realities of the time as backdrop for its actions. For the rest, the everyday material culture of the past fills the mise en scène against which melodramatic romances play out.

A review of *The Strawberry Blonde* foregrounds precisely this kind of reverie for the visual landscape of the past:

> Did you ever wear high button shoes and a broad-brimmed sailor hat? Did you ever go down to the corner saloon for a five-cent schooner of beer and later sing barbershop ballads with a bunch of the gay young blades by the light of the silvery moon? If you did, then you should get a lot of pleasure—lot of nostalgic delight—out of the Warners' lusty, affectionate, and altogether winning 'Strawberry Blonde,' which arrived yesterday at the Strand. (Crowther 1941b)

The nostalgia on offer in *The Strawberry Blonde* is collective, rooted in and activated by the visual, material and leisure culture of the 1890s (Figure 1.1).[9] The review continues: 'Its amiable, infectious quality lies in the serio-comic way it recreates the Eighteen Nineties culture of New York—horse and buggy courtships, dancing at the beer gardens, Sunday afternoon street music and maybe an occasional brawl' (Crowther 1941b). It is not the film's intention to engage with the 'history' of New York during this period but to reconstruct it through reference to the practices, pursuits and visual and aural landscape of everyday life. As such, the film and its reception by Hays and Crowther prefigure the debates about nostalgia and the cinema

Figure 1.1 Rita Hayworth and James Cagney in *The Strawberry Blonde* (1941). Warner Bros/The Kobal Collection/John Ellis.

that were thought to have first emerged in the 1970s. This is not to suggest that the nostalgia film as theorized by Fredric Jameson already existed on cinema screens of the 1930s and 1940s. These earlier films were produced in a social context shaped by a different historical consciousness—a different perception of history and its uses in the present—than that which emerged decades later. However, there is ample evidence that, contrary to conventional wisdom and film scholarship, the 'nostalgia film' of the 1970s was not an entirely new label or type of film.[10] Even the 'decade nostalgia' thought to arise for the first time in 1970s film and popular culture is the focus of 1930s film, fashion and design reviews.

The 'Nineties' was not the only privileged object of nostalgia during the early decades of the twentieth century. The Victorian Era invaded the cultural consciousness and, in the early 1930s, provoked reflexive thoughts on nostalgia itself. In an illustrated three-page article extravagantly titled 'Victorian Days That Beckon Us. A Picture of That Bygone Age of Frills and Furbelows Toward Which, With Strange Nostalgia, We Turn Our Eyes from the Contemplation of

Our Own', P.W. Wilson notes 'a strange and inconsistent dualism ... in the trend of today'. He explains: 'Along with on-sweeping modernism is a looking backward, a nostalgia for a bygone age and, of all periods—to make the contrast as challenging as may be—it is the Victorian Age toward which longing eyes are more and more directed' (Wilson 1933). Wilson suggests that 'Neo-Victorian' nostalgia first appeared in literature but quickly spread to inform fashion, furniture and textile design as well as the habit of collecting old prints. The 'permanence' and 'common sense' associated with the Victorian era functioned as a balm for the 'troubles and stupidity of the twentieth century'. Yet, in the midst of this nostalgic reverie surface important questions and doubt: 'What is it in the Victorian Era that still fascinates us? Why do we wish sometimes that we could turn the clock back and be again as once they were?' One of Wilson's queries even targets the objects of nostalgia: 'How is it that their frills and furbelows ... their friendship's garlands and Venetian blinds still charm us ...?' Wilson admits that '[i]t is of course distance that lends enchantment to our view of the Victorians' (Wilson 1933).

In a layout nearly identical to the lavishly illustrated Victorian spread, Mildred Adams announces how fashion, with its 'special genius' for picturing the 'spirit of the times', is channelling four decades of styles (Adams 1933). The stylish woman of 1933 is 'eclectic and capricious, rummaging in the ragbags of the recent past, trying on the old and pretending it is the new, mixing all sorts of things together in one grand show, for that is the mood of 1933'. Among the privileged items in this ragbag are the styles of the esteemed Nineties, 'a period of great elegance' and one which, it should be noted, 'repeated every cut, every design, every quirk dear to the Eighteen Thirties'. The nostalgic impulse of the 1930s seems perfectly sensible to Adams—given the grave political and economic problems of the era—as does the fashion world's tendency to select randomly styles from 1905 or 1910 without concern for 'purity'.

This kind of nostalgic indulgence in visual pastness was not limited to fashion of the early 1930s (Pope 1940). Furniture and indeed even the fabrication of miniature rooms managed to create a nostalgic atmosphere and permit reminiscence without reference to specific historical eras.[11] Constructing a look of 'pastness' by rummaging through historical styles is a practice centuries old. However, describing this impulse as 'nostalgic' and in a way which mobilizes a wide-ranging set of connotations and conditions associated with 'nostalgia' was another significant development in the history of the concept in the United States. Indeed, these particular uses suggest nostalgia not only entered popular speech far earlier than originally thought by Davis, but also that the aesthetic strategies associated with it—including those later derided by Jameson in his analysis of postmodern films and visual culture—were already at work in a nascent form decades earlier. In fact, I would argue that nostalgia's early uses in the cultural realm prefigured its later understandings and made a substantial contribution to the discourses that shaped and continue to shape its meaning.

'Everybody's Just Wild About ... Nostalgia': Discourse and Debate Since the 1950s

Throughout the 1950s and 1960s nostalgia continued to be used in the service of book, music, film and theatre reviews. It also, perhaps unsurprisingly, began to appear as a theme in American academic literary criticism including, for example, a book length study of Marcel Proust's work (Miller 1956).[12] At this time, a degree of syntactical consistency also started to emerge. Nostalgia was often described as something 'stirred' as in 'the smell of apple pie stirs nostalgia for childhood'. But as its expression became more uniform, the sphere of objects for which one might feel nostalgia expanded. Food, flavours, home décor, knick knacks, buildings, landmarks, railways, cars, sailing ships, airplanes, hairstyles, games, athletes and remarkable sports plays joined the roster of viable triggers of nostalgia. Television too became a vehicle for its proliferation, recreating past worlds and ways of living. The small screen even offered a kind of two-pronged nostalgia by broadcasting and even restaging films from the 1930s which were set at the turn of the twentieth century.[13] With these additions, questions started to surface about how much time must elapse between the initial experience of an object or event and the moment it activates a nostalgic response. In fashion and music, a few decades were thought to suffice, while in politics the passing of a single term might warrant an expression of longing for the 'good old days'. Already in the 1950s nostalgia for the Second World War occupied columnists' and readers' thoughts. This runs against the findings published in sociology, psychology and marketing journals whose authors argue that only recently have we started to experience a shorter turnaround for nostalgia's attachment to cultural and personal objects.

Throughout the 1960s nostalgia became entrenched as the word of choice to describe what was, by then, perceived as a national obsession with the material, visual and popular culture of bygone times. Those very same objects that garnered the attention of nostalgics during the 1950s continued to be celebrated as conduits to both personal and cultural pasts. Despite efforts by proponents of social justice movements to highlight the histories of women's subjugation, imperialist enterprises and slavery, the popular press remained awash with celebrations of traditional—usually rural—lifestyles, the Second World War and African-American culture. Past political eras remained vital in the national imagination from the 'McKinley era' to the 'Eisenhower era' to even Camelot as mourned already in 1967. But, it is not until the end of the 1960s that nostalgia started to become subject to limited exploration in the context of social upheavals. In a lengthy essay published in *Time* that aims to take stock of the decade's achievements and transformations, nostalgia is attributed not just to conservatives lamenting the loss of a sense of duty and patriotism, but also to the counterculture, those disaffected youths who 'like the 19th century romantics, rebelled against a society they felt had become overregulated, oversystematized, overindustrialized. Like their predecessors, they ... revived the romantic faith in human nature and blamed the institutions of society for corrupting it' (16 December 1969). However, despite nostalgia's increasing explanatory power in social and political discourses, it remained firmly entrenched in popular and consumer culture.

As early as 1970 nostalgia was even branded an 'industry', one responsible for marketing and manufacturing products designed to satisfy consumers' appetites for previous eras and, increasingly, the styles of previous decades. These commodities were not limited to cherished objects, the tangible relics associated with the childhood home. They also included the aural and visual fragments of radio, television and film (Sloane 1970). This onslaught prompted reflection of an increasingly critical kind on why it was that nostalgia had grown so quickly into a phenomenon threatening to subsume all aspects of public and private life. However, this criticism was limited in the early 1970s to the rising cost of memorabilia. What once was considered junk and tossed away without hesitation became collectible and too expensive to own a second time around.

The early 1970s also bore witness to the overt politicization of nostalgia in the cultural realm and, specifically, the attempt by conservative ideologues to recruit nostalgia in the service of their own agendas.[14] This had much to do with the sense among conservative Americans that their traditional way of life was under siege. This sentiment manifested itself in cultural criticism in a number of ways. Self-identified libertarian Jeffrey St. John urged his readers to 'welcome the national nostalgia boom as a long overdue backlash and rebuke to irrational art forms'. His problem was with film, theatre, literature, music and art that foregrounded as its subject 'irrational despair' and manifested an 'antiromantic and antilife' attitude. For him:

> It is not escape from reality the nostalgia lover seeks, but the desire to see the expression of ideas and values which have elevating moral values. What nostalgia offers is a sense that life is not what modern intellectuals and artists tell us it is; it is not a collective sewer in which all are condemned to swim and suffer. (St. John 1971)

This is a thinly veiled attack on those advocating social change and those invested in the 1960s social movements. St. John attempts to politicize the art of the counterculture while promoting as natural (and thus preferred) the types of cultural expressions activating his own nostalgia.

This politicization of nostalgia happened alongside what might be called its 'psychologization'. Psychology's interest in nostalgia is certainly nothing new. It shaped the understanding of a dominant strain of nostalgia in late-nineteenth-century Europe and even informed the odd text on juvenile delinquency in America.[15] However, the institution of American psychology did not fully embrace nostalgia as an object of study until the 1950s. Psychology adopted nostalgia just as it was losing credibility as a military concern and thus preserved its viability as a subject worthy of 'scientific' scrutiny. In fact, the growing authority that psychology enjoyed during the early and mid twentieth century, thanks in part to Edward Bernays' skilful marketing of his Uncle Freud in the United States, helped, in turn, to relegitimize nostalgia. This development, bolstered by the increasing acceptance of psychiatry and psychoanalysis in the public and scientific mind, allowed nostalgia to continue its rich double life, one whose two trajectories would eventually converge.

Throughout the 1960s and 1970s, nostalgia garnered as much attention as a cultural phenomenon in the popular press as it had as a psychological phenomenon in academic journals. The cover of *Life* on 19 February 1971 announced that 'Everybody's Just Wild About ... Nostalgia'. And yet, however much the public was enthralled by the relics, styles and stars of the past, this deluge started to take its toll on people's patience. As early as 1973, Russell Baker published a series of letters from readers complaining about nostalgia and, more directly, the media's obsession with nostalgia.[16] The question 'Why is America so nostalgic?', posed only occasionally earlier in the century, became a mantra by the 1970s. It also spawned a series of related queries suggesting a genuine desire to understand the precise nature and potential effects of the phenomenon. Journalists searching for nuanced answers turned increasingly to psychology, enlisting the help of prominent psychiatrists to provide insight for their readers. Columnist Tom Buckley called on Dr E. Arthur Livingston to explain how and why nostalgia came to dominate film, theatre, television and fashion. Dr Livingston's answer, one consistent with the published academic literature, explained nostalgia as a 'retreat from reality, a pervasive mood of depression and anomie, a loss of sense of the self' (Buckley 1974).

Psychology helped nostalgia survive its mid-twentieth-century 'de-medicalization' and 'de-militarization', to borrow Fred Davis's terms. However, it also, I suspect, ensured its survival as a cultural phenomenon by making sense of people's ongoing fascination with the material, visual and aural culture of times past. More importantly, it did so in a way that supported its emerging political uses. By claiming that nostalgia surfaces in response to uncertainty, anxiety and dissatisfaction with the present, psychology gave ammunition to those with vested interests in renouncing the social shifts of the 1960s and 1970s and returning to the supposed stability of the past. Of course, as later critics of these conservative ideologues revealed, the past recalled nostalgically was to a large extent invented.

By the mid 1970s nostalgia became too widespread a cultural phenomenon to escape academic inquiry. Scholarly literature on nostalgia started to trace its history, examine instances of its use across a wide variety of disciplines and explore the extent to which it structured modern Western thought.[17] Motivating the bulk of these inquiries was a desire to grasp the particulars of late-twentieth-century expressions of nostalgia and evaluate their social and cultural effects. With these efforts emerged attempts to define and delimit nostalgia, to restrict what counted as nostalgia and what could evoke nostalgia. Ontological questions about its precise nature led to debates about its status as an emotion, a form of memory or whether it escaped classification altogether.

The most heated debates emerged in response to whether nostalgia had a negative or positive effect on everything from the individual to American society, from popular culture to presidential politics, and from memory to history. Nostalgia was charged with the following: falsifying the past; severing the past from the present; preventing historical continuity; fostering disillusionment with the present; hindering attempts to improve present circumstances; stifling creativity, innovation and progress; commodifying history; and exploiting emotions for profit. These general concerns became contextualized in the 1980s and 1990s and explored more fully through a number of disciplinary lenses. Certain strands of feminist literary criticism were especially critical of the surge of nostalgia in literature. Jean Pickering and Suzanne Kehde's 1997 collection on nostalgia and nationalism and Janice Doane and Devon Hodges' 1987 collection on the nostalgic impulse in fiction both regard nostalgia as conservative and a means of idealizing women's subjugation to patriarchal authority.[18] This is extremely important work that has shown how nostalgia can serve reactionary aims; however, it assumes that the value of the nostalgic experience is determined solely by the value of its object (what nostalgia is nostalgic *for*).

This tendency to assess nostalgia on the basis of its object is not unique to feminist literary criticism. In fact, it informs nearly all attempts to evaluate nostalgia, whether positively or negatively. Dimensions identified as central to 1980s and 1990s uses of nostalgia are treated as inherent attributes of nostalgia itself. For instance, the idea that nostalgia falsifies the past becomes part of the nature of nostalgia itself: nostalgia *entails* the falsification of the past. Analyses that identify the potential value of nostalgia also tend to conflate its object with its experience (the longing for an irretrievable ideal, for example).[19] On the one hand, an ideal past might illuminate the failures of the present and provoke efforts to fix that which is perceived to be wrong. Yet, on the other hand, the *experience* of nostalgia can potentially generate an awareness of the relationship between past and present or an awareness of personal and collective desires, provide fresh insights into the past and function as a model for looking at the past in a way that identifies aspects ignored by traditional historical methods. That is, a nostalgic point of view might focus on what history neglects and lead to new and productive engagements with the past. It might even provide some insight into how history and memory operate by revealing alternative ways of engaging with the past. Moreover, whereas collective nostalgia contributes to the formation and expression of generational identity, personal nostalgia, according to Davis and his followers, contributes to the continuity of individual identity by cultivating 'appreciative attitudes toward former selves'.[20] Nostalgia in this and other accounts has therapeutic potential. It can help society and the individual cope with change, endure loss, deal with alienation and quell feelings of anxiety and uncertainty.

These potential benefits of nostalgia went largely unrecognized in the academic literature of the 1980s and 1990s. Its political and cultural uses—and especially its usurpation by Reagan and his image machine—made it difficult for anyone but staunch Republicans to find value in it. However, very recently attempts have been made to rethink what seems, in retrospect, a much too rapid dismissal of nostalgia. Although nostalgia's purported benefits were addressed in sociology, psychology and even marketing during the 1990s,[21] it took until the turn of the twenty-first century to initiate a change in attitude toward nostalgia in cultural criticism. For Grainge (2002), Moran (2002), McDermott (2002), Cook (2005) and Cashman (2006), dismissing nostalgia for the reasons cited above seemed too simplistic. Instead, they argued for a more nuanced look at how nostalgia actually operated, citing a wide variety of instances in which expressions of nostalgia carried critical potential. It seems however that British cultural criticism has been more willing to embrace its potential than its American counterpart, even when the object of study is American culture. The British academics listed above have all been instrumental in recuperating nostalgia for critical analytic projects seeking to better understand the nature, function and uses of a collective past.[22]

Part of this effort to reevaluate nostalgia involved its compartmentalization into different types.[23] In some cases, this was done to enable the identification of some types of nostalgia as socially valuable while still ascribing to others pernicious characteristics. It was also done in order to demonstrate the complexity of nostalgia, including its diverse functions and expressions. There is a fair degree of cross-fertilization between disciplines invested in unpacking and problematizing the concept. Marketing studies have looked to psychology and literary criticism while cultural studies has often relied on sociological work published on the topic. But understandings of nostalgia are shaped as much by these academic discourses as they are by popular discourses and engagements with it in popular culture. I shall now shift my focus to one specific type or strain of nostalgia, one which has become dominant in contemporary American visual culture.

This particular dominant strain of nostalgia is defined by any combination of the following key features. First, it is constructed in and experienced primarily through the visual mass media including film, television, advertising, magazines, music videos and video games. Second, its triggers are primarily visual in nature and derive from a canon of symbolic material objects, visual tropes and visual styles associated with media representations of the past. Third, these visual triggers are often mobilized in a self-conscious way that signifies the idea of nostalgia without necessarily evoking an emotional response. Films, for instance, have been classified by critics in both the popular and academic press as 'nostalgic' solely on the basis of their visual attributes. This is not to suggest that affect does not have a role to play in nostalgia, only that it is no longer a necessary condition for the nostalgic experience. This is a significant development for it brings under the rubric of nostalgia cultural expressions that not only evoke the sentiment, but explore, probe and critique it as well. Whether or not we actually feel nostalgia in response to nostalgic triggers, we may be prompted to think about the nature and implications of that feeling—for an object or as an emotion in its own right. The fourth feature of this dominant strain of nostalgia is that it has been infected and thus inflected by consumerism. The two have so often been conflated in the visual mass media that nostalgic desire now involves an element of consumption, acquisition and possession. Fifth, and perhaps most importantly, one object in particular seems to dominate both representations and theoretical analyses of this contemporary form of nostalgia—the Fifties.[24] This 'object' can be perceived through filmic or televisual representations or signified (and thereby generated in thought) by its constituent canonical objects. Its prominence in both the political and cultural realm has generated discussion about the relationships between the experience and the object. While an examination of Fifties nostalgia has the potential to expose the problems associated with conflating object and experience (and denouncing the experience on the basis of its object), it also reveals the extent to which a particularly dominant object might leave its mark on conceptions of the experience. Though the Fifties is arguably the dominant object in this contemporary strain of nostalgia, it certainly is not the only one. In fact, a consideration of other privileged objects—Deco and the Roaring Twenties, the Second World War, the Disco era of the Seventies—reveals much about the nature of this strain. Sixth and finally, this nostalgia privileges time over place. When place is involved, as in the 'small-town America' construct, it is situated in a specific moment in time as communicated through a series of visual clues. In the next chapter I will further define this dominant strain and explore how and why the Fifties emerged at its centre. I will also explore the impact that Fifties nostalgia had on many of the concept's other 'key features' noted above.

Notes

1. See Herron (1993).
2. One might wonder if nostalgia was not only used by military and political elites to rationalize behaviour unbecoming to a soldier, but also actively feigned by these soldiers as a form of low-level rebellion or resistance. Many

thanks to the anonymous reader who alerted me to this idea and thus what might be considered nostalgia's radical potential from the outset.
3. This absence is doubly remarkable because Freud spent his early years studying the works that led to definitions of nostalgia, most notably Haller's mechanist hypothesis (Starobinski 1966: 93).
4. See Casey (1987: 372–75) for a detailed description of how fixation (of and to) and three types of regression (temporal, formal and topographic) have a nostalgic structure. See also Starobinski (1966 102–3).
5. According to Zwingmann, nostalgia first appeared in print in the 1819 American edition of the *London Medical Dictionary*. However, it was the Civil War that brought nostalgia to the attention of the medical and military world in the United States and generated interest in European scholarship on the subject. (Zwingmann 1959: 80).
6. Fred Davis speculated that nostalgia, until the 1950s, was a 'fancy word' and that '[e]asy and unself-conscious use of it was confined mainly to psychiatrists, academic psychologists, and relatively few cultivated lay speakers' (Davis 1979: 4–5, n8)
7. Davis insists in his highly influential and frequently quoted 1979 study that nostalgia can only be felt for a past, thing, or event personally experienced.
8. Music's capacity to evoke nostalgia was often heralded in advertisements announcing the release of films. See for example the *New York Times* advertisement for *Smiling Through* (4 December 1941: 33).
9. *The Strawberry Blonde* was not the only film to revel in the 1890s. 'Nineties Nostalgia', as it was more commonly known, was the subject of other productions including *I Wonder Who's Kissing Her Now* (1947). This film managed to earn a favourable review despite offering 'not one stretch of originality in the whole story'. 'Gorgeous' sets and old songs were enough to induce longing for '[t]hose sweet-ballad days of the Gay Nineties' which, to the reviewer, are 'an inexhaustible supply of ideas for Technicolor screen musicals' (*Wall Street Journal*, 25 July 1947: 8).
10. It warrants repeating that the focus here is on the use of the term 'nostalgia' in the first half of the twentieth century and not on contemporary analyses that retroactively attributed nostalgia to films of this period.
11. See for example 'Nostalgic Touch Seen in Furniture' (4 November 1949: 31) and 'Miniature Rooms Nostalgic in Tone' (19 June 1945: 16). The latter prefigures Susan Stewart's argument in *On Longing* (1993).
12. Its scholarly application happens to coincide with the declining popularity of the 'nostalgia poem', a staple of the popular press in decades prior. A series of poems in the *New York Times* entitled, simply, 'Nostalgia' construct as their lost object everything from heaven (23 October 1897: 23) to the South (11 January 1932: 20), blame their suffering on the city (28 May 1923: 14) and yearn for a home defined by 'the taste of milk and cheese and bread, the feel of pine boughs for my bed!' (14 November 1934: 18). In 'Night Nostalgia on the Desert', the sentiment evokes a flurry of fragmented images and sounds of the city to which the poet longs to return (28 April 1912: SM8).

13. Reviews of the 1959 live television production of *Meet Me in St. Louis* foreground its nostalgia (Gould 1959).
14. The ultimate conservative endorsement appeared on the front page of the *New York Times* with Nixon pronouncing himself 'in favor of nostalgia in the theater'. In answer to the question 'What do you think of this nostalgia bit?', Nixon said: 'I personally go for it.' (5 August 1971: 1).
15. See for example the section 'Social Instincts and Institutions' in Hall (1904).
16. See Baker 1973. One reader berated the 'media's insistence on dwelling constantly on nostalgia' and suggested ironically that '[o]nce you media people let America forget that it is up to its ears in nostalgia, things will straighten themselves out again, and life will once again be what it was back in 1946, when—remember that great year?—Bing Crosby was singing 'Symphony' and ...' And yet, following the publication of these angry letters, use of the term in the media increased.
17. For analyses of nostalgia in sociological thought see Robertson (1990); Turner (1987); and Felski (1995). For analyses of nostalgia in certain kinds of philosophical projects see Schrag (1992); Harari (1989); and Fritzman (1993). There are very few examinations of nostalgia from a philosophical perspective. They are limited to phenomenology and include work by Casey (1977 and 1987); Hart (1973); and Galt Crowell (1999).
18. See also Greene (1991) who supports the view that nostalgia is reactionary and differentiates it from recollection, a practice employed in women's fiction that involves creative reconstructions of the past. For examples of sympathetic views towards nostalgia in feminist criticism see Jacobus (1987) and Radstone (1993). They refute the claim that there is nothing in women's history for which women could feel nostalgia and cite the concept of screen memory and the Medea myth respectively as examples that accommodate feminist nostalgia or nostalgia for moments in women's personal and collective pasts.
19. Only Huffer (1998) and Tannock (1995) attempt to separate object from structure or experience. For example, Huffer argues that the structure of nostalgia 'produces a dynamic of inequality in the opposition between a desiring subject and an invisible other' (1998: 29).
20. Davis 1979: 37. See also Wilson (2005) who offers a series of case studies that support Davis' hypothesis.
21. In the 1990s psychology sourced marketing studies of nostalgia and became less interested in the phenomenon in it own right. It is now used to explain consumer behaviour and marketing initiatives.
22. I suspect that (thanks in large part to the efforts of Raphael Samuel) it has been easier to divorce nostalgia from the British heritage industry than to extract nostalgia from its conservative grip in the United States. However, a 2004 issue of the *Iowa Journal of Cultural Studies* has made an attempt to reevaluate and recuperate nostalgia.
23. Various types include existential, aesthetic, vicarious, real, stimulated, simulated, imperialist, anti-imperialist, official, counter, structural,

restorative, reflective, melancholic, individual, collective, simple, reflexive, interpreted, national and cultural as well as conceptualizations of nostalgia as a mood, mode, desire, memory, emotion and type of imagination.
24. For analyses of nostalgia that use the Fifties as an example see: Wood (1974), Brandt (1978), Davis (1979), Graham (1984), Lowenthal (1985), Birkerts (1989), Unger, McConocha and Faier (1991), Jameson (1991), Stewart (1992), Holbrook (1993), Frazer and Frazer (1993), Bassin (1994), Dickinson (1997), Gill (1999), Wilson (1999), Shumway (1999), Carroll (2000), Boym (2001), Dika (2003) and Marcus (2004).

Chapter 2

The Fifties: Nostalgia's Privileged Object and the Origins of its Dominant American Strain

America's appetite for the images, sounds and artefacts of its recent past has been well satiated by the ever increasing number of films, recordings, fashions, television programs and stage productions that have served up a variety of popular historical eras, every decade since the 1890s as well as a whole range of mythic constructs from the Wild West to the urban gangster. By the 1970s one object in particular began to enjoy a privileged status in the nostalgia industry—the Fifties. Since its arrival, this object has managed to leave its mark on the concept of nostalgia, shape the features central to its dominant strain and, as the next chapter will explore, determine the attributes of the 'nostalgia film' as it is commonly and academically defined.

To begin it will be necessary to distinguish between the Fifties and the 1950s. By the Fifties I mean to signify the mythic, nostalgic construct, while the 1950s will be reserved for the actual historical period of time between 1950 and 1959 and all its social, political and cultural complexities.[1] However, this is not as neat and unproblematic a separation as this semantic distinction might imply. There is much about the 1950s that sources the Fifties including the period's images of itself. Throughout the 1950s, mass media representations of everyday life were part of a remarkably intensive and astute self-mythologizing effort that continues to hold sway, even today, over impressions of the decade. As such the Fifties were in part created during—and are thus contemporaneous with—the 1950s.

Following an examination of what constitutes the Fifties and defines its various types, this chapter will explore how the social, political and cultural forces of both the 1950s and 1970s had a hand in moulding this construct. More specifically, I will examine how

1950s television and advertising fashioned a canon of objects and images that fuelled 1970s nostalgia by supplying the raw (but already mythologized) materials that would constitute a potent nostalgic construct. Part of this analysis will necessarily focus on why the 1970s were especially prone to nostalgia for the Fifties. The final section of this discussion will explore the implications of the links between consumer capitalism and nostalgia and between nostalgia and the Fifties.

The Fifties and its Forms

So what exactly is the 'Fifties'? As a nostalgic construct it is borne from an 'afflicted imagination', to recuperate an important facet of Hofer's definition of nostalgia. But to suggest that it is whatever we imagine it to be overlooks the extent to which it operates as a shared, cultural entity and the extent to which general consensus exists about its nature, function and constituent parts. The individual imagination is really only required to perform a curatorial and evaluative function by selecting from its visual and aural envelope the resonant sounds, images and objects of which we believe the Fifties is comprised and branding the resulting construct utopian or dystopian, banal or fascinatingly complex. In fact, regarding the Fifties as loathsome does not require its disassociation from nostalgia. For many cultural critics of the 1980s and 1990s, it simply made good sense to hold nostalgia, which they saw as a regressive impulse, responsible for generating pernicious constructs like the Fifties. Indeed for some of these critics Fifties nostalgia was synonymous with nostalgia itself.

As a product of both the cultural and individual imagination, the Fifties is an invention, a fabrication. And yet it is also grounded in lived social, political and material realities. Its constituent parts include, for example, poodle skirts, tail-finned cars, pink refrigerators, Levittown, paint-by-numbers, Ozzie and Harriet, jukeboxes, speckled turquoise formica, rock 'n' roll, Ike, hi-fi, and Marilyn Monroe. However reified or mythologized, these are nevertheless tangible and, in most cases, consumable things that existed in various concrete and representational forms during the actual 1950s. They were seen, heard, touched and experienced in real and mediated ways and thus became part of individual and collective memory. They were experienced through contextualizing apparatuses, most notably the mass media, which mobilized them to suit Cold War ideology. They were integral to the 'American Dream' and had the capacity to signify the prosperity and stability made possible (so the rhetoric goes) under free-market capitalism. They were ultimately 'good' things with the capacity to embody the virtues of a life lived during the 1950s. But they were, of course, only part of a 1950s reality that also included abject poverty, the neglect and subsequent deteriorization of urban centres, institutionalized and politically-sanctioned racism, lynchings, misogyny, McCarthy witch hunts, the Korean War and nuclear anxieties. Naturally, the distaste that many have for the Fifties has much to do with the way in which it eclipsed the 1950s, obfuscating the details and events that comprised, for some historians, one of the most repressive decades in U.S. history.

These obfuscations are not exclusively the result of later historical or nostalgic omissions, but were already begun in earnest during the 1950s with the proliferation of television and its mythical vision of everyday life broadcast daily into millions of American homes.[2] As such, the 1950s was the first decade to represent itself on a mass scale through a *visual* mass medium. While cinema offered windows on other worlds, on how 'other' people lived, television purportedly reflected its audience back to itself through the representation of the 'ordinary', 'average' American family. Of course, this family was narrowly defined as white, middle-class, usually suburban, God-fearing (typically Protestant), patriotic and enthusiastically capitalist. This capacity for visual verisimilitude was no match for television's precursor, radio, on which some of the domestic sitcoms of the era enjoyed their first incarnation. More specifically, this capacity to reconstruct and champion advertisers' target audiences and to flaunt the visual spectacle that was 1950s commodity culture rendered television instrumental in inscribing social meanings into select products, thereby shaping the signifiers that would later play a central role in the construction of the Fifties.

In this way the Fifties functions as a sanitized ideological construct masking the turmoil and oppressions of the 1950s. Yet, it is not used exclusively in the service of nostalgia and nor is it a homogeneous entity. The visual and aural envelope that contains the Fifties has fuelled the creation of different kinds of Fifties in cinematic, televisual, leisure and corporate contexts. There is what we might call the 'Lounge Fifties' with its emphasis on the objects and activities central to an urban bachelor 'Rat Pack' lifestyle. Porkpie hats, hi-fi, cocktails, Daddy-O!, Playboy, smoky clubs, atom-inspired furniture and cigarette girls contribute to the visual landscape of Lounge in its various contemporary manifestations. Popularized by the movie *Swingers* (1996), 'Lounge Nights', with enforced dress codes and strict (and often gendered) rules of social etiquette were hosted everywhere from The Spoke (a university pub in London, Ontario) to Club Montepulciano (a massive venue in London, England) where only 'retro glamour' would get you through the door.[3] Just recently, George Clooney became so smitten with his own Rat Pack experience on the set of the remake of *Oceans Eleven* (2001) that he proposed to build a Las Vegas casino to recapture the aesthetics (and likely the ethics) of the Lounge lifestyle.

There are no neat divisions between the different Fifties on offer.[4] Many of the props central to Lounge appear in the 'Hollywood Fifties', a noirish vision of urban America that uses silver-screen glamour to cloak the anxieties, fears, and bigotry lurking just beneath the surface. *L.A. Confidential* (1997), *Where the Truth Lies* (2005), *Hollywoodland* (2006) and an episode of *Angel* entitled 'Are You Now or Have You Ever Been' (2000)[5] make use of this variant. A slight twist on the Hollywood Fifties is the 'Suburban Horror Fifties' in which the orderliness and visual perfection of Levittownesque neighbourhoods contrast with the intolerance of its inhabitants. *Edward Scissorhands* (1990) is a particularly good example as it shows how narratives need not be set in the 1950s to achieve this effect: alluding to a kind of 'Fiftiesness' often suffices. These visions of the Fifties, like others too numerous to categorize here, borrow many of their signifiers from what is perhaps the most abundant type, the 'Populuxe Fifties'.

With its origins in the commodity and sitcom culture of the 1950s, the Populuxe Fifties has infiltrated film, television, advertising, music videos, product design and packaging, fashion and fashion photography, postcards and calendars since the 1970s. Coined by Thomas Hine in 1986, 'Populuxe' (a term now recognized by the Oxford English Dictionary) marries the words 'populism', 'popularity' and 'luxury' to describe the material objects produced between 1954 and 1964, a materialistic 'golden age'. This ten year span was 'one of history's great shopping sprees' when 'America found a way of turning out fantasy on an assembly line' and during which products became not only more readily available but also, according to Hine, 'invested with greater meaning'. The exaggerated styling of cars, appliances, furniture, clothing and everyday household objects 'celebrated confidence in the future, the excitement of the present' and the ability of the 'average' family to share in the 'bounty of a prosperous time' (Hine 1986: 3–6).[6] This vision of the Fifties received the most play during the 1950s on television, in print and in politics as part of the period's Cold War rhetoric. And it is the type of Fifties that has been the source for the majority of nostalgic engagements with the postwar era since as well as critical engagements with nostalgia itself. In fact, the Populuxe Fifties played a significant role in shaping understandings of nostalgia in the second half of the twentieth century.

Populuxe describes an attitude toward consumption as well as a new visual flamboyance designed into consumer goods. As such, it evokes a visual language that speaks to a certain set of economic values and preoccupations that helped define the postwar years. It is therefore, at base, an adjective targeting visual culture and one that leaves little room for sound or music (except perhaps in the design of hi-fi systems and album covers). I certainly recognize the importance of music and the revival of 1950s rock 'n' roll as part of the Fifties nostalgia boom.[7] However, whereas music has received a fair bit of attention in film and cultural criticism as central to the evocation and experience of nostalgia, the use of props and visual tropes has not. My aim in selecting the Populuxe Fifties as a point of focus here is, first, to explore how a Fifties nostalgia grounded in visual and commodity culture impacted on cinematic engagements with nostalgia and, second, how the visual creation of pastness on film in the service of nostalgia may speak to more than a regressive, conservative impulse and warrant a reconceptualization of nostalgia itself. In order to arrive at this new understanding of nostalgia, we must begin by asking what exactly created the Fifties and how the 1970s shaped its meaning and significance. As we shall see, television and its relationship to commodity culture plays an important role in this tale.

The Fifties Materializes

By the early 1970s, the Fifties had already managed to eclipse virtually all others as the preferred nostalgic construct of marketers and cultural producers. It was celebrated on the cover of *Life* for 16 June 1972 (Figure 2.1). Inside this issue a heavily illustrated ten-page spread produced a picture of the Fifties through its styles, including the 'Greaser Look', 'Marilyn Look' and 'Preppy Look' as well as Hula Hoops, Sock Hops and the 'Detroit' hair cut—'a flattop with fenders' (1972: 40). The popular press was one of many venues in which the Fifties made its appearance. Although *American Graffiti*, one of the landmark films of the decade, was released in 1973, it was not the first cinematic incarnation of the Fifties.[8] *The Last Picture Show* (1971) and *Two-Lane Black Top* (1971), a road movie featuring a 1955 Chevrolet as its star, predate this Oscar-nominated teen film. So too did the theatrical debut of *Grease* in 1972, a production which prompted one reviewer to observe, somewhat incredulously, that '[t]hey are starting to be nostalgic about 1959 now'. Despite this, the reviewer proceeds to praise its successful suggestion of attitude and period through setting and dress as well as how it managed to capture 'the flavor of its time' (Barnes 1972).

Figure 2.1 'The 50s', Cover of *Life*, 1972. Billy Ray/Time & Life Pictures/Getty Images.

Grease (in both its stage and screen version, the latter released in 1978) and *American Graffiti* capitalized on the period's fondness for 1950s music. *Let the Good Times Roll* (1973), a musical documentary featuring interviews with early rock 'n' roll performers and footage from the era, attempted to situate a series of musical milestones in the political and cultural context of its time. Like its fictional counterparts, it suggested that rock 'n' roll provided both a personal and collective soundtrack of a decade. In fact, its revival started early in the decade with original recordings and original stars of the era commanding increased attention and increased prices. A 1972 report in *Time* claimed that Elvis is now 'in many ways bigger than ever' (19 June 1972).

Television too was quick to cash in on the trend, running the *Brady Bunch* from 1968 to 1974, *Happy Days* from 1974 to 1984, and *Laverne and Shirley* from 1976 to 1983.[9] By the late 1970s, the number one shows three years running included these sitcoms set during the 1950s or ones engaged with a kind of Fiftiesness (see Stark 1997: 84). Fifties nostalgia was also bolstered by the syndication of 1950s sitcoms such as *Father Knows Best* (1954–1960) and *Leave it to Beaver* (1957–1963). The characters of the former even reunited in 1977 for the television movie *Father Knows Best: Home for Christmas*. Of course, these kinds of reunion shows may trade more on the bitter than the sweet of nostalgia as they necessarily register the passage of time on the aging faces of the actors. And yet, like the original episodes in syndication, the nostalgia on offer is real and vicarious, personal and cultural: for the experience of having watched these programs the first time around and for the era constructed and signified by the show. In fact, *Leave it to Beaver*, a domestic sitcom which enjoyed only moderate success during its original run, gained mass popularity in the 1970s (Stark 1997: 83–4). For Baby Boomers, *Leave it to Beaver* offered an idealized vision of their childhood and, in the minds of conservatives, recalled a model of family life and a set of values currently under threat. For the film and television producers of the 1970s, these syndicated sitcoms bolstered and sourced their nostalgic offerings, acting as visual templates for their own visions of the Fifties.

The Fifties as a privileged object of 1970s nostalgia was also mobilized politically, though not, as Daniel Marcus rightly points out, as overtly or to the extent that it would inform the partisan debates of the 1980s and 1990s (2004: 35). Its political potential was often exercised in cultural criticism and, specifically, in thinly veiled attacks on the effects that 1960s social movements had on cultural production. For example, in a review of the 1973 Whitney Biennial, Hilton Kramer celebrated the nostalgia for abstract painting of the Fifties:

> For after a decade or more of the most vociferous anti-art propaganda, with painting again and again pronounced 'dead' in the name of politics or 'life' or movies or sometimes only dumb objects, this resurgence of abstraction is

itself an unmistakable cultural statement. What it affirms is an unshaken belief in the disinterested work of art. What it signifies is a repudiation of all those ideologies that attempted to enlist art in causes beyond its own area of competence and realization. (Kramer 1973)

By branding this 'nostalgia for the abstraction of the fifties' a form of 'esthetic self-recovery' Kramer draws on the already-existing discourse of Fifties nostalgia. Perhaps he hopes his readers' own Fifties nostalgia (or knowledge of its prevalence) will inform their opinion of his argument. This is a well-thought out strategy for a conservative critic invested in discrediting the art and politics of the counterculture.

So, what was it about the United States in the 1970s that led it to adopt the Fifties as its privileged object of nostalgia? While nostalgia of the kind enjoyed in the 1970s was nothing new, this decade did see its exponential growth and development. In the next section I will explore the key political and cultural factors that gave rise to Fifties nostalgia.

Prone to Nostalgia: The Fifties in the 1970s

During the second half of the 1960s through the 1970s consciousness-raising efforts promoted by the Women's Movement, Gay Rights, Civil Rights, Anti-war and Anti-capitalist groups revealed that the consensus and stability promoted as virtues in previous eras were either fabricated or enforced through repression, subjugation and exploitation. They destabilized many of the norms perpetuated by conservative ideology by demystifying a series of 'naturalized' constructs involving gender, sexuality, race and the family. In doing so, they challenged the authority of major social institutions, undermining their capacity to dictate morality and behaviour. Some key social transformations acquired the permanence of law, as in the case of the decriminalization of homosexuality and repeal of sodomy laws across several states during the 1970s and, most famously, the 22 January 1973 Roe vs. Wade decision. This constitutional legitimation managed to permanently entrench what began, in some cases decades earlier, as political and social agitation. For conservative ideologues, and specifically those with vested interests in maintaining white, heterosexual male privilege, the traditions once upheld by the authority of their institutions had eroded to the point that they seemed all but irretrievable, except perhaps in the mass-mediated imagination.

While these social upheavals triggered nostalgia among certain constituencies of society for the white, middle-class, nuclear family celebrated in syndication, a more general and pervasive nostalgia for economic security surfaced in response to a series of events and processes that ushered in the fiscal despair of the 1970s. Economic recession, two oil crises, and stagflation (the result of an increase in the inflation and unemployment rate and a stagnant economy) affected a large cross-section of American society. The Misery Index, calculated by adding the unemployment rate to the inflation rate was, on average, much higher during the 1970s than any decade since its inception.[10] Crucially, Eisenhower's tenure in the White House from 1953 to 1961 coincided with the lowest scores on this barometer of economic and social well-being. Although such indices fail to accommodate the many complex factors determining economic shifts and necessarily oversimplify the root causes of national pessimism or optimism, it is hardly surprising, in the context of a multi-pronged nostalgia for the Fifties, that the postwar period should be revered for its relatively wide-spread prosperity. After all, even significant sectors of the working classes enjoyed increased spending power and some economic security for many of the immediate postwar years.

Political realities and events of the 1970s also found their oppositional counterparts in the Fifties construct. The image of the corrupt politician embodied by Nixon stood in stark contrast to Eisenhower's benevolent paternalism, a character trait stressed and circulated by the latter's PR machine. The 'Good War' myth, reiterated in a variety of forms and media throughout the 1950s, assured Americans of their military superiority during the nascent Cold War years, a power that seemed all but lost with failure in Vietnam. Even the moral certitude that once fuelled the United States' 'democratizing' campaigns eroded in the context of domestic resistance to the Vietnam War. Of course, while the Fifties seemed to offer precisely what the 1970s lacked or lost, nostalgia, quite conveniently, did not attach itself to Sputnik's success, the 1958 recession and postwar nuclear anxieties, however much agency 'duck and cover' government safety reels promised. Moreover, these positive images of the 1950s/Fifties were embellished by the self-mythologizing efforts of the 1950s to construct an image of the United States as economically and politically robust, an image well-suited to Cold War rhetoric. News programs, documentaries, advertising and sitcoms all confirmed for their viewers that those who subscribed to the ethos of consumer capitalism would find themselves living the American Dream.

Expressions of nostalgia for stability, prosperity and military prowess defined the Fifties through specific social, economic and political 'realities'. In these instances nostalgia attaches to 'how things were' on a collective level. However, other objects of nostalgia are also locatable in the Fifties and the 1950s, including, for Baby Boomers, childhood and adolescence and the childhood home. Moreover, as the first teenage generation with an identity distinct from adults, they purchased products created specifically for them, including fashion and popular culture. And as the first teenage generation with purchasing power, they were able to accumulate what would later become the material relics and canonical objects used to elicit nostalgia. All this helped to add a personal dimension to 1970s nostalgia, heightening for this particular demographic a wistful longing for the Fifties. Their longings were well served, thanks in part to their own efforts in film, television, manufacturing and publishing—efforts which made the visual landscape of their childhood available to others.

But why were the Fifties adopted as an object of nostalgia beyond the Baby Boom cohort? And why do those with no connection to the 1950s continue (in the twenty-first century) to consume its images and material culture and even claim to feel nostalgic when confronted with representations of this era? To answer these questions we need to consider a variety of factors, including the role played by the visual mass media, the conflation of nostalgic and consumerist desire and the extent to which the appeal of a particular past—rather than dissatisfaction with the present—facilitates engagements with nostalgia. Doing so will help us to arrive at a clearer picture of why the Fifties left its imprint on the concept of nostalgia and contributed to the formation of its dominant cultural strain.

Predisposed to Nostalgia: The Fifties in the 1950s

Economic prosperity during the 1950s, felt through an increase in disposable income and leisure time, was confirmed by statistics and thus not wholly the result of myth-making enterprises. Likewise, there is something about the visual, material landscape of the 1950s that facilitated its nostalgic appropriation and cultural resonance. In other words, in both the economic and cultural realm 1970s nostalgia for the Fifties is perhaps as much dependent on certain concrete realities in the 1950s as it is on dissatisfaction experienced in the

1970s. Indeed, the two realms are intricately linked. The artefacts that constitute 1950s Populuxe (pink toasters, atom clocks, tail-finned cars, New Look fashions, etc.) embody and signify not just the economic prosperity, but also the social and political values that constitute the Fifties. Moreover, it is precisely this ability to encapsulate and communicate relatively specific meanings that renders the visual culture of the Fifties so potent in 1970s as well as contemporary expressions of nostalgia. It is the sheer ubiquity of these kinds of expressions, often self-consciously promoted as nostalgic, that has contributed to our understanding of nostalgia in its current dominant strain as one that is heavily dependent on the *visual* and intimately tied to the machinations of commodity culture. The emergence of this can, in large part, be attributed to the institutional structures of postwar television and, in particular, the way that television programming participated in the reification of products and the promotion of consumer capitalism through planned obsolescence.

Postwar television was a key site where conspicuous consumption was made visible in its presentation of a model of appropriate consumer behaviour which elevated people's consciousness of commodities, enhancing their desirability and reinforcing their various symbolic meanings. It provided the context in which these processes could unfold, ones which served both the manufacturing industry and Cold War ideology. Select commodities were carefully placed in mise en scènes constructed to foreground the pleasures of everyday life in the 'American Dream'. Here they were granted narrative importance as revered objects desired by the characters with whom the audience was expected to identify. These characters behaved like 'proper' consumers by acknowledging the meanings inscribed in these commodities and their role in constructing a white, middle-class, Protestant identity.

Postwar governments were fully aware of television's potential to influence beliefs, desires and consumer behaviour. They sought to regulate television as much as possible and, to this end, supported the forays of radio broadcasting corporations into television at the expense of the Hollywood studios which were kept out of this new medium. Peter Krämer explains that government legislation denying Hollywood access to television, supporting instead radio corporations' efforts to control the industry, and the 1948 Supreme Court ruling in the Paramount anti-trust case prohibiting vertical integration, severely weakened the studio's defences against television (1996: 33). Hollywood had a history of venturing into territory deemed morally bankrupt and ideologically provocative in the postwar climate, addressing, at times, contemporary social problems that might dampen a buying mood. NBC, on the other hand, whose parent company RCA had its origins in an alliance between General Electric, AT&T, Westinghouse and United Fruit—corporations which enjoyed intimate relationships with various administrations throughout the early twentieth century—could be counted on to nurture consumption and project the image of the United States as a unified, stable, prosperous and dutifully capitalist society. Thus, as might well be expected, the interests of Cold War ideology were deeply entwined with the interests of consumer capitalism on the television sets nestled at the heart of American homes in the 1950s.

Domestic sitcoms were perhaps best at serving these interests.[11] *Leave it to Beaver, The Adventures of Ozzie and Harriet* (1952–1966), *The Donna Reed Show* (1958–1966) and *Father Knows Best* showcased on a weekly basis the morality and prosperity of the 'average' American family, one that was, almost without exception white, Protestant, middle-class, nuclear and suburban. These programs supplied the viewer with specific models of familial behaviour and organization, solutions to problems encountered in the domestic sphere and resolutions to morally ambiguous situations. Avoiding serious subject matter and treating trivial dilemmas as all-important, these programmes represented for their 1950s audiences, if not reality, at least a glorified normality to which they ought to aspire. As Ella Taylor argues:

> Like all representational narrative, television strives to convince us that its words and images reproduce our own experience or that of people like us ... With its visual naturalism, its attention to the quotidian details of ordinary lives in recognizable domestic settings, television has disguised its interpretive character, inviting the viewer to forget that a story world is being constructed. (1989: 38)[12]

Despite this verisimilitude and the ostensible aim to reflect rather than construct reality, very specific moral lessons were being furnished through a series of binary oppositions such as 'self-promotion versus friendship, greed versus thrift, middle-class informality versus the restrictiveness of wealth, homemaking versus careerist isolation, and familial togetherness versus economic self-promotion' (Leibman 1995: 25). These binaries also tended to structure cinematic melodrama during the 1950s, but with one important difference. According to Nina Leibman's meticulous survey of postwar film and television narratives, 'in film the social world becomes the familial, while in television, the familial world operates as an allegory for the social' (1995: 25). The issues and objects granted narrative importance in domestic environments were thereby imbued with social importance. More significantly, they were ones (as the list of binaries suggests) that were economic in nature. This fact was confirmed by empirical data. During the 1950s, one in three domestic sitcom episodes dealt with status, consumerism, economic opportunity and the advantages of industrial capitalism while a remarkable one in eight focused on consumer items (Leibman 1995: 61 and 109). However, in order to understand how these domestic sitcoms produced the objects and props favoured by nostalgic representations of the Fifties by transforming consumer items into canonical objects we must begin by considering their sponsors.

During the 1950s major corporations including Texaco, Kodak, General Electric, General Mills, Philip Morris, Kraft, Nabisco and Buick owned the television shows broadcast by the networks. This arrangement gave them the power to determine the structure of programmes, the narrative content of individual episodes and, in the case of General Mills' *Betty Crocker Magazine of the Air* (1950), to invent programmes that featured their own products. In a format initially devised for radio, they carved up programme time to accommodate commercial breaks, first every fifteen minutes and then eventually every twelve minutes, a shift which signalled the increasing value of advertising.[13] Perhaps even more importantly, these sponsors were responsible for the proliferation of the episodic series.[14] These series, which included sitcoms and Westerns based on the 'twin principles of plot repetition and continuity of characters', gave audiences a chance to become familiar with and develop emotional attachments to heroic protagonists and families represented as morally superior to their own (Taylor 1989: 23-24). However, differences between episodic genres required the development of strategies specific to each. Sponsors of action adventure series set in the past or future, for example, produced commercials associating their product with the protagonist, suggesting that consumption could maintain identification by making the viewer more like the hero. General Mills used the ever popular Lone Ranger and Rocky and Bullwinkle as spokespersons to advertise their products. Action adventure series set in the present could often easily embed their products within the mise en scène but only according to the sponsor's strict guidelines. Sitcoms were especially effective at showcasing sponsors' products, primarily because these products were intended for use in domestic environments. Though sponsors could not be named, they ensured their commodities occupied prominent visual places (Figure 2.2). Ozzie Nelson of *The Adventures of Ozzie and Harriet* recalled that:

> while we were sponsored by Hotpoint, they furnished the kitchen with all the latest Hotpoint appliances, and if we had a choice of where to play a scene we'd move it into the kitchen where Harriet could be cooking dinner or putting dishes in the dishwasher or taking clothing out of the dryer. Or even if we were eating dinner in the dining room the Hotpoint appliances could still be seen in the background. (Nelson in Leibman 1995: 110)

Network reliance on sponsorship translated into corporate control not only over the way episodes narratively and visually contextualized their products, but also over the hiring of actors and writers.[15] Both network and sponsor went to great lengths to avoid even the hint of controversy, taking often drastic measures to insulate themselves from critique. For example, during the early 1950s when television shows were produced by advertising agencies, General Foods fired Jean Muir from a title role in *The Aldrich Family* (1949–1953) upon discovering her name listed in a 1950 publication by 'American Business Consultants' entitled *Red Channels: The Report of Communist Influence in Radio and Television*. With Eisenhower's appointment of McCarthy protégé John C. Doerfer and McCarthy friend Robert E. Lee as successive FCC commissioners in the early 1950s, sponsors could not risk allying themselves with anyone who seemed un-American (Barnouw 1982: 121–56).

Predictably, this repressive environment yielded ideologically homogenous programmes. However, in some instances ambiguities surfaced and narrative explorations of consumerism (as well as gender and race) exposed contradictions. For example, it was difficult for writers to reconcile the Puritan ethic motivating characters in domestic sitcoms with the postwar doctrines of conspicuous consumption and planned obsolescence.[16] Opposing thrift and hard work to greed and credit (increasingly a staple of 1950s consumer culture) seemed to compromise the corporate agenda to convince audiences to part with their money. It was also at odds with Eisenhower's 'You Auto Buy!' campaign designed as a 'psychological offensive against unpatriotic, stay-at-home thrift' (Marling 1994: 133). Nevertheless, television programmes continued to laud Puritan virtues, a practice for which there are several possible explanations. The promotion of these 'virtues' might have seemed the logical response to the fear that television's potential to corrupt young minds could provoke a backlash against its commercialism. Moreover, by supporting a programme that extolled thrift, sponsors could claim

Figure 2.2 David, Ricky and Harriet Nelson with the Hotpoint Stove, *The Adventures of Ozzie & Harriet* (1952–1966). ABC/The Kobal Collection.

that their product was not manufactured to satisfy a desire or want, but rather to fulfil a practical need. Indeed, the contradictions produced by the tension between venerating thrift and promoting conspicuous consumption may have to do with attempts to graft new desires onto traditional values and the hope that the latter would mitigate the negative effects of the former.

These contradictions inherent in consumerist ideology, including the point at which the model of the family as a site of decency and restraint came into collision with conspicuous consumption, can also be explained by structural shifts in the television industry including, for example, changes to advertising strategy (which in turn affected narrative treatments of greed and thrift) and the exclusion of select commodities from moralizing tales. During the mid 1950s networks started to feel the financial strain caused by a sharp increase in advertising expenses. Realizing they could no longer profit under the existing model, networks introduced the 'magazine concept' requiring *several* advertisers to buy commercial time during a single show. This shift in industrial investment affected programme content, transforming a character's desire for a single product into a general desire for consumption. This was reconciled with the Puritan ethic by suggesting that such desires could be satiated by hard, honest work (Leibman 1995: 237). Characters who bought things before they could reasonably afford them were depicted as greedy, while a commodified lifestyle was just fine for those who were financially secure. Thrift itself was redefined in various subtle ways to suit a postwar economic climate. It could involve saving money to purchase a newly desired object at a later date or spending money on tools needed to fix up an older one.

However, some products were granted superior status over others (Leibman 1995: 238), rendering them exempt from these economic lessons. The close and long lasting relationship between the automotive industry and television, as well as the car's place in national myths of exploration, ensured its place among these privileged goods. The latest model of car would sit conspicuously in front of the family home, a Chrysler in the case of *The Adventures of Ozzie and Harriet* and a Chevrolet in *My Three Sons* (1960–1972). In 1958 an article in *House & Garden* speculated (incorrectly) that people would be so enamoured with the beauty of their new automobiles that they would want to create 'living garages' (Figure 2.3) in order to literally live with their cars (Hine 1986: 56). Blueprints accompanying the article illustrated how to include your vehicle in the decorative schemes of these new spaces where the family socialized and ate their meals. (Carbon monoxide with your fish dear?)

Figure 2.3 The 'Living Garage' as featured in *Home and Garden* 1958. Plan59.

By celebrating consumerism and visually foregrounding a selection of privileged commodities, domestic sitcoms functioned as one of the key sites responsible for generating a 'canon' of sorts—a collection of objects with the capacity to signify the Fifties. The symbolic force of these objects and the reliability with which they continue to call to mind this mythic construct also has much to do with their limited numbers, perhaps attributable in part to the participation of relatively few sponsors during the early years of television. For the most part, commercials focused on introducing the latest designs in cars and appliances, revolutionary cleaning products and exciting new ways to prepare food. In accord with planned obsolescence, many of these objects, ones we might now describe as Populuxe, were designed for visual display, to stand out even when not the subject of narrative scrutiny or the target of a character's consumerist desires. The look of these objects, their transformative potential and their social meanings took centre stage in 1950s television commercials. Their qualities were then also reinforced in the context of domestic sitcom kitchens and driveways. In fact, the way in which these commodities were contextualized through placement and demonstrative use, not only in television but also print advertising, supplied a series of visual tropes as potent as the privileged canonical object itself. Mother in her high heels and New Look skirt, immersed in the modernity of her colourful streamlined kitchen, showcasing with a balletic poise the latest countertop scrub guaranteed to disinfect her gleaming Formica surfaces, is but one of many visual tropes which continues to circulate in visual culture, evoking the Fifties for both nostalgic, parodic and political purposes. Father and son washing the new tail-finned car on the driveway of their suburban bungalow, on a sunny weekend afternoon, is yet another.

Television commercials also did their part to naturalize the relationship between their products and the 'idealized' suburban milieu. In one notable example, Chevrolet created a two-minute commercial in 1959 that mimicked the formal and narrative conventions of the domestic sitcom. Starting with a close-up on the license plate, the camera pulls back to reveal a young girl perched on the back seat of a Chevrolet station wagon staring out the rear window. She catches the attention of a young boy walking by and makes a face at him. He reciprocates and when his parents come to investigate what captured his attention, his father sees only the car and not his new playmate to which he is excitedly pointing. The father looks longingly at the car, then pensively, calculating whether or not he can afford it. His wife too is instantly taken with the car, and becomes even more enamoured as she watches the door to their old station wagon open and the groceries comically roll out. The viewer is then offered a series of close-ups on the design features of the car, intercut with reaction shots registering the full gamut of exaggerated, cartoonish expressions from surprise to wonder to desire to finally sheer joy at having made the decision to purchase the vehicle.

This station wagon is clearly the family's second car as well as 'Mother's car', as confirmed by shots of her both in the driver's seat and driving through a suburban neighbourhood. The station wagon's association with the feminine and, by extension, the domestic, is visually reinforced by the design of the showroom. With curtains, lush plants and pictures on the wall, it looks more like a postwar living room than a car dealership. And yet, despite the focus on what is to become 'Mother's car', there are subtle visual cues designed to entice Father too. At various points the new Chevrolet convertible comes into sight. On one occasion, massive tail fins intrude into shots purportedly offering a full view of the station wagon. At other points, an oval picture of the convertible appears, like a thought bubble, suspended over the dealer. There is no dialogue and, until the very end, no narration that speaks to the product on offer. Instead, for nearly the entire length of the commercial a playful allegretto soundtrack punctuates its many comic devices and heightens key moments of anticipation. It is precisely the kind of music that one would expect to hear complementing the innocent antics of the Cleavers or Nelsons.

This commercial reconstructed the mise en scène of the domestic sitcom in order to align the Chevrolet with this world. But when such products were actually embedded in the scenes of sitcoms it was up to the object itself to speak to its own virtues. It was these kinds of product that lent themselves to canonization better than others. Many were motivated signifiers with the potential to communicate their intended symbolic values. Design elements would point the reading of the object in the right direction. On postwar automobiles, rocket-like tail fins signified the futurity, expansionism and technological supremacy central to postwar ideology. The automobile's size and superfluous accessories signified ostentation, prosperity and conspicuous consumption, while constantly changing exaggerated design elements ensured planned obsolescence. These associations were entrenched in the minds of the postwar public with the help of print advertisements using rockets, spaceships and men in flight suits as props to sell cars.

According to Karal Ann Marling, the TV dinner was another such motivated signifier, manifesting visually the postwar tension between science and tradition. The foil container sectioned the food in a manner connoting a scientifically balanced meal and was packaged in a brightly coloured box echoing the dimensions and look of the television set. The container may have quite literally referred to nutritional science and a modern technology, but its contents still signified tradition: turkey was a labour-intensive holiday feast that formed part of the family traditions of Thanksgiving and Christmas (Marling 1994: 232–35). And because the turkey's special status made up for the TV dinner's mode of preparation, the housewife was not seen as shirking her responsibility to provide sumptuous and nutritious dinners or compromising the socially established divisions of labour in the family.

Through sheer ubiquity and repetition, the relationship between canonical objects and their postwar sitcom environments became naturalized to the point where select 1950s commodities now function synecdochally, standing in for the values, ideas and ideology which constitute the Fifties as a distinct mythic entity. Consensus regarding their meaning and role in forming an American middle-class identity was facilitated by the fact that these objects happened to be mass-produced commodities personally owned by many Americans and that their primary contextualizing apparatuses—television and magazines—were consumed by an exponentially growing audience. This also ensured a representational as well as real material access to these canonical props. That same Hotpoint dishwasher seen on the *Adventures of Ozzie and Harriet* (and in print and television advertising) could also be seen and used in the comfort of one's own modern, streamlined kitchen. Hollywood may have long stimulated its audience's tastes in fashion, home décor and furniture, but the practice of mimicking the styles seen on film are necessarily different than the practice of cooking on the very same stove Harriet Nelson used in the service of her postwar sitcom's particular vision of domesticity. Whereas Hollywood was trend-setting and cheap copies were made to imitate movie glamour, the idea that your stove may have come off the very same assembly line as Harriet's facilitates identification not just with the idealized protagonists, but with the world they inhabit.

Materialism and Material Culture: The Conflation of Nostalgic and Consumerist Desire

Mass production and thus mass availability likely made the job of production designers of 1970s sitcoms set in the 1950s much easier.[17] With the proliferation of flea markets specializing in 1950s artefacts, the tools and décor of everyday life became readily, if not always cheaply, available. As part of the growing nostalgia industry, these venues received plenty of attention in the popular press, initiating discussions about the potential for objects to recall the past and debates about whether one could feel nostalgia for periods not personally experienced. Presumably, these flea markets were buoyed by the success of Fifties sitcoms as much as these sitcoms heightened the nostalgia for hula hoops, poodle skirts and pink refrigerators. While this was a mutually beneficial relationship, the availability of 1950s household objects also enabled these 1970s sitcoms to construct a convincing Fifties milieu.

This was of vital importance for two reasons. First, the 1950s, having only recently passed, would remain fresh in many American's memories. Perhaps it still existed in the kitchens, living rooms and basements of those who either gave up on or could not afford to follow the dictates of planned obsolescence. It most certainly would have remained present for those tuned into radio stations playing 1950s rock 'n' roll. Furthermore, it became increasingly prominent in political rhetoric, which, as the decade went on, began to evoke the worlds of 1950s sitcoms in the service of partisan debates. Second, these 1970s sitcoms set in the 1950s shared air time with actual sitcoms from the 1950s. Because storylines and issues dealt with would have necessarily been refracted through 1970s concerns, these programs had to rely more on formal devices to communicate their Fiftiesness. Marion Cunningham's kitchen would be measured against June Cleaver's kitchen. For *Happy Days* to be read by its viewers as set in the 1950s it had to resemble the representations of the 1950s with which the audience was familiar, and which the audience may have been watching simultaneously in syndication. This meant that it had to achieve what might be called a kind of 'televisual verisimilitude'. This had the added effect of reinforcing the Fifties construct borne out of the self-mythologizing practices of the 1950s, of which television was one—but a nevertheless significant—part. It helped to ensure the survival and recognizability of that Fifties canon, further entrenching it in the popular imaginary. In the context of widespread nostalgia for the 1950s, it also helped to legitimate the Fifties on television as a reflection of, and thus a kind of privileged access to, that era. As one *Life* journalist put it in a nostalgic review of the Fifties, 'Ozzie and Harriet are so real—they are the Nelsons—we have only to breathe to imitate them' (1 April 1999: 74).

Gaining access to the past through its objects—in either material or representational form—became an integral part of how nostalgia was understood during the 1970s. As the previous chapter revealed, this kind of access was possible, and indeed even pursued, during the early decades of the twentieth century. However, the almost singular attachment in the 1970s to the Fifties and the specific ways in which it was mobilized as a response to economic decline, social change and political dysfunction, have left their mark on nostalgia. Perhaps even more significant in forcing a reconceptualization of nostalgia is how the Fifties came to be evoked through a selection of canonical objects and the visual tropes used to contextualize them. These canonical objects were first and foremost commodities that played an important role as part of the logic and character of postwar consumer capitalism. They were subject to a series of discursive practices in television, advertising and politics designed to heighten their desirability. Consumers were assured that buying products one did not need was not a sign of greed or the abandonment of that once revered Puritan ethic. Instead, the unnecessary replacement of goods in perfectly working order was an act motivated by patriotism and rooted in a desire to participate in the American Dream—the ultimate model of freedom and democracy that the U.S. government and business were intent on marketing internationally. Moreover, as the marketing of Populuxe promised, buying things was simple good clean fun.

This idea of a harmless and even venerable kind of consumer capitalism—a golden age of conspicuous consumption—is precisely what appealed in the 1970s. As much as the return of hula hoops and turquoise Formica evoked the styles and visual opulence of the Populuxe aesthetic and, for Baby Boomers, the comforts of a nostalgically filtered childhood, they also recalled a different kind of economic reality coloured by the mass availability of consumer goods. Even those who could not participate in what Hine called the postwar 'baroque bender' (1986: 3) likely believed advertisers' claims that *most* were enjoying access to mass-produced popular luxuries as well as politicians' claims that spending was good for you and the nation. This 'benign capitalism' is precisely the kind of quality advertisers since the 1970s relished in their pursuit to distance their products from the realities of consumer capitalism: the economic disasters of the 1970s, the corporate greed of the 1980s and the unethical and corrupt practices that have come to light around multinationals since the 1990s.[18] However, it is this practice of selling commodities through Fifties nostalgia that has provided some of the fuel for critics of nostalgia who claim that it does little more than commodify the past. Or, as Boym says of the current global entertainment industry of nostalgia, it 'tricks consumers into missing what they haven't lost' (2001: 38).

Nostalgia for the Populuxe Fifties was certainly instrumental in facilitating the conflation of consumerist and nostalgic desire.

However, to date, most of the critical literature has focused on the impact of nostalgia on consumerism, on the use of nostalgia to sell products and to create a desire for goods.[19] But while nostalgia has inflected consumerism, consumerism has also inflected nostalgia, pointing to a more complex relationship between the two than previously recognized. The discourses of consumption filter nostalgia, inflecting it through association with, for instance, notions of acquisition, possession and economic exchange. Consumer capitalism marks nostalgia and these marks in turn contribute to reshaping contemporary nostalgia. For example, by transforming individuals into consumers, consumer capitalism has transformed nearly every social act into an act of consumption. Thus, every facet of an individual's social and indeed even personal life is affected to some degree by consumerist and economic considerations. Even memory and experience have come to involve a transaction; they too are commodities that can be bought and sold. Vacations, theme parks, games, music and the cinema are just a few of the commodities that promise experiences and memories for a price.

It is almost inevitable in a society which has conditioned its members to view themselves as consumers, their actions as transactions and their participation in the social world as consumption, that any longing for what is lost in time and space will become coloured by consumerist desire. If nearly everything is a commodity, then nostalgic yearning becomes attached to commodities. If nearly every action and experience involves consumption, then nostalgia cannot escape the structuring influence of consumerist desire that underpins consumption. In fact, nostalgia is especially susceptible because of all it shares with consumer capitalism: a promise of transformation in the present; a fleeting instant of pleasure followed by the return of desire; deferring sustained satisfaction by keeping the ultimate transformative object forever out of reach, while in neither case does such an object actually exist. There is an element of fetishistic disavowal at work here. Both the consumer and the nostalgic subject 'know perfectly well' that purchasing the desired commodity or recapturing the desired past will not fully or permanently satisfy their desire. Yet they nevertheless continue to engage in these pursuits, lending credence to Stewart's argument that nostalgia is a 'desire for desire' (1993: 168).

This entwining of nostalgia and consumerism has become cause for concern. Madison Avenue's use of nostalgia bolstered critics' charges that sentimental uses of the past in popular culture were nothing more than a deceit designed to sell products and lifestyles by manipulating emotions and memories. Any nostalgia felt in response to such advertisements was just as 'inauthentic' as the fabricated pasts themselves. These charges were not only levelled at the retailers and manufacturers who found nostalgia to be a useful marketing tool. It was also levelled against conservative politicians during the 1980s and most notably those involved in the media campaigns designed to get Ronald Reagan, himself a 1950s Hollywood icon, elected. The Fifties, and especially the Populuxe Fifties, was often evoked to bolster support for socially conservative legislation. According to Daniel Marcus, the nuclear family championed by domestic sitcoms took on 'documentary value to illustrate the stable realities of American life before the disruption of the Sixties social movements' (2004: 41).

Reagan's rhetoric about free-market capitalism was also well-served by the model of conspicuous consumption celebrated by the Cleavers and the Nelsons. Although Reagan simply latched on to the already existing groundswell of Fifties nostalgia, he contributed to it in several significant ways. His allusions to the past through television and film were 'highly imagistic, approaching myth rather than history, featuring static tableaux meant to illustrate enduring qualities of the nation rather than to provide causal explanations for historical change' (Marcus 2004: 64). As such, he not only entrenched the Fifties as a primarily visual and mass-mediated construct in the popular consciousness, but also legitimated the Fifties as 'history'. However much Reagan himself straddled the domains of politics and entertainment, of 'reality' and 'fiction', his uses of the Fifties in political rhetoric imbued this nostalgic construct with a kind of historical authenticity.

Critics of Reagan's presidency were quick to point out that his efforts to sell the Fifties as history rivalled the manoeuvrings of Madison Avenue. These critics are certainly right. But in the process of decrying conservatives' uses of Fifties nostalgia, they contributed immeasurably to the growing trend that understood nostalgia through the Fifties. In other words, the critical literature attributed to nostalgia the practices characteristic of Fifties nostalgia, thus conflating object and experience. For some authors, the Fifties were evoked as the example par excellence that revealed precisely how nostalgia operated, though often without acknowledging the extent to which features specific to the Fifties were being written into definitions of nostalgia itself. Although this conflation of object and experience is problematic, it has yielded numerous important studies offering valuable insight into how nostalgia has been mobilized for insidious aims and how attempts to evoke longing for both real and fictionalized pasts are often integral to conservative backlashes against the inroads made by progressive movements. It has also produced some of the key cultural criticisms of postmodernism which seek to explain how nostalgia, as an aesthetic mode, is partly responsible for severing past from present and denying any kind of meaningful access to history.

Object and Experience: The Fifties and Nostalgia

To separate object and experience is something of a philosophical operation. It would require isolating and identifying the essence of nostalgia independent of its object. For a concept that has travelled globally, through centuries and across countless disciplines, this leaves very little for us to work with. It reduces nostalgia to a longing for something lost in time or space. Perhaps this is enough. Such a philosophical operation would allow us to identify nostalgia's many uses in the cultural and political realm. This in turn might enable us to consider nostalgia's benefits, ones that are once again coming to light after decades of suspicion and derision. But what do we lose in this exercise? And is this kind of theoretical distillation even possible given the multiple and highly divergent discursive economies that have moulded nostalgia into a variety of forms during the twentieth century? Might this cause us to lose sight of how its role in certain contexts has shaped and reshaped understandings of the concept? Or, more specifically, might we lose sight of how the dynamics of Fifties nostalgia has informed its uses and produced features key to its current dominant strain? Might we also lose sight of nostalgia's malleability and capacity to register the kinds of desires and different types of roles envisioned for the past in the present? Of the power of its objects to leave their mark on the experience?

Perhaps it is best not to look at this as an either–or question. On the one hand, we need an understanding of nostalgia that is not so beholden to its privileged objects that we fail to acknowledge other creative, productive and critical uses. On the other hand, we need one that recognizes the extent to which these objects acquire the force to restructure our perception of the experience. Adopting this kind of dual consciousness about nostalgia will enable us to realize, for instance, that Fifties nostalgia—its manifestations and effects—is not always inherently conservative, regressive or negative. In fact, the key features of nostalgia's current dominant strain, ones shaped in large part through its grip on the Fifties, have a certain critical potential. For instance, nostalgia's reliance on visual and material culture facilitates recognition of the significance of images of the past in forming and mediating conceptions of history. It also reveals the extent to which history has been inscribed—and can thus be accessed—through material culture. This kind of access to the past might provide fresh historical insights and function as a model for engaging with the past that identifies different aspects of history. It may even speak to the ways in which we experience history and the effects of this on our historical consciousness.

The capacity for the Fifties to signify rather than evoke nostalgia—and thus generate nostalgia's separation into what Grainge (2002) refers to as its 'mode' and 'mood'—also has its benefits. It isolates the emotion as an idea to be scrutinized and facilitates a critical distance that permits explorations of the object of nostalgia. However, as some films (such as *Far From Heaven*) make clear, critical distance need not come at the expense of affective pleasure. While the conflation of consumerist and nostalgic desire may 'trick us into missing [and buying] what we haven't lost', in its overt forms, it draws attention to the machinations of commodity culture. It lays bare the mechanisms through which desire is manufactured and symbolic meanings are inscribed into consumer goods. In some instances these goods—as props in films—can launch effective and stinging critiques of consumer capitalism itself. An examination of Fifties nostalgia also alerts us to the contributions of the past and present in formulating nostalgic objects. Specifically, it reveals that the myths and constructs created out of both the past and present are, in some instances, as important as records of facts and events, speaking to both current preoccupations and the desires that defined previous times.

What follows next is a consideration of nostalgia and film and the ways in which the current dominant strain of nostalgia —as shaped by the prominence of Fifties nostalgia in contemporary visual and popular culture—has manifested itself in the cinema and in film criticism.

Notes

1. This distinction will apply generally to all decades expressed as the 'Thirties', 'Forties', etc., and their numeric counterparts as in the 1930s, 1940s, etc. Moreover, it is worth noting that the Fifties typically extends to 1963 and Kennedy's assassination which signalled, for many, the end of an era.
2. Whereas in 1950 there were less than 5 million television sets in American homes, by 1960, well over 50 million sets had been sold.
3. Academic curiosity got the better of me one evening in 2000 and so, in the interest of 'research', I experienced what *The Independent* branded 'the future of clubbing' and met countless Playboy bunnies and Vegas Showgirls as well as a score of Marilyns, a plethora of Franks and even a few Deans at a Montepulciano event.

4. Likewise, the line circumscribing the Fifties from the 'non-Fifties' was often crossed. Public debate about the potential for rock 'n' roll and Hollywood to promote juvenile delinquency and immoral behaviour meant that whereas for some, icons like Elvis and Marilyn Monroe threatened the sanctity of the Fifties, for others, they were integral components of a vibrant, prosperous and free culture. However much the self-mythologizing efforts contributed to the construction of the Fifties, they remain only one stage in this process which was to resume with great force amidst the nostalgia boom of the 1970s. The refinement and entrenchment of privileged objects and images within what might be called the Fifties canon, emerged during this later decade. Any ambiguity surrounding that which seemed provocative or even indecent during the early years acquired a kind of innocent charm in the wake of the 1960s sexual revolution.
5. This particular Angel episode could also be classified as part of the McCarthyite Fifties which includes *Fellow Traveller* (1989), *Guilty By Suspicion* (1991), *Citizen Cohn* (1992), and most recently, *Good Night and Good Luck* (2005).
6. It is important to note that Hine does recognize how exclusionary this construct of the average American family is (1986: 6).
7. See for example Shumway (1999).
8. The 1970s produced approximately thirty films set during the 1950s.
9. There was also of course *M*A*S*H* (1972–1983), set during the Korean War. Though clearly not a *domestic* sitcom, it did deal with 'everyday life' sorts of issues. However, unlike its counterparts, the 1950s setting was used to remove the show from its actual object of critique, the Vietnam War.
10. The Misery Index began in 1948 and its data can be accessed at www.miseryindex.us.
11. According to Nina Leibman, 'domestic comedies' should not be confused with 'family comedies' which were not restricted to suburbia and did not feature exclusively white, middle-class and Protestant characters (1995: 8)
12. Then, as now, these televisual images of everyday life were interpreted as suggesting at least a degree of truth. According to a study by Lynn Spigel, domestic sitcoms continue to shape perceptions of women's lives during the 1950s. Her subjects, American college students who watched these shows in syndication in the 1990s, initially believed that they reflected the reality of the period (1995: 16–33).
13. This growing importance is also reflected in the increase in revenue from US$57.8 million a year in 1949 to US$1.74 billion a year in 1962 (McClure 1963: 222).
14. By the 1958/59 season, nine out of ten shows were episodic series.
15. Dress rehearsals in the days of live television were even supervised by company officials (Taylor 1989: 20).
16. The importance of making cautious investments and saving money was the subject of numerous episodes of *Leave it to Beaver* ('The Bank Account', 'Stocks and Bonds' and 'The Credit Card'), *Father Knows Best* ('Art of Salesmanship', 'Bud, the Millionaire' and 'Bud, the Willing Worker') and the

Donna Reed Show ('The Football Uniform', 'The Merry Month of April' and 'A Penny Earned').
17. According to the makers of *Down With Love* (2003), eBay is the best source for period props today.
18. Since the 1980s countless studies have been published in consumer research journals which find that evoking a nostalgic response in the audience typically means that this audience will have a favourable attitude toward the product and come to desire it.
19. Holbrook observes that 'consumer behaviour involves ... phenomena based on emotionally-charged associations with product-related experiences from the past' (Holbrook 1993: 82). Another study finds that nostalgic elements in adverts help to achieve the goals of advertising (exposure, attention, comprehension, receptiveness and retention) and that comprehension for example, may be 'augmented by employing nostalgic elements to create cognitive associations between images of bygone times and product characteristics' (Unger, McConocha and Faier 1991: 346–47).

Chapter 3

The Nostalgia Film in Practice and Theory

It is with some hesitation that I title this chapter 'The Nostalgia Film'. This designation seems to imply that what follows is an engagement with genre, an argument for why films or sets of practices related to the production and consumption of a group of films should be circumscribed by this label. Certainly issues addressed by genre theory including the entrenchment and circulation of codes and conventions, the evolution of genre types and sub-genres, and the ways in which a specific genre might respond to sociohistoric realities seem rather pertinent to the analyses of films that follow this chapter. Indeed they are. Fifties nostalgia films might well be categorized as one of many sub-genres of the 'nostalgia film' which make use of a defined set of narrative and formal conventions. I suspect a case can even be made for 'Fifties nostalgia' as a genre that exceeds the cinema, working through the Fifties Populuxe canon across visual and material culture. However, this involves constructing an argument that, while illuminating in some respects, requires a shift in emphasis away from how cinematic engagements with nostalgia have the potential to provide critical insight into the operations of visual pastness. Mobilizing the term 'nostalgia film' as a generic category also makes it difficult to include the seemingly marginal yet compelling uses of a single prop or specific actor for engaging and evoking nostalgia. Despite the recent nuanced conceptualizations of genre which acknowledge its elasticity, genre labels continue to suggest a degree of coherence and singularity markedly absent from the various ways in which nostalgia's relationship with the cinema can be theorized.

So why use the term 'nostalgia film' at all? In part, I suppose, to have my cake and eat it too. While I do not plan to explore the ways in which theories of 'genre' might structure an analysis of nostalgia and the cinema, I hope that issues raised in the context of genre theory, including those mentioned above, will be addressed in the questions I formulate about the films under consideration here. Perhaps this allusion to genre might help carve out a terrain for future explorations of, say, Eighties nostalgia or Second World War nostalgia or any number of nostalgic constructions currently under-served in film criticism. But my main reason for preserving this label has to do with its roots in Fredric Jameson's analysis of postmodern aesthetic modes. Jameson's definition of 'the nostalgia film' has nurtured a full continuum of scholarly literature on cinematic nostalgia from that affirming his position to that which finds fault with his valorization of modernist forms of creative expression as well as his failure to acknowledge the merits of postmodern cultural production. As such, perceptions of the 'nostalgia film' as a theoretical concept tend to be dominated by the attributes assigned to it by Jameson including, for example, its 'depthless' recreations of past styles at the expense of meaningful engagements with history. Although quite limited in scope given the myriad of ways in which the cinema has dealt with nostalgia over the last few decades, I want to take up Jameson's definition, for it targets precisely the kind of nostalgic expressions discussed in the chapters that follow.

However, before examining Jameson's 'nostalgia film', his debate with Linda Hutcheon over the critical potential of select postmodern aesthetic modes and the recent attempts by Vera Dika and Paul Grainge to recuperate nostalgia, I would like to review some of the ways in which nostalgia enters into a relationship with the cinema beyond the visual creation of pastness.[1] I do so not only to acknowledge the extent to which nostalgia has permeated all facets of the cinema, but also to suggest how the various components of a film can work together to reinforce or deconstruct the nostalgia on offer. It is important to emphasize the discursive role played by both individual films and film theory in shaping conceptions of nostalgia and the extent to which Fifties nostalgia occupies a privileged space in both these domains.[2]

Nostalgia and the Cinema

Beyond the Film

This section surveys some of the ways in which nostalgia as a mood or feeling is activated by the cinema. Starting with the cinema (broadly defined so as to include what lies outside the filmic text) I will enlist Svetlana Boym's two types of nostalgia—restorative (which involves attempts to restore how things were) and reflective (which reflects on what has been)—to classify the kinds of practices engendered by deep investments in films, stars and theatres. I will then turn to the filmic text itself and consider how narrative strategies, music, montage sequences and period casting have all been deployed in the service of nostalgia in popular Hollywood film.

Curiously, restorative nostalgics do not think of themselves as nostalgic but rather as individuals tasked with recuperating the past for some kind of national or cultural interest (Boym 2001: 41). For them, longing for a lost home, however broadly defined, spurs the production of monuments and myths in an effort to recover past 'truths'. A modified and more personal version of this impulse is at work in those who seek to inhabit particular filmic worlds and the personae of actors, characters or, perhaps more typically, amalgams of the two. In these instances, nostalgics seek to reproduce what they perceive to be the essence of these lost and, in many cases, impossible objects. This seemingly fruitless impulse is one supported and encouraged by well-organized fan societies and the nostalgia industry.

Take, for example, Tony Alleyne's project to replicate, in his flat, the interior of the Starship Enterprise. This may have enabled him to feel part of the *Star Trek* world—to inhabit a fictional futuristic realm—but it also left him bankrupt. Considerably less extreme is the promise by American furniture manufacturer Thomasville that their 'Bogart Luxe Collection' will infuse your living space with Hollywood glamour, Art Deco style and all that Humphrey Bogart himself connotes. There are a number of slippages and mediations at work in this example which permit Thomasville's promotional material to work on several levels. Art Deco, a style which has itself endured for decades as a privileged object in the nostalgia industry, is here mediated by Hollywood. Of course, this is not a new association but one nurtured during the interwar years. Art Deco style made its Hollywood debut with the 1928 release of *Our Dancing Daughters* and continued to inform spectacular set designs throughout the era of Classical Hollywood cinema (Massey 2000: 25). It was mediated by Hollywood long before Thomasville decided to ask its potential customers to think Deco through Bogart and his films.[3]

Indeed it is also difficult to imagine Humphrey Bogart divorced from his iconic roles, most notably *Casablanca*'s (1942) Rick Blaine, *The Maltese Falcon*'s (1941) Sam Spade or *The Big Sleep*'s (1946) Philip Marlowe. Certainly this is the point. 'Humphrey Bogart' is as much a construction as 'Rick Blaine', one predicated on a specific kind of film noir masculinity. But it is difficult not to also read Bogart as 'real'—as an actual person. Thus, while evoking a 'Bogart style' rather than a 'Casablanca style' infuses Thomasville's campaign with a kind of 'truth' or 'reality', there remains the expectation that 'Bogart' be read through his contextualizations in various fictional realms.[4] Who, except for die-hard fans, would know how Humphrey Bogart actually decorated his house? The spaces inhabited by Bogart that are recognizable to a wider film-going audience are the ones constructed by the art directors working on his more famous films (Figure 3.1). It is these spaces that Thomasville now offers to consumers who wish to restore and experience for themselves the filmic worlds once inhabited by a silver-screen icon. This is a clever marketing ploy which engenders all types and degrees of identification by offering a way to restore a lost and (ostensibly) irretrievable set of nostalgic objects and by appealing to fans of Bogart, his films, film noir, Hollywood glamour, Art Deco and specific constructs of masculinity.

An expressly stated nostalgia also drives attempts by some fans to recreate themselves as Audrey Hepburn and the type of postwar femininity signified by Hepburn as a star construct. This is the subject of Rachael Moseley's fascinating study of the fan practices adopted by different generations to express their investment in this cinematic icon.[5] These practices typically involve dressing and accessorizing in a way reminiscent of 1950s and 1960s fashion in order to look like

Figure 3.1 Mary Astor and Humphrey Bogart in *The Maltese Falcon* (1941). Warner Bros/First National/The Kobal Collection.

Hepburn. Moseley discovered that while 'slightly older' women were interested in Hepburn's look in a performative and retro way, younger women (in their 20s) were 'invested in a highly nostalgic way in the innocence and romance of the era represented in the films and by Hepburn's stardom' (2002: 174–75). Although Moseley sets up a distinction between retro performativity and a post-feminist, conservative nostalgia (thus reinforcing the alignment of nostalgia with regressive and reactionary impulses), she does acknowledge that a 'range of readings are produced around Hepburn's image in which feminist sensibilities sit in negotiation with a nostalgic retreat from the contemporary' (2002: 197). Despite acknowledging the role of postmodern play in structuring participation in a retro economy, it seems clear from the interviews that the 'slightly older' women were just as motivated by nostalgia as their younger counterparts.

This deep investment in Audrey Hepburn and her look was confirmed recently by the astronomical sum that her 'little black dress' (designed by Hubert de Givenchy) fetched at a Christie's auction in London on 5 December 2006. One of three dresses of its kind, it was expected to raise £70,000 for a Calcutta-based educational charity, but ended up drawing a winning bid of £410,000 (Auction Frenzy over Hepburn Dress 2006). This may have also had something to do with its staged return on Natalie Portman on the cover of *Harpers Bazaar* a month earlier, an act which further fetishized both the dress and Hepburn herself. Audrey Hepburn has also been used by The Gap which inserts original film footage of the star dancing into its television commercials as well as by Longines which calls on her glamour to sell its watches.

While the above examples involve acts of restoration, attempts to retrieve in material form the vestiges of cinema's past, reflective nostalgia (which thrives in wistful longing according to Boym), also structures ways in which people have engaged with the cinema. The cinema—in its physical and psychic manifestations—has functioned as an object of this reflective kind of nostalgia. Threats to tear down old cinema theatres often incite passionate debate about their value. This value, attributed to both their architectural qualities and social significance, is one shared with other public community venues like sports stadiums, exhibition centres and fair grounds.[6] Already during the mid twentieth century efforts to preserve such sites were, according to the popular press, fuelled by nostalgia. Their social significance, then as now, had much to do with the age-old belief that physical structures functioned as containers for memories. Demolishing buildings would thus sever access to these memories—memories of experiences marked by excitement, anticipation and community.[7]

The significance of the cinema theatre (and the practice of 'going to the pictures') to the formation of cultural memory is the subject of Annette Kuhn's remarkable ethnohistoric study of cinema going in 1930s Britain. She reveals the key role played by the cinema as a social site and the importance of memories of movie palaces, individual films and the range of social practices related to the consumption of films, including walking to the theatre, sharing responses to films and bartering with jam jars to gain entrance to a show (Kuhn 2002: 41). Though Kuhn does not deal with nostalgia directly,[8] interviewees' responses are shot through with many of its most basic attributes as commonly understood: the present is inferior to the past in several respects including being less safe or characterized by a diminished sense of community; memories are bittersweet because of the realization that the past cannot be regained except in memory; reminiscence involves relishing sense memories of smell, sounds and the feel of surfaces; and positive aspects are recalled and celebrated at the expense of acknowledging negative aspects, except when hardships are remembered for being overcome by resourcefulness.

Old movie palaces and past spectatorial experiences are just two of the objects of nostalgia which have inspired private wistful longing. Reminiscences are also shared publicly in a variety of forums from fan clubs to websites whose participants are united in their desire to recall or recapture these and other practices connected to the cinema. Here, extinct or outmoded genres, styles of acting, constructs of glamour and elegance as well as different ways of speaking and behaving have prompted both reflective and restorative nostalgia in ways that blur the distinction between these two types. What the cinema beyond the individual filmic text meant (and continues to mean) to people, groups and cultures across history, and the various kinds of feelings, memories and practices it engenders, certainly deserve further study. However, this is well beyond the scope of this current project which can only begin to address certain points of intersection between nostalgia and the cinema. As such, I would like to shift focus to the filmic text itself to explore narrative structure and music—two strategies for engaging nostalgia well-documented in the literature—and opening montage sequences and period casting—two strategies as yet unacknowledged.

Narrative

In its most ancient form, nostalgia's 'narrative' involves a state of being which seems Edenic from the vantage of the present. Through the passage of time, this Edenic state is lost. Such loss initiates mourning, longing and attempts to retrieve or recreate (in memory or reality) the desired prelapsarian condition. This trajectory bears some striking similarities to the narrative of classic Hollywood cinema in its most basic form, which is itself based on the narrative structures of fairy tales and Bildungsroman. And despite the many and varied experiments with narrative, we continue to see this structure underlying contemporary popular Hollywood film. On the one hand, the Eden-loss-retrieval trajectory is *structurally* similar to the equilibrium-disequilibrium-equilibrium trajectory of narrative. Typically, the world of the story is introduced as enjoying a state of equilibrium. This state is then threatened and disrupted, forcing characters to restore order to their lives and their environment. But it is not so much the original state that is successfully recovered by the ending credits as the stability with which that state is associated. Closing scenes reestablishing equilibrium present a world different and often evolved from the first. On the other hand, there are certain equivalencies between the terms of the tripartite structures that seem to facilitate the translatability of nostalgia to the screen. The original state of equilibrium is akin to nostalgia's object. When lost or altered, both inspire searches for and attempts to regain times and places thought to be superior to the present. And in both instances, when retrieval is finally acknowledged to be impossible, the goal shifts to reestablishing the stability and certainty thought to reside in the past.

The stability and certainty defining the initial state of equilibrium and the object of nostalgia renders them retrospective constructions. The feeling of nostalgia reshapes the past to address concerns and desires specific to the present. In the cinema, everything is already at once past, and not only in terms of the absence signified by each cinematic image. Narrativization entails a process of selection and interpretation that can only take place after the passage of time has transformed the present into the past. Although events represented during the initial state of equilibrium unfold as present in the spectator's present they have, of course, been carefully organized to offer a certain ordered view of the fictional world. They are also determined by what happens next during the subsequent stage of disequilibrium. An opening sequence might emphasize political stability rather than familial stability if political instability characterizes the state of disequilibrium, and vice versa if later scenes represent infidelity or divorce. This is not to suggest that an initial focus on familial stability could not lead to a story about political intrigue. The nuclear family, as a site that effectively articulates patriarchal relations, can function as a model for the political. After all, we recall from chapter 1 that the Oedipal trajectory is itself structured by nostalgia and structures literally and metaphorically much narrative screen fiction.

Like narratives structured by nostalgia, narratives ostensibly *about* nostalgia can take several forms. One popular variation involves protagonists acting on their nostalgic longings for childhood by returning to the site of their childhood home. Though they eventually come to realize that the past cannot be regained, sites mnemonically connected to childhood often function as portals granting some kind of access to this past. Pilgrimages to rediscover these places provide opportunities to physically and, by extension, mentally, inhabit these objects of nostalgia, ones shaped and interpreted by memory and the imagination. How these sites function is best explained through what Anthony Purdy identifies as a 'mnemotope'.

Drawing on Bakhtin, Purdy defines a mnemotope as a 'chronotopic motif that manifests the presence of the past, the conscious or unconscious memory traces of a more or less distinct period in the life of a culture or an individual' (2002: 447). Whether accessed physically by visiting the childhood home or mentally through flashbacks, these objects of nostalgic longing are often represented to the spectator as manifesting the presence of the past. This is accomplished by marking these sites with 'memory traces' established as significant within the film or ones that have general cultural significance. Purdy not only accounts for both individual and cultural mnemotopes but also for how they may be 'inflected by attitudinal values ranging from nostalgia and desire through obsession to horror and denial' (2002: 447). Naturally, the concern here is with nostalgic mnemotopes and their narrative function in film. Although these sites—or more accurately the nostalgically inflected memories of these sites—fuel protagonists' journeys, discovery of them rarely yields the transformative experience anticipated. Instead, the journey itself assumes narrative importance, often leading to self discovery and the knowledge that, while the past cannot be revisited, the memory of it as imprinted upon mnemotopic sites can function as a utopian model for the future. That is, the past envisioned today functions as the blueprint for a better tomorrow.

A nostalgic desire to revisit what is constructed in *Hearts in Atlantis* (2001) as an 'individual mnemotope' motivates Bobby Garfield (David Morse) and structures the narrative trajectory of the film. This desire to return home is triggered by the acquisition of a baseball glove following the death of an old friend. Initially surprised by the state of disrepair in which he finds his old house, he begins to reflect on his feelings, asking: 'Why is it that we always expect home will stay the same?' The camera follows Bobby as he inspects the marks of the passage of time, taking note of the peeling paint, the growth of vines and later the rust on a discarded wind chime. He wanders through the empty house, stops at his bedroom window, and looks outside. Physically occupying the very same space he once did triggers a somatic memory of a ritual performed there whose reenactment initiates his nostalgic reminiscence. First as an adult, and then as an eleven-year-old boy, Bobby fogs the pane of glass with his breath and draws two parallel lines in the condensation. This action separates the present from his nostalgically remembered past, as do a number of other formal strategies and conventions employed to ensure the spectator too is aware of the nostalgia on offer. Bobby's flashback, which comprises nearly the entire film, concludes with his move to Boston. This flashback begins with a significant colour shift as the vibrant, warm and sun-drenched world of the nostalgic memory replaces the cold, bleak, monochromatic present which opens the film. However, at the very end, as Bobby abandons his childhood home for what is presumably the last time, warmth and colour enter the mise en scène of the present. This signals the return of childhood optimism to the adult self, something confirmed by the voice-over narration recounting the lessons learned from his visit home and from replaying his memories of the past. His renewed hope for the future is emphasized visually in the final shot by the melding of adult and child, present and past: middle-aged Bobby driving his car morphs into the young Bobby riding his bike across the very same landscape.

In a variation of the return narrative, the past is revisited by the protagonist in his or her present form, not mnemonically, but physically—typically with the help of a time machine. Pat Gill suggests that in films like *Back to the Future* (1985), *Terminator* (1984), *Terminator 2* (1991) and the television series *Quantum Leap* (1989–1993) this actual return is fuelled by 'nostalgic disavowal'. Gill explains that this form of fetishistic disavowal 'makes the "I know perfectly well, but nonetheless" displacement mechanism of disavowal into both an amelioration of the past and a standard of comparison in the present: "I know perfectly well that I can't undo or recapture the past, but if/when I do, my present life will be more comprehensible and pleasant"'(1999: 164). However, there are important differences between returning to the past in memory and actually doing so which call into question the ways in which the past revisited operates as a nostalgic construct.

While returning physically to the past transforms the present, revisiting the past through memory transforms the characters' (and therefore the spectators') *interpretation* of the present. As a key attribute of detective films, flashbacks often contain information relevant to a present mystery or the motivation for continuing whatever search the character has embarked on. And while the return to the past is fuelled by nostalgia, the past returned to is not a nostalgic construct. The story world may very well appear as a nostalgic object and there may be the expectation that the audience consume it as such, but it is experienced as present by the character's present self. It does not involve the memory of a past self in a past time and place. Moreover, because nostalgic reminiscences originate in the character's present, they are filtered through and structured by the present, something reinforced and often literalized by voice-overs. Through voice-overs, the characters maintain a kind of presence throughout the memory, interjecting at points to interpret the past from the vantage of the present. As such nostalgic flashbacks are inhabited by both the former and present self. In *Stand by Me* (1986) and *Inventing the Abbotts* (1997), for instance, the voice-over fades as the action begins but returns on several occasions to remind the spectator of the presence of the present and to draw attention to the split in time. Nostalgia may prompt both physical returns to the past and flashbacks illustrating memories of the past, but only the latter functions as a nostalgic construct for both the protagonist and the spectator.

Music

Like narrative, music too enjoys a double-layered relationship with nostalgia. According to recent film scholarship, music can be nostalgic as a trigger evoking nostalgic longing in its listener and in its structure. For David Shumway, the use of popular music on film soundtracks has the capacity to generate nostalgia because it is 'widely shared' and can 'constantly keep the viewer located somewhere else' (1999: 40–44). A song can function as a mnemonic prompt by calling to mind experiences from the time it was first heard or the time during which it was most often listened to. Because of music's capacity to stir deeply felt memories of the Proustian variety, films often use well-known tracks deliberately to provoke nostalgic responses at key moments in the narrative. One strategy designed to increase the likelihood that most members of the audience will hear something personally meaningful involves excerpting verses from several songs to create an aural montage.

Forrest Gump (1994) uses this strategy in a way that calls into question the power of the visual relative to the power of the aural in shaping interpretations of a scene. Vietnam combat sequences are accompanied by a sampling of Aretha Franklin's 'Respect', Bob

Dylan's 'Rainy Day Woman', Jimmy Hendrix's 'All Along the Watchtower', the Doors' 'Soul Kitchen', the Mamas and the Papas' 'California Dreamin', Jefferson Airplane's 'Volunteers', Credence Clearwater Revival's 'Fortunate Son' and Buffalo Springfield's 'For What its Worth'. Most of these songs are explicitly anti-war and thus reflect the countercultural impulses of the late 1960s and early 1970s. However, *Forrest Gump* selects lyrics that, out of context, obscure the political message of the song. Hearing only the first few lines of 'Fortunate Son' ('Some folks are born to wave the flag; Ooh, they're red, white and blue; And when the band plays 'Hail to the chief ...'; etc.) while images of platoon camaraderie occupy the screen suggests the music reflects rather than criticizes the events represented. Moreover, choreographing the action (and at times the editing) to the music reinforces this fabricated and delusive harmony between the content of the song and the content of the image. Given the film's practice of evoking nostalgia for mainstream America (from the Fifties to entrepreneurial capitalism in the 1980s) while deriding the aims and actions of the counterculture and, given the practice of sampling from a variety of songs, the Vietnam sequence anaesthetizes an appalling episode in American history. Using popular music to evoke nostalgia for personal experiences while illustrating the Vietnam War is tantamount to requesting that spectators suspend their critical faculties and indulge in private reminiscence during the representation of a horrific event in which the hero of the film (mainstream America as embodied by Forrest Gump) is implicated.

Carol Flinn's study of the use of music in popular film has a slightly different focus. Her interest lies in the structural connection between nostalgia and scores inspired by the late Romantic traditions of Richard Wagner and Richard Strauss. She argues that, while independently music and utopia are associated with nostalgia, the type of non-representational music used in classical Hollywood film has 'the ability to generate great degrees of affect' and connote an 'impossible, plenitudinous and nostalgic condition' (Flinn 1992: 10). Films like *Gone With the Wind* (1939), *The Sea Hawk* (1940) and *The Adventures of Robin Hood* (1938), depend on their musical scores to 'restore an original quality or essence currently lacking ... within the text, the apparatus, or the moment of consumption' (1992: 48).[9] These scores are structured around a musical desire to return to an earlier moment through a series of melodic forays that stray from the original key only to return to it in the end. For Flinn, they enact the attempt to return home and the return to origins that characterizes the nostalgic experience. Drawing on the work of János Maróthy, Flinn shows how these returns are often fraught with obstacles in the form of 'foreign elements', ones whose expulsion lends 'special force to the final tonal achievement of a piece' (1992: 94). She also suggests that film score music uses a variety of formal devices to lengthen individual notes and sequences as a way of stressing the 'irretrievability of the object' (1992: 94).

While the nostalgia on offer through classical Hollywood film scores may be a subtle one, working at the level of the subconscious, these kinds of scores also function as cultural codes to evoke a Hollywood golden age, specific genres, or even that elusive construct—Hollywood glamour. The importance of specific soundtracks to particular genres has naturalized their association to the point where a few bars can evoke a type of film or narrative event. This capacity for certain arrangements to signify (melodramatic) heartbreak or loss, for example, emerged through consistent repetition and thus in a way similar to a genre's iconography or the Fifties canon. This is not to suggest that these signifiers cannot also point to countless and even contradictory meanings or signify nostalgia for the purpose of critique. Rather, when associated with other cues, they are particularly adept at confirming a film or scene's engagement with nostalgia.

Opening Montage Sequences

Popular music is an important component in montage sequences that introduce films set in the past. Several films have made use of this strategy including *Going All the Way* (1997), *Blast From the Past* (1999) and *L.A. Confidential*. As the opening credits appear a series of still photographic shots or clips flash on the screen to the rhythm of the musical selection. Typically, they remain on screen for a few seconds and represent the social milieu of the filmic world. In some instances they make reference to historical events and the material culture of an era to situate the film temporally and to communicate the social status of its characters.

The opening montage of *Going All the Way* evokes a postwar middle-class milieu through a series of illustrated images depicting men drinking beer on a patio, children playing in a cherry-red truck parked in a driveway, a corner store, a boy staring into a toy shop window, a suburban bungalow, a son and his parents admiring a new car, and a woman being shown the latest fashion by a friend while her husband pretends to fish in the living room. No one image is privileged or framed as having greater semiotic significance than another. Their import lies in what they share: recognizability as wellworn visual tropes that speak to the leisure culture and domestic bliss at the heart of the Populuxe Fifties.

Likewise, in *Blast from the Past*, defining images of the Atomic age including mushroom clouds, gas masks, family fallout shelters and photos of Kennedy, Khrushchev and Castro flash on screen to the tune of 'Accentuate the Positive'. However ironic this juxtaposition may seem, it becomes clear by the final credits that accentuating what the film identifies as the positive aspects of early 1960s American life (e.g., politeness, respectfulness, etc.) and reintroducing them thirty-five years later has a positive impact on the present. In this way, the opening sequence foreshadows the film's message.

L.A. Confidential uses its introductory montage to a similar end. It even uses 'Accentuate the Positive' and does so also for ironic effect. But, whereas *Blast from the Past* supplants the initial irony generated through the juxtaposition of images and music with a moral tale extolling the virtues of postwar life, *L.A. Confidential* does the reverse. Here, what initially appears to be a celebration of 1950s Los Angeles—and Fifties America as a nostalgic construct—turns into an indictment of the corrupt forces at work in the city. Already by the end of the opening montage sequence, the lyrics and images are at a far remove from one another, offering a stark, ironic juxtaposition that effectively sets the tone for the film. Sandy beaches, orange groves, suburban bungalows, backyard swimming pools and people working appear as Danny DeVito's voice-over describes how land is cheap, jobs are plentiful and American families are happy. He tells us that we can 'have all this and, who knows, maybe even be discovered' as movie stars like Marilyn Monroe and Frank Sinatra flash across the screen. He continues: 'Life is good in Los Angeles. Paradise on earth … That's what they tell you anyway.' So ends the first half of the opening sequence, comprised of found footage of familiar scenes and familiar personalities that appear and disappear at a relatively steady rate of every two or three seconds. These fragments, mined from newsreels, home movies and postcards, appear in varying types of colour and black and white, thus retaining the aesthetic cues that identify their media type and alerting us to their status as representations.

The images that comprise the second half appear at an irregular rate and often include multiple viewpoints of a single scene. They also paint a very different picture of Los Angeles as a city plagued by organized crime. References to Hollywood inaugurate this portion as the narrator admits to the disparity between the reality of Los Angeles and its promotional myths: 'they're selling an image, they're selling it through the movies, television.' From here on in found footage is mixed with images from the film's reality as we are introduced to some of its characters and their crimes. These latter sequences often include zooms and pans and remain on screen for much longer than their documentary counterparts. They are crisp and clear and lack the marks of past representational technologies— the graininess of 16mm or the amateurish jerkiness of home movies. As such, the film's reality becomes privileged as somehow more authentic, more 'real' than the extant documentary sequences here foregrounded as representations and as false, nostalgic images. By this point 'Accentuate the Positive' is fully out of sync (both musically and in terms of content) with the rapid flashes of bloodied, bullet-ridden corpses, and the nostalgic construct of Los Angeles that initially complemented the soundtrack is revealed to be just that—a construct.

Period Casting

On the director's commentary for *Sin City*, Robert Rodriguez enthuses that Carla Gugino was perfect for the role of Lucille because she somehow seems 'displaced in time'. In other words, Gugino looks like a 1940s film noir actor. Likewise, Sandy Powell, the costume designer on *Far From Heaven*, was both challenged and thrilled by Julianne Moore's pregnancy throughout the shoot. On the one hand, it meant constantly adjusting the seams of her elaborate costumes. But, on the other hand, her body type resembled that of the more voluptuous actors of the 1950s. In both these instances, the look of an actor was credited with lending the film a kind of period authenticity as well as what we might describe as a kind of filmic or generic authenticity. After all, Gugino and Moore may not resemble one's family photos of the period, only the looks promoted by Hollywood studios at that time. This practice of selecting actors based on their resemblance to film stars of times past is what I call 'period casting'.

An actor's association with a specific period can be based on several factors. In the case of Carla Gugino her face and body type were thought to resemble the construct of beauty favoured for the femme fatale of postwar noir. Voice too can also help situate a character in a past era. Patricia Clarkson (*The Green Mile* [1999], *Far From Heaven, Good Night and Good Luck, All the Kings Men* [2006]) does not sound contemporary, but rather convincingly historical. The grain of her voice,[10] the subtle inflections of tone and the rhythm of her delivery are striking in their pastness and call to mind outmoded ways of speaking. They do so in a manner similar to the way a few bars of music can instantly turn our thoughts to past movie moments, scores and genres. David Strathairn (*L.A. Confidential, Good Night and Good Luck*) both sounds and looks as though he stepped out of the 1950s, but only as the occasion demands. Make-up, hairstyle, costume and eyebrows tweezed in a particular way can do much to transform a good character actor into a star of the 1920s, 1930s, 1940s and so on.

Actors who do not naturally look displaced in time can also become period typecast through repeated association with specific eras. For example, Josh Hartnett has become aligned with the 1940s or, more accurately, various Forties through his appearances in *Pearl Harbour* (2001), *Sin City* and *The Black Dahlia* (2006). *Good Night and Good Luck*, a film deeply invested in historical authenticity, is populated by characters (Figure 3.2) who have given convincing performances in films set around the mid twentieth century: Patricia Clarkson and David Strathairn as noted above; Jeff Daniels in *Pleasantville* (1999), Robert Downey Jr. in the American version of *The Singing Detective* (2003), and Matt Ross in *Down with Love*. George Clooney too belongs to this list, but for other reasons as well. He actively pursues film projects that are set in, or allude to the styles of, the postwar past including *Oceans Eleven, Oceans Twelve* (2004), *Ocean's Thirteen* (2007), *The Good German* (2006), and *White Jazz* (2008) as well as other historical periods like the 1930s (*O Brother Where Art Thou* [2000]) and 1920s (*Leatherheads* [2008]). Clooney has also made a concerted attempt to model his star persona on the leading men of the 1950s and members of the Rat Pack like Dean Martin and Frank Sinatra. And as noted in the previous chapter, he even sought to build a 1950s—or, more accurately, Fifties—style casino that would permit its gamblers to inhabit this era. Thus, Clooney's pastness stems as much from his roles as it does from his off-screen behaviour, attitude, style and pursuits.

Past performances inform subsequent ones, either to the detriment or to the benefit of belief in the story world. While Cate Blanchett may effectively emulate Greta Garbo, Ingrid Bergman or Marlene Dietrich in her role as Lena in *The Good German*, she may also echo her own past roles as Katharine Hepburn (*The Aviator*), Meredith Logue (*The Talented Mr. Ripley* [1999]) or even Galadriel (*The Lord of the Rings* Trilogy [2001, 2002, 2003]). However aligned with specific eras certain actors may seem, period casting cannot guarantee that audiences will call to mind the appropriate role. Such is the case with Tobey Maguire. Viewers of *The Good German* familiar with *Pleasantville* may note a striking similarity between Bud's do-good all-Americaness and that of Tully as he attempts to manipulate Jake (George Clooney) and mask his deeply disturbing sociopathic malevolence. In fact, this particular connection is apt to generate awareness of the roots and geopolitical implications of this do-good

Figure 3.2 Robert Downey Jr., Patricia Clarkson, George Clooney, David Strathairn and Matt Ross in *Good Night and Good Luck* (2005). Warner Independent/2929 Productions/The Kobal Collection/Melinda Sue Gordon.

all-Americaness, yielding, in the process, a kind of analytical pleasure. However, one reviewer recalls hearing fellow audience members burst into laughter at the sight of Spiderman having sex. Despite these inevitable slips, period casting can help situate a narrative in a specific era by recalling past performances, genres, films, star personas or constructs of glamour. As such, the actor—through looks, voice as well as mannerisms and movement—can do much to evoke and carry into a film nostalgia for these facets of cinema's past and the mythic or historical realities it purports to represent.

This survey has attempted to shed some light on the range of ways the cinema—in its widest application—uses and activates nostalgia. It is worth stressing that however potent popular music or opening montage sequences may be in generating longing for times past, rarely do films rely exclusively on just one strategy to induce nostalgia. As such some of the practices noted here will necessarily receive attention in the chapters that follow. For the remainder of this chapter, however, I will turn to theorizations of the nostalgia film and pay special attention to how visual pastness is identified as a defining feature and source of debate.

Nostalgia in Film Theory

For Fredric Jameson, *American Graffiti* is the inaugural nostalgia film (1991: 19). And, a quick glance at the scholarship confirms that Jameson's discussion of *American Graffiti* is the seminal text on the nostalgia film. It certainly remains one of the most cited passages, a theoretical cornerstone for countless engagements with nostalgic representations of the past and one that has left its mark on understandings of the concept. However, it is not the first. That distinction belongs to Marc Le Sueur, who published his 'Theory Number Five: Anatomy of Nostalgia Films: Heritage and Methods' in a 1977 issue of the *Journal of Popular Film*. Le Sueur's 'theory' is worth reintroducing to film studies, not only for how it prefigures Jameson, Boym and Grainge's definitions of nostalgia, but also for its characterization of 'deliberate archaism', a term ripe for recuperation in light of the surge of non-representational aesthetic or cinematographic codes in recent releases. It is the perfect term to describe the practice of filmmakers who make films to look like they have been made decades earlier (e.g., *Far From Heaven* and *The Good German*). Moreover, Le Sueur remains one of the early voices in cultural criticism who finds at work in nostalgia (including cinematic nostalgia) the potential for more than just reactionary fantasies obfuscating truth and history.

For Le Sueur, nostalgia is a 'concept of history', one for which 'few have attempted to establish the general working principles' (1977: 187). It is a way of engaging the past and bringing into the present that which other approaches to history ignore. He challenges criticisms issued during the 1970s in the popular American press that frame nostalgia as an exclusively conservative phenomenon, arguing instead that it is 'sometimes allied with very vital and assertive social and political currents' (1977: 188). Thus (and for the most part), he avoids conflating object and experience, pointing to both nostalgia's reactionary uses and its 'very important social effects'. To accommodate such politically divergent applications, Le Sueur splits nostalgia into two types: restorative and melancholic. 'Restorative nostalgia', much like Boym's term, represents a somewhat aggressive impulse motivating attempts to recapture and revitalize the past. He suggests that nostalgia attaches itself to aspects of the past which have not fully exhausted themselves, including practices and desires which continue to have relevance to the present. 'Melancholic nostalgia', like Boym's 'reflective nostalgia', is escapist in nature and characterized by wistful longings for what has become lost to time.

According to Le Sueur, Hollywood is the main purveyor of nostalgia and especially nostalgia of the melancholic kind. Defined by its 'essentially uncritical methodology [that] ... often creates a body of semi-truths', melancholic nostalgia tends to be escapist, presenting a highly romanticized image of the past and providing little analysis of these previous eras represented (1977: 189–92). However, like restorative nostalgia, it can also initiate new ways of interpreting and understanding history. In some instances a filmmaker or artist's nostalgic view of the past 'can force the viewer to a new awareness of the past by overcoming preconceptions one may have of certain epochs' (1977: 192). In other words, films can change what people think and how people feel about past events and eras. Like nostalgia itself, cinema's ability to persuade is not necessarily either inherently dangerous or inherently positive. While it may allow formerly suppressed histories to emerge in the public consciousness, it may also, as in the case of *American Graffiti*, supplant one set of myths with another: the 1950s as 'complacent' with the 1950s as 'optimistic' (1977: 192).

Le Sueur elaborates on Hollywood's melancholic nostalgia by charting how it induces wistful longing for times past. It does so, first and foremost, by emphasizing the 'prosaic clumsiness' of 'an archaic point in evolution' (1977: 189). In other words, nostalgia is experienced for eras historically unremarkable, devoid of momentous social or political events and, thus, characterized by simplicity and stability. For Le Sueur, the 1950s 'would seem to be the quintessential archaic period in and of itself' (1977: 191). Simplicity and stability certainly do figure into *mythic* conceptions of the 1950s. And nostalgia does indeed become attached to moments immediately preceding significant change. However, nostalgia also becomes attached—in the Hollywood imagination—to key historical conflicts like the American Civil War and the Second World War. As such, it is also aligned with the transformative events that bring about eras perceived (rightly or wrongly) to be stable and prosaic.

Thematic content is not the sole means by which a film participates in the construction of a melancholic nostalgia. Le Sueur identifies two key aesthetic strategies which also play an important role in evoking nostalgia: 'surface realism' and 'deliberate archaism'. Surface realism is produced through the use of period markers such as dress, cars and setting and is indicative of the obsession with period details characteristic of all nostalgic art (1977: 193). Flea markets and antiques fairs source the mise en scène of these films for which period verisimilitude is of utmost importance. Surface realism is an apt term for it suggests some doubt as to how 'real' the realism is or, more accurately, how deep it runs. On the surface, a film set in 1957 and populated with objects produced during this year might seek to claim the mantle of period authenticity. And yet, the public and private spaces of 1957 were not constituted by objects produced solely in 1957. A living room from that year (or 1927, 1977 or any other) would have inevitably contained items and traces from previous years and decades. This kind of surface realism may seem artificial and unsettling if one actually thinks about it. But I doubt this alone would be enough to disrupt belief in the authenticity of the world represented. Given the widespread practice of basing twentieth-century period recreations on mass media images, a mise en scène's realism may have more to do with its recognizability than anything else. That is, we may evaluate the realism of a 1950s setting on the basis of whether or not we recognize the objects within it as ones already contextualized by films or television programmes that identify the 1950s as their subject. Ironically, a Fifties milieu constructed with worn 1930s or 1940s objects to suggest poverty or thrift may not be read as authentic. For example, *Bastard Out of Carolina* (1996) clearly identifies the 1950s as its timeframe, but eschews all Fifties signifiers and nostalgic visual codes in favour of a dull and desaturated mise en scène to reinforce the poverty and violence suffered by a young girl in the rural South. However much it might authentically recreate one facet of postwar life, it may not be read as such by audiences used to a certain image of the 1950s.

'Deliberate archaism' describes the practice of creating what Le Sueur calls 'new-old films'. These films, which mine the 'memories of media forms' strive to recreate not only the look and feel of the period in question but also the appearance of art from that distant time (1977: 193–94). *American Graffiti*, for example, uses what Le Sueur describes as a garish jukebox aesthetic by reproducing the look of a 1950s film. To this we might add several recent variations of the practice including obsessive and faithful recreations of past media aesthetics. *Far From Heaven* mimics Douglas Sirk's postwar palette and use of colour for (melo)dramatic effect. *The Aviator* digitally replicates specific two- and three-colour Technicolor processes. *The Good German* was shot through 1940s lenses and with a single camera in order to look like a 1940s film. We should consider subtle allusions to past media aesthetics as accomplished by *Starship Troopers*' (1997) visual nod to early 1960s science fiction film or *Schindler's List*'s (1993) black-and-white aesthetic that seems to borrow from both 1940s documentary and fiction. The blending and retooling of past media forms—as foregrounded in *Sin City*'s 'B-noir meets comic book meets pulp novel cover' look and *Sky Captain and the World of Tomorrow*'s (2004) 'sepia tone meets full colour' look— also warrant a place among deliberately archaic practices. These kinds of cinematographic manipulations, ones employed in an effort to achieve visual or media pastness, is precisely what Jameson decries in his work on the nostalgia film. However, for Le Sueur, deliberate archaism does not necessarily entail that the film surrenders its capacity for critical exploration. Although he does not pursue this point further, he states that *American Graffiti*'s garish jukebox aesthetic either 'entails a healthy re-examination of old techniques and formats' or can 'result in a stylistic calcification' (1977: 195).

Le Sueur's willingness to acknowledge, however hesitantly, the potential for deliberate archaism to initiate healthy reexaminations of the past was considerably ahead of its time. As noted in chapter 1, it is only really within the last decade that cultural theorists and historians have started to reevaluate and recuperate nostalgia by recognizing its critical potential. Prior to this shift, two basic tendencies dominated analyses, ones by no means abandoned in light of these more recent reconceptualizations of nostalgia. The first aims to show that a film is nostalgic through its use of intertextual devices or flashbacks meant to evoke nostalgia in the spectator (Wollen 1991; Lury 2000). Often, the object of nostalgia is identified as a purportedly lost or threatened ideal such as a specific construct of nation, community, masculinity or femininity. Common also in literary criticism, this approach tends to focus on how narrative trajectories enact nostalgically motivated returns to past times and places.

The second tendency, originating out of Fredric Jameson's derisive commentary on postmodern nostalgia, involves evaluating the relationship between history and the nostalgia film. For Jameson, films that represent the past do so through assumptions and stereotypes rather than engaging with history in any sort of meaningful way. He argues that nostalgia films and nostalgic aesthetic modes (such as irony, parody and pastiche) displace 'real' history with the history of aesthetic styles. *Body Heat* (1981) and *American Graffiti*, for example, merely imbue the present with the quality of pastness (alluding to the 1930s and the 1950s respectively) but do not actually engage with the historical realities of these decades. Instead, they evoke an impression of what Jameson describes as '30sness' or '50sness' through the fashions and the styles of these eras, through surface realism and deliberate archaism. Jameson indicts postmodernism's aesthetic modes because they are deeply implicated in consumer capitalism and have managed to replace the modernist forms of art that once provided its viewers and readers with access to the past.

In an attempt to rescue postmodernism's aesthetic modes, Linda Hutcheon challenges Jameson to acknowledge that films using parody and irony to show the distance between the present and a past they purport to represent have the potential to reveal that 'there is no directly and accessible past 'real' for us today' (1989: 113). There is no 'real' (Marxist) history for Jameson to access in the first place. She explains that postmodern parody is a 'value-problematizing, de-naturalizing form of acknowledging the history (and through irony, the politics) of representation' (1989: 94). These films do not constitute evidence that contemporary society inhabits a 'perpetual present', as Jameson suggests, but instead reflect an obsession with history and a desire to find a way to know the past. But, while Hutcheon attempts to salvage parody from Jameson's dismissal of it as nostalgic escapism, she equates pastiche with nostalgia and labels both impotent in the pursuit of understanding history and our relation to it. For Hutcheon, pastiche is little more than an allusion to the past and lacks parody's capacity to interrogate the nature of our access to history.

Hutcheon's challenge to Jameson initiated a debate which has since become a popular reference point for discussions of nostalgia films. However, their debate is not about nostalgia itself, but rather which postmodern aesthetic modes should be classified as nostalgic. They *agree* that nostalgia fails to provide access to history and to the questions surrounding the role and nature of historical inquiry. Consequently, analyses, like Martin Hunt's work on Terence Davies' films, which ascribe epistemological or historiographic value to cinematic representations of the past (thereby supporting Hutcheon's view) are reluctant to identify these representations as nostalgic. Moreover, labelling serious engagements with the past 'parodic' or 'historiographical metafiction' and not nostalgic suggests that these are mutually exclusive, even oppositional categories. Reluctance to acknowledge nostalgia's presence also hinders investigation into how nostalgia works in tandem with other postmodern aesthetic modes. Nostalgia's critical potential is thus overlooked, facilitating its continued use as a pejorative adjective to describe the commodification of the past or meaningless allusions to historical eras and events.[11]

Whereas Paul Grainge has made an attempt to move beyond this debate in his study of how black-and-white images facilitate explorations of the politics of memory, Vera Dika rejects wholesale dismissals of nostalgia in favour of identifying resistant and oppositional practices at work in these films. Central to both these accounts is a focus on visual style and the visual image as the site and source of engagements with nostalgia. As such, they take as their starting point Jameson's definition of the nostalgia film. However, rather than join the chorus condemning its effacement of history, they explore the potential for nostalgic representations to teach us about the present's uses of the past.

Grainge provides a framework for thinking about a 'nostalgia mood' (which involves loss and longing) and a 'nostalgia mode' (which is devoid of affect and functions purely on an aesthetic level) with reference to American visual culture of the 1980s and 1990s. Though not mutually exclusive, Grainge's interest lies primarily in the nostalgia mode and how monochrome, as a non-representational code, is used in news magazines, global advertising, Hollywood film and syndicated television 'to establish and legitimate particular kinds of memory in American cultural life' (2002: 3). He rejects Jameson's critique that 'amnesia and historicist crisis' necessarily follow the creation of visual pastness (2002: 6). Grainge rightly points out that Jameson's model fails to take into account how audiences negotiate meaning and instead argues that 'meaningful narratives of history or cultural memory can be produced through the recycling and/or hybridization of past styles' (2002: 6).

Vera Dika suggests that nostalgia films which rework past genres and images in oppositional ways have the capacity to 'construct a new system of meanings through the critical displacement of its elements'

(2003: 121). In *Last Exit to Brooklyn* (1989) there is a disconnect between the visually recognizable Fifties and the narrative which 'foregrounds the ills of the 1950s' (2003: 142) According to Dika, this 'shatters the viewer's expectations' and 'allows us to reconsider some of the representational constructions from that era' (2003: 146). In other words, it forces us to acknowledge that the Fifties is a construct, a fabrication at odds with both cinematic and historical narratives involving race, gender and class. Key to Dika's argument is the location of nostalgia in the image, the result of what she identifies as the 'renewed status of the image' in contemporary culture (2003: 18). In fact, there is nothing outside the film's Fifties mise en scène that warrants its description as nostalgic. Surface realism alone is responsible for its classification as a nostalgia film.

This orchestrated disconnect between parts of a film to facilitate critical and oppositional readings is something Andrew Higson identifies in the crop of British heritage films produced during the Thatcher years (1979 to 1990). He argues that in films like *Chariots of Fire* (1981), *Another Country* (1984), *A Passage to India* (1985) and *A Room with a View* (1985) 'the past is displayed as visually spectacular pastiche, inviting a nostalgic gaze that resists the ironies and social critiques so often suggested narratively by these films' (1993: 109). For some critics, like Robert Hewison (1996), these films are simply part of a larger 'Heritage Industry' which has commodified an imperialist, upper-class past purged of social and political complexity. As a construct of 'nation' it has also been used in the service of conservative political rhetoric to distract from the economic turmoil of 1980s Britain and present a homogenized vision of Britishness at a time when multiculturalism was acknowledged as an integral and important part of national identity. However, as Higson argues, 'it would be wrong to suggest that these films resonate unequivocally with Thatcherite politics' for they are, in his estimation, 'too ambivalent to sit easily in such an equation and in various ways propose more liberal-humanist visions of social relations' (1993: 110).

In both the British heritage film and the American nostalgia film the components of surface realism (props and costume) and deliberate archaism are charged with sourcing spectacle, commodifying history and constructing escapist, reactionary visions of the past. But while they may invite classification as nostalgia films on this basis, according to Dika and Higson they retain the capacity to provide critical insight only through the use of carefully strategized narrative subversions. For Dika, *Grease* and *Badlands* (1973) share with *Last Exit to Brooklyn* the use of the Fifties as a visual construct to signify nostalgia but rely on character behaviour, dialogue, and narrative actions to analyze and deconstruct historical myths. In fact, she suggests that the 'emotional tone' of these films 'is better described as rage or despair' (2003: 55). However much rage and despair seem odd bedfellows for nostalgia, her assessment is consistent with Grainge's belief that nostalgia as an aesthetic mode is one wholly devoid of sentiment, longing or desire. Certainly this speaks to one important facet of contemporary nostalgia: the idea that it can be signified visually and without the generation of affect. This is indeed part of how we think about and use nostalgia today and how the label is deployed in film reviews published in the popular press and online. But in order to further develop our understanding of the nostalgia film, it is also necessary to reevaluate how visual strategies (beyond Grainge's black-and-white image) might provide critical insight into the relationship between the past and the present. That is, we need to consider how the visual dimensions of the cinema might be the source of both its nostalgic label *and* its critical consciousness when bolstered or even impeded by narrative and thematic content. We also need to think about films that seek to activate a nostalgia mood through aesthetic strategies in order to see how feeling and critical insight, as Richard Dyer (2007) has recently argued, are not necessarily divorced.

Jameson was half right in his condemnation of the nostalgia film. It is indeed very much about the visual. But, the visual—through the practices of surface realism and deliberate archaism—can be put to creative uses that initiate engagements with history, nostalgia and the uses of the past in the present. It can reveal something about our own historical consciousness and what we expect history to do for us. Even if not used in explicitly critical ways, the visual components of a 'nostalgia film' can often be read critically and oppositionally in a way that draws on the kind of history Jameson and others have thought evacuated from these kinds of representations. This is the aim of the following three chapters which discuss props, costume and deliberate archaism in turn.

Notes

1. The aspects of film responsible for visual pastness will be the subject of the following chapters.
2. With the help of the Internet Movie Database I have managed to compile a list of over 300 English-language films released since 1970 that have engaged in some ways with the Fifties and/or 1950s. In fact, the number of productions more than doubles each decade from about 30 in the 1970s to

over 60 in the 1980s to nearly 150 in the 1990s. Close to 100 have been released between 2000 and 2006.
3. Massey (2000) explains how Art Deco was one of several styles mediated by Hollywood which have also influenced style and design practices.
4. This slippage between truth and fiction is most forcefully articulated through the descriptions offered for the pieces for sale which provide information about Humphrey Bogart the person, his characters, the films in which he appeared and the film industry itself. Consider the text accompanying the 'Del Mar Floor Mirror': 'Del Mar is a famous thoroughbred racetrack where Bogart and other big-name celebrities spent time watching the races and betting on the horses. Del Mar's seaside locale near San Diego was an easy getaway from the prying eyes and cameras of Hollywood. Thoroughbred racing was one of the most glamorous of sports, and along with Santa Anita and Hollywood Park racetracks, Del Mar was popular with the Hollywood set of the 1930s and 40s.' The text and furniture is pitched primarily to male consumers, speaking to male experience, except in descriptions of bedroom furniture. The 'Leading Lady Vanity Stool' is contextualized by the following: 'Bogart's many movies included a Leading Lady of the calibre of Bette Davis, Katherine Hepburn, Audrey Hepburn, Gina Lollabrigida, Jennifer Jones, Claire Trevor, June Allyson, Ingrid Bergman, Barbara Stanwyck, Lizabeth Scot and more. But it was the young actress, Lauren Bacall that became Bogart's most famous leading lady and wife after they fell in love in 1945 while making the movie *To Have and Have Not*' (www.thomasville.com).
5. See especially Chapter 6, 'Audrey Hepburn, Nostalgia and Postfeminism in the 1990s' in Moseley 2002: 170–213.
6. See for example the following *New York Times* reports: 'Doomed City Palace Only a Ghost of Old' (14 April 1963: 391) and 'Tour into Nostalgia Recalls Splendors of Movies Palaces (25 September 1961: 35).
7. Nostalgia for the movie palace and viewing experience of yesteryear have been the subject of several films including *The Last Picture Show, Cinema Paradiso* (1988), and *The Long Day Closes* (1992).
8. Although Kuhn does not use the term in her analysis of cinema-going experiences, she does use nostalgia once to describe how the narrative of *Maytime* (1937) finds its equivalent in its audiences' bittersweet longing for an unattainable object—its now deceased stars (2002: 212).
9. For a discussion of these specific films see Flinn 1992: 108–110.
10. I take this expression from Barthes (1977).
11. For examples of pejorative uses of the term in cultural criticism see Wood (1974), Graham (1984) and Birkerts (1989).

Chapter 4

Sin City: Reading the Tails of a Populuxe Prop

Outside the city limits of Amarillo, Texas on land owned by helium tycoon Stanley Marsh III, ten Cadillacs are buried in a row—fins up (Figure 4.1). Known as the 'Cadillac Ranch', this site-specific installation was commissioned by Marsh in 1973 and completed in 1974 by Ant Farm, a collective of artists whose core members included Chip Lord, Doug Michels and Curtis Schreier.[1] These ten Cadillacs represent the evolution of the tail fin from 1949 to 1963, a sculptural catalogue of ten model changes that resulted in ever higher fins until 1959 when they gradually started to shrink.

Cadillac Ranch is a testament to conspicuous consumption that simultaneously critiques and celebrates its product. For the members

Figure 4.1 Ant Farm's 'Cadillac Ranch', 1974. The Art Archive/Global Book Publishing.

of Ant Farm who vividly recall much anticipated trips as children to witness the arrival of the latest models, the Cadillac tail fin embodies the imaginative—almost utopian—design impulse that characterizes their own works of radical architecture and design. Chip Lord describes Cadillac Ranch as a 'tribute to the tailfin and tailfin culture in a kind of loving way'. But he also suggests that it functions as a critique of planned obsolescence, one communicated most aptly and directly through the act of burial. Ant Farm members (as well as their critics) speculate that Cadillac Ranch is perhaps the best-known work of public art, owing to its proximity to Route 66, a series of promotional ventures initiated by the artists and, perhaps most importantly, the 'cultural baggage' attached to the car (Lord, in Lewallen and Seid 2004: 71).

This 'cultural baggage' is at the root of the tail-finned car's ubiquity and longevity as a filmic prop. Along with poodle skirts and colourful streamlined appliances, it is instantly recognizable as belonging to the Fifties and, more specifically, the Populuxe Fifties. Its cultural baggage is its dominant cultural meaning which, thanks to the logic of postwar conspicuous consumption, is inscribed quite clearly in its form. As noted in chapter 2, the tail-finned car functions as a motivated signifier. Elements of its design mimic those of a rocket, eliciting connotations of futurity, expansionism and technological supremacy. Its monstrous size and superfluous chrome betray an indulgence in ostentation and abundance. Bright, flashy colours speak to postwar optimism, signalling an end to the serious and grim war years, while frequent design changes conferred status on those dutiful consumers who wished to communicate their prosperity and, by extension, their patriotism by changing their car regularly.

That this specific load of cultural baggage should remain so firmly attached to the tail-finned car has much to do with its place in the discourses of postwar consumer capitalism and futurity as well as the way in which these two discourses intersected. Postwar America's interest in the future was not purely scientific. It was also political and economic. A passion for space travel, deliberately encouraged by the government-run space programme, translated into the promotion of a certain brand of Cold War political ideology. The space race and conspicuous consumption were of equal importance to defeating the Soviets. 'Conspicuous' is significant here because it reveals the reliance of postwar economic logic on the visual attributes of consumer goods. Products had to look the part. They had to flaunt their own obsolescence and convey the idea that a society replacing its cars and major appliances on the basis of colour alone *must* be prosperous. This sentiment was further reinforced by a marketing rhetoric that trumpeted the wide reach of prosperity. The explicit message was that everyone in the United States owned a suburban bungalow filled with the newest domestic technologies and proudly parked the latest model of car in the driveway for all to see. These 'good citizens' heeded their patriotic duty to spend, to select for purchase goods that visually proclaimed progress, prosperity and faith in the future.

However, objects and images signifying futurity were also tempered by traces of the past. Madison Avenue responded to fears about too much newness by providing assurances that however innovative the product on offer, it remained linked to tradition. Some of these links were accomplished aesthetically by incorporating familiar design features like streamlining which, by the 1950s, was already retro-futuristic. Others were accomplished by stressing the object's traditional function. For example, aspects of the tail-finned car's design may have seemed futuristic, but its function to provide increased mobility was hardly anything new. Attempts to equate driving with space flight and space exploration appeared to be little more than subtly revised versions of the frontier myth. Rugged individualism, unhampered mobility and conquest of an untamed nature were central elements of this mythology and were often evoked in the automobile advertising of the period.

The present chapter will focus on the tail-finned car as a key prop in order to suggest how its cultural baggage (or 'cultural significance' as I will explain in a moment) plays an integral role in generating meaning and facilitating critique. I will begin with a few comments on the state of prop scholarship in order to carve out a place for the type of canonical object employed in film *because* of its cultural baggage: specifically, reified commodities that have circulated widely in nostalgic representations (including films) and the nostalgia industry. Then, following a brief discussion of how films released since the 1970s register shifts in this prop's use, I will focus on how *Sin City*'s tail-finned cars bring the Populuxe Fifties into visual (and, to a point, ideological) collision with other nostalgic constructs mobilized in the film. *Sin City* is an easy target for criticisms of the Jamesonian variety including intertextual indulgence and the displacement of real history with the history of aesthetic styles.[2] However, I will explore how the visual strategies that identify it as a nostalgia film also have the capacity to initiate oppositional readings. Specifically, I plan to trace the (economic) logic attached to the tail-finned car through the *Sin City* world. Doing so reveals how this prop functions as a conduit to the meanings, myths and histories that serve to demystify Populuxe itself and, in the process, yield analytical and archaeological pleasures for the engaged, critical spectator.

Props and Their Cultural Significance

Props rarely take centre-stage in film criticism. Instead they enter into discussions about mise en scène, production design and genre categories in narrative fiction film.[3] In these analyses collections of certain types of props are said to define and distinguish Westerns from, say, science fiction or film noir. A key prop may function as the object of a quest or become associated with a specific character. Such props become invested with particular meanings through the course of the film, functioning as clues to plot direction and providing insight into characters' states of mind.[4] But however significant, visually isolated or narratively foregrounded certain props may appear, they also interact with other elements in the production of meaning. Gibbs stresses that while it is 'important to consider each element's potential for expression ... it is worth remembering from the outset that these elements are most productively thought of in terms of their *interaction* rather than individually—in practice, it is the interplay of elements that is significant' (2002: 26).

As part of the mise en scène and as falling under the jurisdiction of the production designer, props (whether key or filler) are indeed only one component of the overall look or 'visual concept' of a film.[5] They tend to be mobilized in conjunction with other cinematic strategies to serve distinct narrative ends, to say something about a place or to convince us of the authenticity of a particular historical period. However, as C.S. Tashiro rightly points out, props, as objects, also 'exist independently of a story ... and have their own string of associations' (1998: 9). As such, 'there will always be a number of interpretative possibilities attached to them that have nothing to do with their narrative function' (1998: 11). Latent meanings may even disrupt narrative continuity or introduce unexpected 'semantic sour notes' (1998: 11).

My interest here is in the sorts of props whose latent meanings become manifest by virtue of their very nature and design as well as how they are visually and narratively foregrounded. Rather than introduce unanticipated 'sour notes', these props arrest narrative continuity in a way that provides viewers with the opportunity to consider the strings of associations attached to them and how these associations might generate additional layers of meaning. In the case of the tail-finned car, for example, these associations have been inscribed into the form of the object and reinforced through relatively consistent uses in film, television and print since it first rolled off the assembly line. In Fifties nostalgia films, the car's association with the Fifties and its privileged place in the visual grammar and economy of nostalgia make it useful in the production of both meaning and affect. Whether employed as a prop for the purposes of nostalgic indulgence, exploration or critique, the tail-finned car is the kind of object that cannot easily shed its associations or the traces of meaning it accrued through its travels across various temporal and media contexts. Nor can it be wholly divorced from its original function as a commodity signifying the logic of American postwar consumer capitalism. Moreover, depending on the spectator's investment in the car and the Fifties, the sight of tail fins can evoke nostalgia, signify nostalgia or enable an awareness of the type of feeling one is being coaxed into experiencing.

At this point it is useful to turn to design history and briefly address the ways in which objects and design features accumulate meaning. Whereas print advertisements juxtaposing cars with rockets demonstrated in no uncertain terms the source and significance of the tail fin, other, less literal adaptations also grant access to specific sets of meanings and histories. For example, Dick Hebdige has shown that streamlining can mobilize a whole set of ideologically charged connotations with meanings encoded both at the design and production stage (1988: 58). In other words, streamlining signifies more than just futurity. It also speaks to its own history and the factors enabling its development including advancements in pressed steel technology (stamping), the emergence of new consumer markets, and the force with which curvilinear design served as a response to the ruling functionalist orthodoxy. Hebdige elaborates:

> The fact that stamping technology made it easier to produce curved forms ... meant that this innovation and the increased rationalisation of the production process which went with it could literally *declare itself in form*, could advertise through its very newness those quantitative and qualitative breaks that had been made in the production process, in the scale of production and in the size of the potential market to which 'streamlined' products were to be directed. (1988: 63, emphasis added)

With this, Hebdige manages to heed an important warning directed against design historians by Adrian Forty in his influential book, *Objects of Desire* (1986). Forty argues that the tendency to confuse art and design or talk about designers in the same way *some* art historians have talked about artists obscures the role that social and economic pressures play in the construction and manufacture of designed goods. Where social contexts are considered they are done so unsatisfactorily and the 'history' offered remains, for the most part, 'ornamental' (Forty 1986: 8). In these analyses the designer is privileged as the 'author' of the object, the source of its look and meaning. This results in a failure to consider how objects are related to their historical context and how they reflect the myths and desires of the society that produced them. The designed object's power to communicate myths and meaning has much to do with the fact that 'unlike the more or less ephemeral media, design has the capacity to cast myths into an enduring, solid and tangible form, so that they seem to be reality itself' (Forty 1986: 9).

Forty's study provides ample evidence of how the social, political, economic and cultural context in which an object is produced comes to bear on the design of the object and thus how the object reflects—through its visual qualities—the conditions of its production. However, his account fails to consider how an object's circulation in specific contexts inflects and informs the various meanings, myths and histories inscribed in its form. In other words, Forty's account does not extend to the object's life after production or how the passage of time and the passage of the object through a variety of contexts leave their mark on it. Admitting an object's multiple and potentially divergent uses certainly complicates any attempt to arrive at its meaning. This is a problem Hebdige acknowledges through a series of questions he poses at the outset of his analysis of the Vespa. He asks how it is we might arrive at a comprehensive understanding of an object's multiple meanings, functions and values as well as how we might provide an account of what it means to groups of users separated geographically or temporally (Hebdige 1988: 80).

Hebdige answers these questions with a convincing account of how dominant meanings emerge to define an object's 'cultural significance'. His interest is specifically in the Vespa as a semiotic sign and how this sign is consumed in the British national imagination. He offers a detailed history of the conditions of production and marketing of the Vespa, reviewing the factors driving its invention and the reasons for its popularity in Italy. Hebdige then traces the Vespa's export to Britain and suggests how its meaning was derived from the various ways in which it was received, whether with esteem or derision, as well as how its crossover into a new geopolitical context resulted in additional connotations, most notably 'Italianness' and 'Continental style'. A variety of factors, including its streamlined design, its technological strengths and limitations, the increased autonomy it offered women and motorcycle enthusiasts' denunciation of it as inferior all fed into the 'Vespa myth' or, in other words, the scooter's full cultural significance: 'the sum total of all the choices and fixings made at each stage in the passage of the object from conception, production and mediation to mass-circulation, sale and use' (Hebdige 1988: 82).

Like the tail-finned car, the Vespa has also enjoyed a notable career as a key prop in the cinema. Its iconic status renders it instantly recognizable in films produced on both sides of the Atlantic, from the 1950s through to the present, including *An American in Paris* (1951), *Roman Holiday* (1953), *Alfie* (1966, 2004), *American Graffiti*, *Absolute Beginners* (1986), *Austin Powers* (1997) and *The Interpreter* (2005). Drawing to varying extents on its Italianness or Sixties countercultural Britishness, these films depend on its cultural significance (or 'cultural baggage') to tell us about the characters who ride them and the worlds they inhabit. In these instances, the Vespa has the potential to speak its history and meanings, shaped in part by its life and uses as a material object and by the various contexts in which it has appeared. Its interaction with other elements in the mise en scène as well as its cinematographic framing and narrative contextualization will inevitably inflect its meanings in any given scene or film. However, like the tail-finned car, it comes attached to a string of associations that cannot be easily discarded. Like the tail-finned car, it is used so often precisely because of its reliability in communicating a set of dominant meanings.

Tail Fins Through Tinted and Critical Lenses

In one particularly rich and, given the focus of this discussion, auspicious example, a tail-finned car and a Vespa come into collision figuratively (and nearly literally) in the opening scene of *American Graffiti*. A stilled image of Steve (Ron Howard) leaning against his prized tail-finned car in the parking lot of Mel's Drive-in provides the backdrop for the opening credits. The first *moving* image tracks Terry the Toad (Charles Martin Smith) as he rides his Vespa past Steve and crashes it into the vending machines positioned near the entrance of the diner. These vehicles are used to say something about the characters with whom they are associated. Steve is self-assured and popular, the high school president, the kind of 'all-American' teenager who has a beautiful girlfriend with whom he is destined to live the American Dream. Terry is a quintessential nerd without any discernable smarts, uncomfortable in his own skin, clumsy, socially awkward and resigned to living a life marked by humiliation and insecurity. While Terry's friends drive meticulously detailed tail-finned cars and souped-up trucks,[6] Terry is stuck driving what has been coded through use and representation as a 'girl's bike', one that he is incapable of controlling; according to Debbie (Candy Clark), it is 'almost a motorcycle'.

These vehicles contribute more to the film than confirming character personalities, qualities and social position. They also reinforce its narrative engagement with nostalgia. As George Lucas explains, *American Graffiti* is a movie about cruising, a uniquely American sociocultural phenomenon that defined teenage culture during the 1950s.[7] Polished chrome and freshly waxed (*car*) bodies are displayed by males as the plumage to attract females in this rather bizarre mating ritual. By focusing on this activity specifically, Lucas aimed to document for posterity a facet of personal and collective history. Indeed *American Graffiti*'s 'natural' performances and use of Techniscope for its visible grain and desaturated colours contribute much to the film's 'documentary' feel. And while the film's diegetic and non-diegetic use of recognizable popular songs contribute to its period authenticity, cars too remain central to its construction of surface realism. In fact, the majority of the movie takes place either in or around cars. They are fetishized through long-held shots and close-ups and talked about at length by the central characters. They also have transformative power. After Steve entrusts Terry to look after his car, Terry gains confidence and attracts the attention of a beautiful woman (Figure 4.2). For Lucas, whose main concern is with the experiences of young heterosexual men, the film centred as much on the relationship between these teenagers and their cars as it did on their relationship with rock 'n' roll.

The film's use of popular music has been heralded as an innovation in filmmaking and one of the key factors determining its classification as a 'nostalgia film'. As such analyses have tended to privilege soundtrack over props, only acknowledging the car radio as the source of 1950s hit songs. This ignores other, more important connections between music and tail-finned cars. According to Lucas, one of the central aims of the film was to acknowledge the distillation of 'old innocent rock 'n' roll' by the British invasion. This clash of cultures is not articulated musically or narratively. It is communicated entirely through the juxtaposition of Terry's Vespa and Steve's tail-finned car.

The image of Steve leaning against his car in Mel's parking lot is instantly recognizable as a snapshot of Fifties (and 1950s) youth culture. It documents a moment in time captured and preserved. But the drive-in diner and tail-finned car, framed for contemplation, accompanied by 'Rock Around the Clock' and dimly lit by the fading light of dusk, belong to an era about to pass.[8] Time itself is arrested, but only temporarily. Whatever reminiscence this frozen image evokes is abruptly disturbed by the injection of movement—Terry's crashing entrance into the scene. The Fifties is intruded upon by the Sixties and specifically the British counterculture, signified and embodied by the Vespa. Here the Vespa functions as the harbinger of a sudden change in music and teen culture. It signals to the audience of 1973 (and audiences since) that rock 'n' roll, diners and cruising would all be supplanted by new sounds, originating primarily from the UK, and new sets of social practices. *American Graffiti* activates the strings of associations accrued by the Vespa through its use in British film and youth culture, ones often closely associated with Swinging London: Mods, sexual promiscuity, the hedonistic lifestyles popularized by films like *Alfie* and *Casino Royale* (1967), the music of the Beatles and the Rolling Stones, and fashion trends such as Mary Quant's miniskirt.

Figure 4.2 Charles Martin Smith as Terry the Toad driving Steve's tail-finned car in *American Graffiti* (1973). Lucasfilm/Coppola Co./Universal/The Kobal Collection.

While the tail-finned car represents the (American) Fifties as it was constructed and propagated in the nostalgia economy of the 1970s, the Vespa signifies the start of the invasion of the British counterculture and the inevitable adulteration of a 'pure' American way of life. Through its association with Terry, the Vespa also presages what the film implies is the emasculation of Fifties American culture by the 1960s. However, British music and Vespas alone did not comprise this 1960s threat. The American Women's Movement, Gay Rights and Civil Rights Movement that sought to challenge the hegemony (and normativity) of the white heterosexual male hover at the edges of the film as unacknowledged sources of protest against the Fifties. Whether by foreign or domestic forces, Terry is eventually reemasculated at the end of the film. After enjoying a flirtation with status and virility enabled by his guardianship of Steve's tail-finned car, Terry returns to his Vespa and, we surmise, his original socially awkward and insecure self. Almost immediately thereafter we learn of his participation in Vietnam and thus his involvement in the conflict that severely eroded confidence in the United States' military prowess. *American Graffiti* mourns the loss of the virile masculinity embodied in the tail-finned car and the way of life it represented. It also laments the impossibility of living the American Dream in a 1960s world inalterably changed through social protest. According to the film, Steve and his car no longer have a place in this new America.

American Graffiti helped to reinforce the dominant cultural meanings inscribed in the tail-finned car. It appealed to and underscored its cultural significance in a way that placed it firmly within the robust Fifties nostalgia economy of the early 1970s. This film also helped make possible the car's later central role in critiques of the Fifties and nostalgia itself. For example, the tail-finned car's recognizability and reliability as a signifier for postwar prosperity and optimism (among other things) rendered it a potent prop in horror films and an easy target for those angered, frustrated or bored by the ubiquity of the Fifties.

Stephen King's *Christine* (1983), starring a homicidal 1957 Plymouth Fury, is one of the earliest examples of this tendency.[9] The film opens with a flashback set in 1957 in a Detroit car assembly plant (Figure 4.3). Christine's bright, rich red colour immediately stands out in this hazy, nostalgia-coded milieu.[10] The car's appetite for murder is established at the outset as is its practice of playing a 1950s pop song just before the kill. Like Terry the Toad, Arnie Cunningham (Keith Gordon)—a name that instantly evokes the Cunninghams of *Happy Days* fame—is transformed through his possession of the car. Once a hapless social outcast subjected to constant abuse by high school bullies, ownership of Christine transforms him first into a confident and assertive individual and eventually into a ruthless killer.

The murderous rampages executed by Christine are all the more shocking because of the car's association with the Fifties and, by extension, the ways in which the Fifties circulated as a Golden Age in the popular and visual culture of the 1970s. Despite the film's simple use of contradiction to heighten the horror, certain cinematic strategies complicate the effect, including how the Fifties permeates the film. As Arnie becomes increasingly attached to Christine he transforms not only his behaviour, but also his look to accord with the styles and fashions of the 1950s. In other words, he is seduced not just by the car, but by the era the car represents. The fact that his investment in the Fifties leads him to lose his moral compass serves to critique the wave of early 1980s Fifties nostalgia, especially Reagan's use of the Fifties as a beacon of morality.

However, the film also suggests an awareness of the mediated nature of the Fifties including its origins and uses in film and television. The knife fight in shop class early in the film recalls a similar confrontation staged in *Rebel Without a Cause* (1955). Buddy

Figure 4.3 The 1957 Plymouth Fury on the assembly line in *Christine* (1983). Columbia/The Kobal Collection.

(William Ostrander) looks and behaves like the quintessential Greaser, smashing what Keith Gordon describes as Arnie's 'Buddy Holly glasses'—thick black rimmed glasses held together with tape. Arnie's friend Dennis (John Stockwell), the handsome all-American jock who bears more than a passing resemblance to the 1950s teen stars, comes to his defence. But this sequence alludes to more than just *Rebel Without a Cause*. It also directly references *American Graffiti*. Arnie is Terry resurrected who, as noted, becomes transformed through his possession of a tail-finned car. Steve and Dennis are the unlikely friends of social outcasts who feel compelled to protect them. John (Paul Le Mat) and Buddy are the Greasers, tough and threatening, but ultimately harmless. *Christine* thus recycles the iconic sequences and characters of 1950s cinema as well as 1970s nostalgic representations of the Fifties (e.g., *American Graffiti, Happy Days* and *Grease*). That *Christine* is set in the late 1970s rather than the film's own present just a few years later is particularly telling and further aligns the film with Fifties nostalgia from this decade.

These strategies and intertextual references suggest a degree of self-consciousness about the Fifties as a mediated, nostalgic construct. That the film's critique of this construct is effected through the visual and material culture at the heart of the 1970s nostalgia industry, facilitates an engagement with nostalgia itself and an awareness of the capacity for key props to generate critique. This critique may ultimately fail to provide a nuanced assessment of some of the Fifties' more insidious uses. Nevertheless, *Christine* does represent an important first step in cinematic deconstructions of Fifties nostalgia by using the canonical objects with which it is associated.

A more sophisticated critique of the Fifties as a nostalgic construct is launched through the tail-finned car in *The Reflecting Skin* (1990). Here the use of the car helps to challenge and deconstruct its conventional signification. The film replaces the Fifties with an image of 1950s America that resembles a catalogue of deviance, from behaviour considered taboo in certain times and places (such as the expression of female sexuality) to acts universally condemned (such as child murder). The arrival of the tail-finned car initiates a series of crimes committed by its passengers and by the inhabitants of the small rural town they visit. It is the first distinct period marker in a mise en scène devoid of 1950s signifiers and thus its 'newness' stands in stark contrast to the 'oldness' of the milieu. It is a harbinger of horror that exposes the violence, misery and cruelty marring the type of landscape represented as idyllic in the majority of films that announce their setting as 1950s America. Yet, the tail-finned car's recognizability as a signifier of the Fifties is what permits it to function as a site of contestation. As an object culturally inscribed with consumerist desire it can be fetishized through framing in order to render explicit this desire for the purpose of critique. Long-held shots that survey its form from every angle to foreground its desirability and fetish potential render it strange and sinister in a narrative about unchecked desires ruthlessly pursued.

As a privileged object in the construction of the Fifties (and especially the Populuxe Fifties), the tail-finned car has travelled widely across popular visual media. The remarkable force with which it communicates its cultural significance has ensured its continued survival. Its uses are varied and have shifted between eliciting nostalgic experiences to criticizing nostalgia and its constructs. One might expect these shifts to compromise its semiotic force, to redefine it as a free-floating signifier. However, this has not yet happened. Critiques of nostalgia may animate the tail-finned car as a sinister force or help characterize its passengers as malevolent. But this does not depend any less on its connection to the Fifties as a nostalgic construct than do unabashedly sentimental celebrations of the car. The tail-finned car also retains its semiotic force for another reason. While its diverse associations may impress themselves on viewers familiar with *Christine* (or, say, Marilyn Manson's video for 'Tainted Love') informing subsequent encounters with this prop, many recent releases—including those expressly intertextual—have opted to ignore its more critical uses. This is the case with *Sin City*.

Sin City: Femmes Fatales, Tail-finned Cars and the Clash of (Nostalgic) Constructs

Sin City (co-directed by Frank Miller and Robert Rodriguez) is a faithful cinematic translation of three of Frank Miller's graphic novels (*The Hard Goodbye, The Big Fat Kill, That Yellow Bastard*) with a fourth short story, *The Customer is Always Right*, providing the source for the prologue to the film. The film exploits the aesthetic and narrative conventions of B-noirs like *Detour* (1945) and *Kiss Me Deadly* (1955), Will Eisner comics and pulp novel covers of the same period. It also revives, in caricature, the characters that populated these dystopian postwar worlds as well as their ways of speaking and interacting. However, it is rarely classified as neo-noir or considered in relation to *Chinatown* (1974), *Body Heat, L.A. Confidential* or *Hollywoodland*. Instead, it attracts the label 'hyper-noir' to suggest an over-the-top, excessive indulgence in the conventionalized visual and narrative tropes of noir.[11]

Little is left unstylized in this film. The cinematography, editing, characters, acting, dialogue, action sequences, violence and mise en scène clearly emanate from the hyperbolized world of comics, a quality Rodriguez was keen to preserve. For him, *Sin City* dialogue 'doesn't sound like screenplay dialogue' and the film 'doesn't move like a normal movie would'. The camera often tilts or tracks upward to capture in 1.85:1 aspect ratio the portrait orientation of many of Miller's drawings, a strategy which emphasizes the verticality of the space. Though predominantly black and white, the film's monochromatic palette rarely fades from consciousness as it might in *Good Night and Good Luck*. Injections of saturated primary colour, the use of white silhouettes against a black background and shifts in the degree of tonal contrast all ensure that the 'black and whiteness' of the film remains foregrounded (Figure 4.4).[12]

Admittedly *Sin City* may seem an odd choice for a case study in a book about nostalgia. Critics quite rightly and accurately describe it as a 'deeply unwholesome guignol fantasy' (Bradshaw 2005), 'an inhumane film' (French 2005), one dominated by 'gleeful sadism' (Chocano 2005). It is also disturbingly misogynistic in its violence and characterizations. Nevertheless, it satisfies recent definitions of the 'nostalgia film' as discussed in the previous chapter. For example, it exhibits features of Grainge's 'nostalgia mode' through its use of black and white as a non-representational code. In this instance monochrome may not perform a legitimating function; however, it does engage with the politics of memory and operates in ways that suggest the nostalgia mode in a film that is ostensibly all style need not be divorced from the nostalgia mood. Despite the film's palpable inhumanity, the nostalgia mode facilitates a nostalgia mood for past aesthetic forms and the variety of worlds and social relations described by them.

Sin City's deliberate archaism and use of visual cues to signify a series of mid-twentieth-century moments also situates it within a contemporary nostalgia economy. And like *Last Exit to Brooklyn*, these visual strategies may allow us to reconsider some of the representational constructions that emerged during the eras to which the film alludes (Dika 2003: 146). Rather than simply offer a series of disconnected samplings of noir, comics and pulp novel covers as an exercise in postmodern quotation, *Sin City* mobilizes visual references to these forms in a way that reveals (likely unintentionally) how each of these genres was part of a larger, interconnected system of representation that registered wartime and postwar anxieties about gender and sexuality. Whereas Lucille (Carla Gugino) and The Customer (Marley Shelton) are modelled on the femmes fatales of film noir, Wendy/Goldie (Jaime King) and Gail (Rosario Dawson) stepped off the covers of pulp novels and the pages of comics, respectively. They speak to the ways in which the femme fatale stereotype has necessarily been inflected by the formal and narrative conventions of the media forms it inhabits. However, as we shall see, *Sin City* mobilizes its representational constructions in a way that is arguably more complex (and convoluted) than *Last Exit to Brooklyn* which, as we recall, pits a nostalgic-looking Fifties against a series of characters and narrative events at odds with this Fifties world. *Sin City* offers up a varied array of visual styles, props and character types that fade in and out of alignment with one another, at times creating cohesive 'film noir' sequences while at other times fusing the conventions of Japanese Samurai films, postwar automobile advertising, contemporary video games and monsters from the Marvel comic universe.

Whether the act of foregrounding the femme fatale's multiple and divergent expressions ultimately demystifies or celebrates this particular construct is, at points, difficult to ascertain and ultimately depends on individual viewers' readings and investments. *Sin City* is often overwhelmed with shots designed to fetishize breasts and legs, to link sex with death, sadism with sexual pleasure. But by virtue of its sometimes faithful evocations of the language of film noir, it facilitates recognition of the ambiguity surrounding the empowerment of its female characters. In some instances this arises out of deliberate attempts to frame women, most notably the prostitutes of 'Old Town', as self-governing warriors with agency. They exist as a kind of post-feminist, hyper femme fatale, women dressed in S&M fetish gear whose power is derived from sex and their resolve to indiscriminately shoot or dismember those who threaten their autonomy.

In other instances *Sin City*'s deconstruction of the femme fatale seems almost accidental. Despite Rodriguez's delight that Brittany Murphy 'nailed the [film noir] genre', her performance as Shellie is highly uneven, resulting in a series of individuated moments that run the gamut from captivating to wrenching to laughable. This inconsistency, resulting as much from her forced acting style as from the inane dialogue written for her, generates two distinct effects. Her delivery of lines functions as a misplaced comic diversion that jarringly detracts from the menace of Jackie Boy (Benecio del Toro) and the disturbing ways in which he degrades, threatens and physically assaults Shellie. However, it also renders strange, and at times wholly unbelievable, her nonchalance about 'being slapped around' (as she says), thus drawing attention to the excessive use of this trope in *Sin City* and its status *as a trope* in postwar film noir. Perhaps, in the end, Murphy's acting, which is difficult not to read as spoofing rather than imitating noir acting, functions as an alibi that seeks to excuse the film's coarse misogyny. It also announces as particularly and peculiarly filmic that which remains for many a brutal reality.

However much *Sin City* may ostensibly cater to a series of heterosexual male fantasies, some juvenile, others perverse and discomfiting, the film does present, arguably in spite of itself, opportunities to read against the grain, to read into the film's femmes fatales their cinematic, literary, and comic book origins and to see them as over-determined constructs. Likewise, *Sin City*'s use of the tail-finned car—itself somewhat over-determined—may also provide insight into the complex and critical uses of nostalgic constructs in film. But my reason for introducing the femme fatale in a discussion about the tail-finned car stems from more than a desire to argue for how both function ambivalently and in a way that has the potential (albeit at times slight) to demystify certain ideological constructs. It also stems from a desire to make sense of the effects of the film's distinct gendering of the cars as well as from the filmmakers' classification of female characters as props(!).

'Booze, Broads and Guns: The Props of *Sin City*' is the title of a special feature on the recut and extended DVD version of the film, which takes it name from another of Frank Miller's graphic novels. This special feature, like several others including 'Trench Coats and Fishnets: The Costumes of *Sin City*', 'Making the Monsters: Special Effects Make-Up' and the 'All Green Screen Version', attempts to shed light on how the look of the film was achieved. Prop coordinator Steve Joyner explains that while the props used are 'based on life', they all have a '*Sin City* twist' to them. He suspects that there is 'probably not a single off-the-shelf product in the movie'. And while it certainly seems as though the property team manufactured every object encountered in the *Sin City* world from weapons and torture devices to the odd piece of mid-century modern furniture, one group of props did in fact come directly 'off the shelf'—the cars. These cars are not mentioned in this segment, but according to the filmmakers they deserved their own featurette: 'A Hard Top With a Decent Engine: The Cars of *Sin City*'.

The featurette stresses what a single viewing of the film confirms: the cars are important characters in the story. They are subject to close-ups, long takes, pans and tracking shots that survey their form and design elements from every angle. They are named, described, discussed and provide some of the few moments of colour in this otherwise black-and-white film. Most cars are from the 1950s, especially those associated with key characters. Hartigan (Bruce Willis) drives a 1955 Buick Convertible, Dwight (Clive Owen) a 1959 Cadillac Convertible and 1957 Ford Thunderbird, Nancy (Jessica Alba) a 1957 Chevy Nomad, Wendy a 1955 Porsche Spyder Convertible and Jackie Boy a 1957 Chrysler Imperial. Virtually every key character is filmed driving and, without fail, driving a vehicle unique to them. These cars are vitally important in conveying to us information about the characters and help us to determine their place in the *Sin City* world. And crucially, this is accomplished in part by appealing to the cultural connotations associated with specific vehicles.

Cars are used in each of *Sin City*'s three main stories to varying degrees and effect. What remains consistent throughout the entire film however, is how these key props inform a distinct series of intersecting binary oppositions that pit masculine against feminine, foreign against domestic, vintage against modern. Female characters tend not to drive the kinds of 1950s American tail-finned cars associated with male characters like Dwight, Hartigan, Jackie Boy and Bob (Michael Madsen). Wendy drives a small European car and Dallas a backless, hearse-shaped 1941 Chevy. In the recut, extended version, Lucille is seen driving a vintage Volkswagen Beetle. Only Nancy, arguably the female protagonist in *Sin City*, drives a tail-finned car. Hers, however, is a Chevy Nomad station wagon, a car coded feminine by postwar advertising (as discussed in chapter 2) and its uses since (e.g., *Far From Heaven*).

With the exception of Jackie Boy, the villains of *Sin City* drive foreign cars and, typically, ones removed in period or styling from the 1950s. For instance, Roark Jr. drives a 1962 Jaguar (British), Mr Shlubb a 1989 Ferrari (Italian) and the corrupt Priest a 1990 Mercedes (German). All solicit negative comment. The Jaguar is faulted for its 'short-lived durability' and capacity to provide only 'cheap thrills'. The Ferrari is described as impractical by Klump who asks, 'Where in this most streamlined and trunkless of transports ... are we to deposit our recently deceased cargo?' And the Mercedes prompts Marv to complain, 'modern cars—they all look like electric shavers'.[13] Thus, while central male characters tend to drive 1950s American-made cars, female characters and the film's villains are associated with foreign automobiles or ones characterized as too 'modern' (from the late 1980s and early 1990s) or too old (from the 1930s and early 1940s). This draws on existing and already well-entrenched binaries that equate, in certain facets of the American popular and cultural consciousness, Europeanness with the feminine and, by extension, Americanness with a kind of virile masculinity.[14]

While the types of cars used reinforce a series of (highly problematic) binary oppositions, the colouring of select vehicles also implicates the film in mythic, nostalgic and *historical* discourses. To further this discussion, I will focus on one story, 'The Big Fat Kill'. But before that, I would like to emphasize that while some of the filmmakers' intentions with respect to the inclusion of colour or framing will be noted, I am more interested in the effects generated by their decisions. In particular I want to explore how foregrounding culturally loaded objects as props with their own cinematic and social histories can initiate critical engagements with the Fifties and nostalgia. In other words, it is of little use to this discussion than Rodriguez and Miller admit constructing shots for no other reason than they would 'look cool' or use colour, as they vaguely claim, 'to highlight an idea'. Moreover, the effects generated by allowing Dwight's Cadillac to remain red are far more interesting that Rodriguez's seemingly disingenuous reason for abandoning black and white in this instance. He explains that red-coloured objects turn a mid-tone grey and risk disappearing into the scene. However he fails to explain why other red cars are not afforded the same treatment.[15]

'The Big Fat Kill' centres on Dwight's quest to protect Shellie and the prostitutes of Old Town, first from Jackie Boy (a corrupt cop) and then from the various criminal elements who see Jackie Boy's death in Old Town as an opportunity to wrest control of the city's sex trade away from Gail and her associates. Dwight's internal monologue spells out his motivations, reactions and intentions and provides a constant narration of the onscreen action. The rhythm of his speech and his choice of words (women are 'dizzy dames') are a clear pastiche of the Philip Marlowesque protagonists of hard-boiled detective fiction, a convention which also surfaces in neo-noirs like *Body Heat*. At times, his performance descends into parody, helped in large part by the overuse of 'hero shots' as Rodriguez calls them. Dwight is often filmed from below, quickly zoomed in on and dramatically lit in half-profile. Gail refers to him as Lancelot, though this is as much an intertextual reference to his participation in *King Arthur* (2004) as it is a description of his character. Despite his various missteps in his quest to protect 'the women', the camera sees and constructs Dwight as a 'knight in shining armour'. The armour, in this story, just happens to be a bright red 1959 Cadillac convertible.

Our introduction to this 'armour' is very dramatic, presaged even by a close-up of Dwight's red running shoes as he sets out on his pursuit of Jackie Boy. Thus, when we see the red Cadillac in the next shot, filmed from above to accentuate its size and especially its length, we recognize it as Dwight's car. Its status as a key prop is immediately confirmed not only by its vibrant colour and centre-frame position, but also by its relationship to another car that drives past. Although this second vehicle clearly belongs the monochromatic world, its softer greys and subtler tonal variations set it apart from the stark black and white of the streets and sidewalk, isolating it from its context and encouraging a comparison with Dwight's car. Such a comparison points to a number of differences between the two vehicles, ones which in turn point to the key signifying elements of the Cadillac.

Several things mark this second car as distinctly older than Dwight's vehicle. Its soft grey colour recalls a kind of filmic pastness that precedes the Technicolor vibrancy embodied by the Cadillac. It is illuminated, but not shiny, and the brightest light falls on its much less prominent tail fins, alerting us to its embryonic status in the evolutionary development of this design feature. In fact, most aspects of its design, including its length, front grill and headlights, are far less pronounced than those adorning the 1959 Cadillac, commonly regarded as the pinnacle of automobile and Populuxe ostentation and extravagance.

What this comparison reveals is subsequently highlighted through cinematographic strategies that foreground aspects of the car's cultural significance. Following a quintessential 'hero shot' of Dwight driving—one filmed from the vantage of the front of the passenger seat—the camera cuts to a close-up of the back end of the Cadillac. Shot with a slightly distorting wide-angle lens, rocket-like fins and bullet-shaped brake lights and reverse lights, encased in a chrome nest resembling the exhaust system of a space shuttle, virtually fill the frame.[16] After a moment to digest visually this spectacle of fins and chrome, the camera cranes over the car until it is situated centre-frame, pausing there for a few seconds before continuing around and down until the front end fills the screen. Again the camera pauses, this time focussing on the massive chrome grill, before simultaneously craning and zooming up over the hood. It stops when a close-up of Dwight occupies the right half of the screen and a single red tail fin the left.

This manoeuvre, designed to survey the car from almost every possible angle, borrows heavily from the visual language of automobile advertising. It is a strategy that shows the object in motion, navigating otherwise deserted streets with speed and agility. It also foregrounds its design features, ones which have little if any bearing on its actual performance. Thus, this scene reads like a car commercial, framing this key prop as something deeply entrenched in the logic of consumer capitalism and as an object of consumerist desire. Indeed, the confidence, optimism, aggression, status and virility written into the car through its postwar promotions and nostalgic appropriations reinforce Dwight's heroism as he embarks on his 'noble' quest.[17]

Colourizing and fetishizing Dwight's Cadillac in this way calls on its cultural significance and reinforces its association with the Populuxe Fifties. In fact, the mere presence of this 1959 model—the embodiment of Populuxe itself—is likely enough to announce the postwar optimism and (suburban) prosperity it was expected to signify. However, in a film world dominated by the aesthetics of postwar underground cultural forms (B-noirs, pulp novels, comics), colourized tail-finned cars are visual and, to a point, ideological anomalies. Whereas these underground forms registered postwar anxieties about gender, sexuality, race, foreign relations and capitalism, the Populuxe Fifties (then and now) masked and repressed these anxieties. This is not to suggest that the Populuxe Fifties is not also deeply implicated in the patriarchal discourses that sought to regulate gendered identities, only that it did so in different ways and through normative rather than nihilistic visions of the Fifites. Thus, by using colourized tail-finned cars, *Sin City* brings into collision disparate visions of the same construct, fracturing the Fifties into its constituent parts. This is something rarely seen in mainstream cinema. Films tend to focus only on one of the 'Fifties' types at their disposal: the noirish Hollywood Fifties in the case of *LA Confidential*, the Suburban Fifties in the case of *Inventing the Abbotts* or the Lounge Fifties in the case of *Swingers*. Rarely do films acknowledge the ways in which these constructs (each with roots in the postwar period) intersect, compete and contribute to the complexity of that time and the mythic visions it produced. By bringing together the kinds of carefully circumscribed objects that source contemporary nostalgia, *Sin City* helps to erode the distinctions between them and permits us to read one against the other.

A simple commutation test best reveals what this injection of Populuxe accomplishes. Without the tail-finned car—especially without a full-colour, fully fetishized tail-finned car—*Sin City* would be an exercise in cultural forms that explores crime and corruption in a postwar urban environment. With the tail-finned car at its disposal, *Sin City* makes possible an engagement with the multiple forms of expression that continue to circulate and contribute to perceptions of postwar America including, most notably, two rather different visions of capitalism: the 'benign' consumer capitalism of the Populuxe Fifties and the unbridled, ruthless entrepreneurial capitalism at the root of crime and corruption.

The mythic benign capitalism written into the Fifties is certainly at odds with the *Sin City* world where state institutions from the law to the church are rife with corruption and rotten to the core. In the 'Big Fat Kill' especially, the pimps, the mob, the police and the prostitutes engage in a bloody battle over control of Old Town's brothels. Free-market competition is violent and unstructured and all who participate pay exorbitant prices for very little return. There is nothing in place to protect those vulnerable in this libertarian society where defence of person and property is an individual responsibility. This kind of economic logic is at odds with the promises of easy fortune made through the tail-finned car just like the anxieties about capitalism etched into postwar underground cultural forms are at odds with the visions of prosperity promoted by *Leave it to Beaver* and *The Adventures of Ozzie and Harriet*.

Though visually dominant and thoroughly fetishized, Dwight's Cadillac seems at times wholly out of place in *Sin City*. Its look as well as what it signifies conflicts with that which visually and narratively surrounds it. Through its presence, however, we are permitted a chance to consume it visually and analytically, to think through its cultural significance and how its meanings inform and inflect the ideological, visual and economic logic of the *Sin City* world. It brings nostalgic constructs into collision with one another and in a way that can reward the engaged and critical spectator. This clash fosters reflection on the competing representational practices that comprise the Fifties, encouraging us to consider the way that they work. Furthermore, it directs us to think about the relationship these practices have to the 1950s and the subsequent eras that resuscitate them.

Notes

1. Those involved in the conception, creation and sponsorship of Cadillac Ranch are: Chip Lord, Hudson Marquez, Doug Michels, Stanley Marsh III, Roger Dainton and Wyatt McSpadden.

2. It is also an easy and deserving target of many other criticisms. However, my interest here is in how different kinds of spectatorial experiences might stem from engaging critically with the meanings generated and stories told through other components of the film, from reading the film oppositionally.
3. See for example Tashiro (1998), Gibbs (2002) and Barnwell (2004).
4. At times, props may also loom large in our memory of particular films, defining for us the sequences that function synecdochally for the complete filmic text. Consider for example *Star Wars*' (1977) light sabers or *Citizen Kane*'s (1941) Rosebud.
5. Barnwell usefully defines the production designer as the person responsible for 'giving a film or television production a visual concept' (2004: 125).
6. Kurt (Richard Dreyfuss), the bohemian intellectual, arrives in the first scene in a 'cool' European car. However he parks it and joins his friends to cruise the streets.
7. Comments made by directors and members of the production crew on this and subsequent films discussed here and in the following chapters are (unless otherwise noted) from the special features accompanying the film's DVD release.
8. The film is actually set in 1962, the year before Kennedy's assassination and the official end of the 'Fifties' as an era rather than a decade. This is particularly telling and reveals that Lucas was tuned into the sense that life changed not in 1960, but in 1963.
9. According to the producer, Richard Kobritz, King chose the 1957 Plymouth Fury because it was one of the only cars of its generation that had not yet been celebrated in literature or on film. Kobritz also explains that unknown actors were cast so as not to upstage the car.
10. FujiFilm was selected as the stock for this sequence for its soft, sepia look.
11. This use of 'hyper-noir' is different from how Phil Powrie defines the term in relation to French film of the 1990s as a 'new noir sensibility', one darker than its predecessors and combining the 'paranoia of the political thriller and the violence of the postmodern and naturalistic thriller' (2007: 55–56).
12. Rodriguez's decision to enlist different visual effects companies (CafeFX, The Orphanage and Hybride Technologies) for each of the three stories also resulted in slight but noticeable shifts in the look of the film.
13. The Yellow Bastard drives an American-made car (a 1937 Cadillac) but only after the transportation co-ordinator discovered it would cost $100,000 a week to rent the Bugatti originally scripted as his vehicle.
14. The other dominant period is clearly the Forties of noir as the filmmakers describe it. And yet, despite the frequent references to this decade and genre, *Sin City* seems just as indebted, both stylistically and narratively, to the B-noirs of the 1950s. This speaks to the film's reliance on perceptions of past media forms more than any actual history of genre or cinematic technology.
15. For example, both Mr Shlubb's Ferrari and Hartigan's Chevy were originally red as confirmed by the film's green-screen version.

16. This wide-angle lens also has the effect of stretching the distance between the chrome and Dwight's head, thus further elongating the car.
17. Jackie Boy's car also appears in colour and specifically a shade of cerulean blue. But as a villain's car it is filmed in a rather different way and without reference to the fetishizing language of advertising. Its finish is dull and, compared to Dwight's car, it is much smaller and boasts far less prominent tail fins. As it turns into the shadowy alleys of Old Town, its colour drains, returning only for an instant with the sporadic flash of lightning.

Chapter 5

Far From Heaven: Creative Agency, Social History and the Expressive Potential of Costume

Whenever *Sin City*'s visual styles and props fall out of alignment with each other—when B-noir clashes with Populuxe—the film can be opened up and its cultural sources subject to inspection. Actively considering the implications of these visual and conceptual clashes makes possible a critical reading of the film (and of history and myth) that can reward the engaged spectator. There is a certain analytical pleasure that can be derived from reading against the grain or from attempting to follow the logic of *Sin City* until it folds in on itself and inadvertently demystifies the objects of its own indulgences. However, the very same pleasure can be had from reading *with* the grain in *Far From Heaven*, a film that puts itself on display as a visual and cinematic spectacle. Cinematography, acting, dialogue, music, setting, lighting, props and costume all announce themselves as rooted in, and specific to, a particular brand of Hollywood filmmaking. They announce themselves as signs to be read and interpreted and the source of an intellectual and emotional investment in Sirkian cinema, 1950s American social history, Fifties nostalgia and the endurance of the past in the present.

Set in 1957 and 1958, *Far From Heaven* stars Julianne Moore as Cathy Whitaker, a suburban middle-class housewife who develops an attraction to her black gardener, Raymond Deagan (Dennis Haysbert), and whose husband Frank (Dennis Quaid) initiates an affair with another, younger man. Written and directed by Todd Haynes, *Far From Heaven* pays tribute to the films and film style of Douglas Sirk, director of *Magnificent Obsession* (1954), *All That Heaven Allows* (1955), *Written on the Wind* (1956) and *Imitation of Life* (1959). Initially dismissed as a purveyor of the most excessive brand of Hollywood melodrama, Sirk was eventually celebrated in the pages of *Cahiers du Cinema* as a great ironist and astute critic of postwar America. His critiques were often effected visually, as a way of subverting the Production Code but also as a way of indulging his fascination with the image. In his 1950s films he transformed the surface of the screen into a visual spectacle of garish, complementary colour in order to unsettle the audience, to facilitate, at key moments, a critical distance and, more simply, to suggest that something might be a little off in the world represented—the world of white, protestant, middle-class housewives and 'organization men' celebrated by the 1950s mass media. Yet as an offering of twenty-first-century film culture, *Far From Heaven* can and does explicitly address the once closely regulated triumvirate of sexuality, race and gender. Production Code-era films could only ever surreptitiously hint at homosexuality, interracial relationships and sex or the possibility that a desire to break with rigidly prescribed gender roles was healthy and acceptable. *Far From Heaven* foregrounds and narrativizes what Sirk could not, but it does so using Sirk's distinct palette that (in addition to carefully selected props and rehearsed mannerisms) confirms for the spectator that what Haynes offers is, at heart, a Fifties melodrama.

Haynes has claimed that he is not really interested in the actual 1950s but only with Sirk's cinematic vision of the United States at mid century.[1] He found his 'Hartford, Connecticut' setting in Patterson, New Jersey because, to him, the old downtown core looked like a Hollywood sound stage. He aimed to make locations resemble sets and create what he called a 'hermetically sealed fictional realm'. And this he certainly managed to achieve. *Far From Heaven* makes only a limited number of judiciously selected references to the official history of the 1950s, the kind that privileges dates and declarations, transformative events and the exploits of public figures over the particularities of everyday life and the experiences of those marginalized by grand narratives. And yet, despite the film's conscious attempt to avoid engaging with the history rehearsed in introductory textbooks and popularized by mainstream historical films (e.g., *Pearl Harbour*) and documentaries (e.g., CNN's *Cold War* [1998], or History Channel offerings), *Far From Heaven* provides insight into more than Sirkian cinema. It provides insight into how we access and experience history and shows that those very same period signifiers and visual strategies responsible for the film's 'surface realism' and 'deliberate archaism' also happen to be the source of its engagement with history. *Far From Heaven*'s production design—and especially its creative and sophisticated use of costume—does more than refer to Eisenhower and Little Rock to articulate the way in which race, gender and sexuality were regulated and negotiated in 1950s America.

Populuxe Props and Technicolor Aesthetics

Far From Heaven could quite easily have worked as the key case study for either the previous chapter on props or the next one on deliberate archaism. It mobilizes specific props including tail-finned cars in ways that draw on their dominant meanings and general cultural significance. Cathy drives a blue and white two-tone station wagon, a vehicle coded as feminine. Advertised during the 1950s as a middle class necessity, it provided Mother with a means of transport to perform the errands central to suburban life at the same time as it signified Father's corporate success and financial security. In fact, these intended uses are catalogued in the opening sequence of the film as Cathy picks up her daughter from dance lessons in the city of Hartford and drives home to the suburbs where she unloads groceries from the back of the car (Figure 5.1). As she does, Cathy's friend Eleanor pulls up in her tail-finned car to finalize the plans for the Whitaker's annual cocktail party. Hers, too, is specifically 'feminine'. It is a medium-pink tone and not quite as large or long as those geared toward male consumers of the period. (But it is not a station wagon and thus functions as one of a series of clues suggesting Eleanor may be childless.)

In this way the film's opening scene relies on the meanings encoded in the cars to convey information about the characters and their lives. It also confirms that this film is centred on women's experiences. Here and throughout the film primary and secondary female characters are seen driving with far more regularity than any male character, moving themselves and, by extension, the viewer, through the suburbs, Hartford and the narrative. Frank never appears behind the wheel and is only ever seen walking to and from his (unseen) car. In fact, he relies on Cathy to drive him home after his 'mix-up' with the police. Cars facilitate a degree of mobility and permit women like Cathy—the white, middle-class, suburban housewife—to enter spaces otherwise physically and socially off-limits: downtown Hartford at night and the black neighbourhoods of the city. But while these props assist in the film's engagement with the complex nature of an enacted and embodied postwar femininity, they also contribute to *Far From Heaven*'s cinematic artifice. Too clean and too new, the cars exist as visual spectacle and as part of Haynes's carefully orchestrated colour palette. They seem somehow

Figure 5.1 Julianne Moore and Viola Davis unload groceries in *Far From Heaven* (2002). Killer Films/The Kobal Collection.

perfectly suited to speak to the essence of postwar America's ideological investments in appearance and newness.

Far From Heaven's deliberate archaism performs a similar function. Modelled on the palette of Sirkian melodramas of the 1950s, Haynes' 'technicolor aesthetic'[2] lays bare the way in which Sirk used colour to heighten the emotional intensity of a scene as well as facilitate the kind of Brechtian distancation necessary to demystify the American postwar bourgeois realm, usually in order to render explicit the ways in which this realm contained and oppressed women. Like *The Aviator*, *Far From Heaven* grants access to cinematic history on an affective and analytical level. And as a strategy that alerts audiences to these films' self-reflexive and contemporary consciousness, the practice of deliberate archaism in these instances brings the past into collision with the present in ways that prompt comparison and evaluation. As Haynes hoped, *Far From Heaven* does indeed force us to ask how far we have really come from the sexism, homophobia and racism entrenched in the social fabric of postwar suburban America.

Nostalgia Isn't as Bad as it Used to Be

For these reasons *Far From Heaven* has been something of a critical favourite, used as a key example in several recent productive endeavours to rethink postmodern pastiche, nostalgia and intertextuality. For Pam Cook, it is an overtly nostalgic film, but one that mobilizes nostalgia to challenge history and accepted versions of the 1950s. It does so by enabling a 'nostalgic gaze' at carefully crafted elements of its production design to illuminate issues of authenticity, memory and identity and draw attention to itself as representation and as a cinematic reconstruction that 'recognizes the gap between the source material and its representation with the knowledge of hindsight' (2005: 14). In doing so, *Far From Heaven* reveals what Cook rightly describes as the complex relationship between history and memory and the potential for nostalgia to realize new forms of history (2005: 17).

In a similar fashion, Lynne Joyrich and Amelia DeFalco's readings of *Far From Heaven* explore how intertextuality and reflexivity allow for critical reflection. Joyrich argues that the film allows us to consider how the media might shape our desires, anxieties, identities and positions (2004: 191). DeFalco, on the other hand, shows how it manages to 'exploit the confusion of actual and imaginary lost objects to create a purely cinematic revisitation of the past that calls these categories into question' (2004: 28). More specifically, it asks whether there is any 'real' history outside the film world. Like the textualized remains of Linda Hutcheon's historiographic metafiction, the past styles and forms at play in *Far From Heaven* show us that access to history is only ever granted through a collection of fragments and representations. But according to DeFalco, the self-consciously mediated nature of this film world does not preclude it from generating nostalgia. She argues that a 'non-experiential nostalgia' is indeed possible and that this kind of nostalgia enabled through 'contact with representations … lays bare the fundamental textuality of the recollected site, its underlying constructedness' (2004: 30).

The capacity for *Far From Heaven* to function critically and analytically as well as generate a deep emotional impact is also of interest to Richard Dyer in his reassessment of pastiche. The film makes us acutely aware of its status as a film, encouraging us to consider how the cinema mediates our relationship to history and to acknowledge 'that what we know about how things felt in the 1950s comes—problematically but only—from cultural artefacts (and in this case films)' (Dyer 2007: 178). The film enables us to acknowledge what Dyer calls 'the historicity of our own feelings'— the fact that how we respond emotionally is not only the result of personal experience but the cultural, social and historical contexts in which we participate.

The Sirkian pastiche, intertextual references and self-reflexivity on offer in *Far From Heaven* are identified by these analyses as the source of both its critical and affective power. The film's application of these strategies shows that postmodern aesthetic modes and the visual creation of a cinematic pastness do not necessarily stand in the way of meaningful engagements with memory and history. Pastiche, nostalgia and intertextual play are not antithetical to critique and historical knowledge but can grant access to the past as well as presuppositions about the past in a way that interrogates its uses in, as well as its relevance to, the present. These are important insights that are well worth pursuing.

The following explores how costume, as a key element of *Far From Heaven*'s mise en scène, contributes to the film's visual pastness at the same time that it performs a myriad of other important meaning-making roles. Specifically, I will explore its function in communicating what oppressive social conventions prohibit characters from articulating verbally, thus granting characters a kind of communicative and creative agency as well as a means through which to express their desires. By doing so, costume makes possible a kind of access to the social conventions governing verbal and sartorial expression in postwar America. This history also seeps in through the New Look-inspired dresses and grey suits as the kind of canonical props and motivated signifiers that grant access to the ideological impetus behind their creation. In the context of a film explicitly concerned with representation and the semiotic power of colour, props and set design, these costumes point back to their past cultural and cinematic uses.[3] The self-reflexive nature of *Far From Heaven* alerts us to the centrality of representation as a structuring concern of the film that encourages consideration of almost every scene as something to be consumed and felt as well as something to be thought through, read and actively interpreted.

Costume and Creative Agency

Given the importance of costume in cinema, there are still, sadly, too few studies devoted to the subject and fewer still that analyze its uses outside classical Hollywood cinema or British heritage drama. However, works dealing with Hollywood and British heritage drama have been satisfyingly thorough in their engagement with the multiple ways that costume operates in film, the history of the role of key costume designers and the links between the fashion and movie industries.[4] They address costume's ability to tell us about characters, their conscious and unconscious desires, their place in the filmic world, their perceptions of themselves, their relationships with others, and how they transform or develop over the course of the film. Costume can confirm or subvert expectations generated by the diegesis, contribute to the cohesiveness of the world represented or, in the interest of visual spectacle, pleasure and the profit margins of the fashion industry, suspend narrative continuity and disbelief. It can demand our attention and an engagement free from narrative concerns and, as Stella Bruzzi argues, 'impose rather than absorb meaning' (1997: xiv). As a key ingredient in surface realism it can also convince us of the historical or cultural authenticity of the period or place on offer. And as central to identification, it can, as several authors have argued, permit spectators to inhabit new or different identities, crossing boundaries of nation, class, gender and time (see, for example, Cook 1996).

Far From Heaven manages to catalogue and explore these and other roles assumed by costume in the cinema. Like the sets, music and lighting, costume speaks for the characters. It expresses visually what characters cannot express verbally. It provides insight into the feelings and desires prohibited by the strict and oppressive social conventions governing life in Hartford. For Cathy it functions as a creative outlet, the means by which she expresses her (limited) agency and her resolve to negotiate rather than wholly subscribe to the prevailing model of femininity adhered to by those in her social circle. For example, during their second encounter, Raymond returns Cathy's mauve scarf that had been swept away earlier in the day by a strong autumn wind. He does so with the simple compliment that the colour suits her. Cathy takes this to heart and the next day wears a soft bluish-grey skirt and fitted tweed jacket with a hint of mauve in its weave as well as a small purple hat. Then, following a violent confrontation with Frank, she sports a cardigan in a colour similar to her scarf and a skirt one shade lighter, signalling her increasing closeness to Raymond and thus her attempt to distance herself from Frank. In fact, after deciding to accept Raymond's invitation to drive in the country, Cathy collects her two-toned purple coat and her mauve scarf which now amount to five variations of the shade that elicited Raymond's initial compliment. This medley of purples and mauves speaks to a kind of desperation of half-conscious attempts to solicit Raymond's further approval and at a kind of fractured and incomprehensible set of competing desires.[5] However, following their 'date', Cathy's resolve to acknowledge her feelings for Raymond and to express the intensity and purity of her desire is done so visually rather than verbally through the rich mauve silk dress in which she appears the next day. As such, Cathy's sartorial choices manage to chart the development of her feelings and express desires prohibited in 1950s Hartford.

Cathy's wardrobe certainly helps to articulate her unspoken desires. However, it does much more than this. We catch the first glimpse of Cathy's mauve scarf as she greets her girlfriends arriving for an afternoon cocktail. Each woman is dressed in warm autumnal colours that complement the setting (Figure 5.2): Eleanor wears a shimmering orange-yellow raw silk dress with a pale moss green coat; Nancy (Olivia Birkelund) and Doreen (Barbara Garrick) are in various shades of saturated orange, red and salmon; and Cathy, quite appropriately given the subject of the dialogue, is in sangria red. (Eleanor speaks of Cathy's left-leaning sensibilities whilst in college and quips that 'they used to call her Red'.) Though dialogue helps to establish Cathy's politics and difference, so too does her scarf. As the only cool colour in this otherwise warm rich palette, it interrupts the surface of the screen and sets her apart. Once Cathy loses this scarf to the wind, she may seem to 'fit in' with her social circle. But this visual harmony masks deeper-rooted differences in both values and experiences, ones which become painfully apparent as she half-heartedly feigns to understand her friends' complaints about their husbands' sexual appetites and demands.

Whereas in this instance, costume speaks to social inclusion and exclusion, it also registers shifts in characters' social roles and connects them to wider historical discourses involving fashion. After Frank leaves Cathy she abandons her billowing New Look skirts for a narrow pencil-skirt suit, signalling a shift in her perception of herself, her responsibilities and status. For Pam Cook, Frank's grey suit functions as his disguise, permitting him to blend into his corporate milieu (2005: 14). Crucially we are to read this as his decision, his conscious attempt to avoid sartorial signifiers that express his sexuality. But at the same time, it is difficult not to see his grey suit as a reference to *The Man in the Gray Flannel Suit* in its book and 1956 film forms (which offer more than a few parallels to *Far From Heaven*) and as a now common shorthand expression for the discontentment bred by postwar materialism and conformity. Thus, certain costumes appear both diegetically and non-diegetically determined, as signifiers contributing to and circumscribed by the narrative, but also as ones allocated to forge connections beyond the story world to historical texts, discourses and representations.

Figure 5.2 Olivia Birkelund, Barbara Garrick, Patricia Clarkson and Julianne Moore in *Far From Heaven* (2002). Killer Films/The Kobal Collection.

Raymond's clothing operates in a similar way. On one level, it simply makes sense for him as a gardener to wear casual clothes and a checked flannel jacket. The warm greens, reds, oranges, yellows and browns that he wears connect him to nature, to the sunny autumnal gardens and forests of Hartford. But they connect him to other Sirkian characters too: Rock Hudson's Ron Kirby, the gardener in *All that Heaven Allows* as well as Hudson's Mitch Wayne in *Written on the Wind*, the geologist whose plaid jacket also echoes the autumnal hues that surround him. In this way costume can, as Sarah Street argues, '"exceed" the demands of the narrative by suggesting intertextual connections and allude to star identities which have been forged outside the narrative system of that particular film' (2001: 32). But instead of alluding to the star identities of its performers, *Far From Heaven* connects its characters to the star personas of Sirk's films. By doing so, the film not only establishes one character through another, thereby complicating our understanding of 'Raymond', but also draws our attention to the star construct itself as an amalgamation of performance and reality—of Ron Kirby and Rock Hudson. In this way, the film invites into its world what the audience might know of 1950s cinema and its characters as well as what viewers might know of the publicity surrounding its stars.

Costume's Cultural Significance

This link to realities and discourses operating outside the filmic text means that costumes often function as those kind of props (like the tail-finned car) that carry into the film a relatively stable and familiar set of meanings. To borrow Bruzzi's phrase again, they impose rather than absorb meaning. *What* is imposed by the women's dresses in *Far From Heaven* is worth pursing further for it gets to the heart of how aspects central to the construction of the film's visual pastness—its nostalgia mode—offer up for examination 1950s personal and collective histories in a way that makes explicit their persistence in and impact on the present. In other words, the dresses worn by Cathy and others are motivated signifiers that have stitched into them postwar desires and fears. These desires and fears are called upon and situated in relation to the pasts—both 'real' and cinematic—in which they circulated and the present in which they continue to exist as nostalgic commodities and potent signifiers of a Fifties femininity subject to reverence, contempt and ridicule in almost equal measure. The image of women and more specifically Mother in her New Look-inspired dress and high-heeled shoes is a highly charged and contested one, an image saturated with the politics of domesticity, femininity, motherhood and family.

That we are to read Cathy in her New Look-inspired dresses as an 'image' invested with meaning and central to the film's engagement with representation is established early on in the film. Certainly the bright colours, luxurious, textured and reflective fabrics are captivating in their own right and stand out as a spectacle for visual (and, I would add, analytical and historical) pleasure. During her interview for the local society paper Cathy's status as an image is foregrounded. The flash of the camera announces Mrs Leacock (Betty Henritze) and the photographer's arrival, catching Cathy unaware. Despite Mrs Leacock's insistence that 'candid views are always the best', she instructs Cathy to pose by the fireplace for a series of shots (Figure 5.3). Her pose and smile are transparently artificial, imitating the types of print advertisements often seen in magazines of the 1950s, including the one framed on the wall behind Cathy. This advert, featuring Cathy and Frank as 'Mr and Mrs Magnatech',[6] remains in the background throughout the interview and even appears in close up as Mrs Leacock praises Cathy for 'posing at her husband's side'. Its composition mimics the staging of the diegesis: in both, Cathy wears a blue dress fanned out around her and is seated next to a television set. Given the prominence of the television, this doubling of the image announces Cathy as image and specifically as a constructed and mediated image.[7] She is presented to be read and consumed.

Figure 5.3 Dennis Quaid and Julianne Moore photographed for the Hartford gossip magazine in *Far From Heaven* (2002). Killer Films/The Kobal Collection.

Cathy's blue dress is visually dominant in both instances and thus an important component of each image. It is a New Look-inspired creation of the kind that dominated not only Hollywood, television and advertising of the 1950s but also nostalgic constructions of the Fifties since. But it is one that has a longer history worth pursing, a history inscribed in its design and instrumental to its transformation by Hollywood into what Maureen Turim (1990) calls the Sweetheart Line. In fact, the way in which *Far From Heaven* catalogues costumes' myriad uses and potential seems to directly engage with how Hollywood mobilized the meanings inscribed in the design of the New Look. The film thus exploits the historical specificity of this design style as well as its cinematic presence and contributions in 1950s Hollywood.

Essentially, the Sweetheart Line dress is the Hollywood or Populuxe version of Christian Dior's New Look. Although the New Look was designed in France by Dior in 1947, it is one example of the type of object that Adrian Forty warns should not be treated as the product of one artist's unique and personal vision. Marling (1994), Cawthorne (1996) and Turim (1990) each explain how it emerged as a response to the privations of war. The vast amount of fabric required to make the skirt was a response to fabric rationings while its flower-like effect was meant to celebrate a femininity that was supposedly denied in the standard asexual suits. Furthermore, the use of vibrant colour was a direct response to a wartime palette of khaki and navy blue (see Marling 1994: 8–49). The fact that such a full skirt could never have been made during the war rendered it a potent symbol for the end of war and its deprivations. As a result, it signifies not only a specific historical moment, but the change, optimism and consumerism actively promoted as its defining characteristics.

Comprised of a 'tight bare bodice, a nipped-in, accentuated waist, a full, billowing skirt', the Sweetheart Line is Dior's New Look infused with a hint of 'period nostalgia' (Turim 1990: 212, 217)[8] which exaggerated its proportions and added a touch of flamboyance. However, the Sweetheart Line differs most from its predecessor in its longevity. The New Look dominated Parisian fashion only during 1947 and 1948 while the copies created by the costume-design supervisors of the major studios remained *the* style, not only in film, but also in mass/popular fashion until the mid 1950s (Turim 1990: 215–17). The garment industry copied the Sweetheart Line to such an extent that it became the most popular style for wedding dresses, prom dresses and even the attire of housewives in the advertising of the decade (1990: 220–22). What the Sweetheart Line preserved—and ultimately reinforced—of the New Look was its general cultural connotations. It too functioned as a potent symbol, not only of the affluence and abundance suggested by its design, but also of a 'proper' postwar femininity. It was a necessary component of a specifically American discourse of the feminine that privileged frivolity over practicality and ornament over function. It replaced the practicality of Rosie the Riveter's comfortable trousers as Rosie's model of femininity was increasingly seen as a threat to the employment prospects of returning soldiers and the patriarchal authority they sought to reclaim. With the help of the accompanying high heels, the Sweetheart Line restricted the movement of women and transformed them into spectacle. However, efforts to promote this passive vision of femininity did not mean that all women accepted its restrictions or adopted this look.

The Sweetheart Line acquired further, quite specific connotations as it was mobilized in Hollywood film. Drawing on examples from *All About Eve* (1950), *June Bride* (1948), *Father of the Bride* (1950), *Gentlemen Prefer Blondes* (1953) and *A Place in the Sun* (1951), Turim shows how the Sweetheart Line was used in character development to signify the 'princess', 'true-woman', 'debutante' and the 'bride' and was worn by characters to signal either their transformation or entrance into the realm of femininity (1990: 217). She argues that '[t]hese connotations were sewn into the style not only by the history of fashion but by the way Hollywood costume design seized upon it, prolonged its life, and positioned it as a reinforcement of narrative ideas' (1990: 217).

Costume as Film and Social History

While costume changes reinforce narrative progress and character development, in *Far From Heaven* they also serve two additional aims: describing (and at times anticipating) the nature and experience of social spaces, and establishing the importance of appearance and newness. Characters in *Far From Heaven* are extremely mobile, constantly on the move from one room to another, driving the streets of Hartford and moving between interior and exterior. Though this mobility ultimately belies the restrictiveness of the place they inhabit and especially the lack of choices available to Cathy and Raymond, it also sets up opportunities for a series of complex interplays between costumes and mise en scène. In fact, despite the regularity with which Cathy changes, we tend to see each outfit in at least two different settings. This creates at least two distinct palettes which gives us a good sense of the different kinds of relationships she has with each space. For instance, Cathy's purple ensemble clashes with the autumnal hues and

Raymond's gardening attire as the two stroll through her yard. Here, costume establishes Raymond's connection to nature and Cathy's distance from an environment that, in postwar America, she was supposed to inhabit—the space of the home. After a walk in the woods they travel to Raymond's favourite neighbourhood restaurant for lunch. Upon entering, both remove their coats, revealing Cathy in purple and Raymond in green. This visual contrast, suggesting rather heavy-handedly a clash of opposites, is mirrored in the restaurant's interior which too is predominantly purple and green. In fact, it seems as though their choice of dress predestined them to end up here. This is the only social space that, however reluctantly, tolerates their presence together. They appear to fit in but in doing so contribute to a palette of contrasting hues that effectively generates feelings of anxiety and unease.[9]

Cathy routinely puts on and takes off her coat as well as gloves and scarves. She does so almost instinctively, as though following a set of deeply ingrained rules governing appropriate dress. But performing these rituals also draws attention to the frequency with which she changes costume and thus the limitlessness of her wardrobe. It is wholly unbelievable that a postwar suburban *middle-class* housewife should have such an extensive collection of dresses. This kind of sartorial extravagance is typically reserved for the rich and the cinematic. Thus, on one level, Cathy's changes contribute to the film's cinematic self-consciousness. It is one of several strategies designed to expose *Far From Heaven*'s own constructed and mediated nature and its engagement with films (rather than the reality) of the 1950s including, especially, the fashion spectacles offered up for consumption in classical Hollywood film.[10] At the same time, the frenetic pace with which Cathy changes into always new, perfectly ironed dresses suggests the premium placed on appearance and the pressure to consume conspicuously. The rate with which she changes is impossible to sustain and one cannot help forecast her (and the United States') eventual consumer burnout. That Cathy is already willing to use dress to creative ends and to express prohibited desires suggests her inevitable revolt against the construct of femininity written into her skirts through film, television and advertising of the 1950s. It also speaks to the possible negotiations of femininity, the performativity of feminine identities, and ways of making do with what was at women's—albeit white, middle-class and heterosexual women's —disposal at that time.

Costume is thus one of the ways in which history—and, in the above example, the postwar pressure to perform a certain kind of femininity through dress and conspicuous consumption—seeps into

Haynes's hermetically sealed fictional realm. Indeed it has the potential to provide as much access to the 1950s as the film's other injections of 'historical realities'—the mention or appearance of events and personalities belonging to both the characters' and the audience's reality. These injections are rare in a film explicitly concerned with 1950s cinema, but noticeable and noteworthy as a result. However, rather than ground the film historically or lend it a degree of historical authenticity, they manage to expose the failure of history to grant access to affective truths and insight into everyday lived experiences determined by race, gender and sexuality.

For instance, actual footage from Eisenhower's 1957 speech on the enforced desegregation of a Little Rock high school plays on the Whitaker's bedroom television set. It is a significant news event but one to which neither Cathy nor Frank pay much attention. This broadcast succeeds in making us aware of the event (and likely aware of our mediated access to the event), encouraging us to rehearse whatever knowledge we have of it, Eisenhower and the Civil Rights Movement. In comparison with how the film fictionalizes the everyday life of Raymond and Cathy and the impact of racism in its unconscious, subtle, overt and violent forms, this 'real' history seems somehow incomplete, ineffective and in-*affective*. It is exposed for the historical shorthand that it is, a documented and well-rehearsed event that eclipses the collective and individual struggles that comprised everyday experience in postwar America. While *Far From Heaven* is certainly unable to offer any kind of comprehensive analysis of racism (nor would I suggest that this is what the film aims to do), it does manage to reveal the limits of 'official' history as a collection of dramatic events.[11] It suggests that understanding racism in the United States requires an attempt to grapple with how it might have been experienced and felt daily and in a variety of ways, from Hutch and his friends' assault on Sarah to Cathy's request that Sybil, her black maid, sign an NAACP petition on her behalf. Indeed, through its engagement with postwar melodrama, *Far From Heaven* seems to suggest that Sirk's veiled critiques of class, race and gender in America provided valuable (and now historical) insight into the realities of 1950s bourgeois life. In short, Haynes makes a compelling cinematic argument for film as history.

Far From Heaven exploits the potential of costume to articulate desires and fears, signal inclusion and exclusion, recycle postwar cinema and its stars and connect the film to a broader American social history. It also reinforces the film's (and the 1950s') investment in visual spectacle and appearance and alerts us to Cathy's consciousness of herself as an image, as a constructed, mediated representation. As a key period signifier, costume keeps us grounded in the Fifties while offering up for examination and comparison aspects of the historical 1950s including the social conventions governing the expression of gendered, racial and sexual identities. And as part of Haynes' meticulously designed colour scheme, individual costumes play an important part in articulating the relationship between characters and the spaces they inhabit. Many of these uses for costume are at work in one final scene that I wish to consider involving a chance encounter between Cathy and Raymond at Hartford's Modern Art show.

The (Modern) Art of Dress: Colour, Form and Feeling

Costume plays a pivotal role in this scene in both a visual and conceptual opposition between warmth (kindness, humanity) and coolness (cruelty, intolerance). At first glance, a distinct coolness permeates the gallery space, achieved in part with bluish grey walls, blue streams of light, dark suits worn by men and various shades of dark, dull greens worn by virtually every woman in the scene. Cathy, too, is dressed in dark green but, as will become significant later, her outfit boasts goldenrod-coloured trim and buttons on its fitted velvet jacket and goldenrod sections of pleats nestled in its full skirt.[12] Initially she appears to 'fit in', to belong to Hartford's bourgeois social set. However, traces of this warm hue hint at an underlying difference, one established earlier when her mauve scarf separated her from her friends and articulated her closeness to Raymond. In this scene, Modern Art—as another form of visual representation—also has a part to play.

Near the beginning of the scene, a tracking shot crosses the room to show visitors looking at a series of green and blue abstract artworks. The camera comes to a rest on Cathy engrossed in a painting composed of red and orange patches. Her rapt attention is interrupted by the flash of a camera and Mrs Leacock's observation, spoken as a newspaper headline: 'Wife of Hartford executive caught communing with Picasso?'[13] This reinforces, yet again, Cathy's status as image, and one among many in this particular scene. It also sets up the appearance of Raymond, announced through the first substantial intrusion of warm colour. As Cathy turns to face Mrs Leacock, colour cues us to notice Raymond and Sarah positioned almost perfectly centre-frame and in focus. Their faces and upper torsos are bathed in a diagonal band of orange-red light streaming in through the stained glass window of the community centre. Once they catch Cathy's eye, she excuses herself, walks toward them and directly into the warm, red light. As she does, the goldenrod sections of her dress glow orange, outshining the dull dark green that initially signalled her connection to the remainder of the art show visitors (Figure 5.4). In the presence of Raymond and his daughter—who also wears the same colour trim on her hat and collar—Cathy's tentative signifiers of difference are illuminated. That Raymond brings out what is purportedly her 'true' and warm inner essence is confirmed by the painting behind them. Positioned centrally in the frame and flanked by Cathy and Raymond, this painting functions as a visual analogue for the staging: the taller black figure clearly mirrors Raymond while the shorter *red* figure functions as a substitute for Cathy.

Whereas in this shot, the art visually reinforces the narrative, in the next shot, the art becomes the subject of the narrative and in a way that foregrounds the potential for colour and form, as part of a non-representational visual language, to provoke deeply felt emotional responses. Following a short sequence outside the gallery, a close-up of a Miró painting materializes on screen. The camera then pulls back slowly and positions itself (and the spectator) just behind Cathy and Raymond. As they discuss the merits of 'Modern Art' the camera shifts to position us in the place of the painting, but cutting away at times to capture the various disapproving glances thrust upon them. Cathy and Raymond remain unaware of this attention and are instead mesmerized by Miró as well as each other. Cathy says of this 'Mira'

Figure 5.4 Julianne Moore, Dennis Haysbert and Jordan Puryear at the Modern Art show in *Far From Heaven* (2002). Killer Films/The Kobal Collection.

(as she mispronounces it), 'I don't know why, but I just adore it, the feeling it gives. I know that sounds terribly vague'. To this Raymond replies in true melodramatic fashion as the camera scans the surface of the painting, 'No, no, actually it confirms something I've always wondered about modern art, abstract art. That perhaps it's just picking up where religious art left off, somehow trying to show you divinity. The modern artist just pares it down to the basic elements of shape and color. But when you look at that Miró, you feel it just the same.' Their reverie is rudely interrupted by a loud cackle, presumably in response to Raymond's observation. The scene abruptly cuts to an elderly woman commenting to Eleanor: 'To tell the truth, I've always preferred the work of the Masters. Rembrandt, Michelangelo.' 'Master' of course has a double meaning here, evoking the history of slavery and the racism that permeates Hartford's still segregated society. It speaks to a binary that separates white and black, conservative and progressive and, in the realm of art, representational and abstract.

Though the film's visual pastness distances the art-show patrons' racism from the present, certain strategies encourage an awareness of the contemporary social and cultural lenses through which we interpret the action on the screen and evaluate the bigotry of Haynes's Hartford against the bigotry that persists in the United States today. What maintains our consciousness of the present is Raymond's assessment of Modern Art. His comments are as relevant to what we see as they are to what he sees. In other words, Raymond's observations on the capacity for abstract forms and colours to elicit deeply felt emotion seem as much directed toward the various mise en scènes he and Cathy inhabit as they do to the Miró. In this scene especially the clash of warm and cool colours oppose passion and compassion to malice and callousness and help to articulate the resolve with which Raymond and Cathy seek comfort in each other in the face of social prejudice. Colour, costume, art and light collaborate to elicit both sympathy and empathy for Raymond and Cathy.

A strong emotional response is not the only thing that abstract forms evoke. One of the points I have tried to make throughout this discussion is that visual signifiers, practices and codes can be entrusted with several functions simultaneously and that complexity does not necessarily compromise the force of the meanings or sentiments they generate. The use of Miró is a testament to this. While Cathy and Raymond's observations on the painting acknowledge the affective potential of form and colour, the Miró painting seems to comment on Cathy and Raymond's relationship. Though not a formal member of the Surrealists, Miró's paintings mobilized sexual symbolism in an effort to delve into the fantasies of the unconscious, prompting André Breton to proclaim that he might be 'the most Surrealist of us all'. Miró's link to Surrealism and thus to sex, fantasy and unconscious desires is highly relevant to the palpable sexual tension between Cathy and Raymond and to their practice of displacing their passion for each other onto art. Miró's abstract composition does more than evoke Cathy and Raymond's passions or communicate the affective power that non-representational codes, like those mobilized in *Far From Heaven*, might yield. It also reminds us that colour and form can function as the source of particular, historically specific meanings that potentially enrich a scene conceptually, offering not just visual, but analytical pleasures.

Far From Heaven is a film that facilitates engagements with nostalgia on several levels. It makes use of the visual language of Fifties nostalgia by practicing deliberate archaism. Tail-finned cars, New Look-inspired skirts, vintage television sets, and mid-century Modern furniture mined from the canon of quintessentially Fifties props help to construct its surface (or cinematic) realism. These two strategies connect the film to others of its kind—a broader generic category—and to a wider nostalgia economy where these very same privileged objects and aesthetic conventions circulate in television, advertising, music videos, calendars, postcards and internet sites. By rehearsing the visual grammar of 1950s cinema, and thus the highly mediated source of many contemporary nostalgia films, *Far From Heaven* operates according to the logic of Grainge's nostalgia mode which is itself grounded in Jameson's understanding of nostalgia as a postmodern aesthetic mode.

Far From Heaven's self-conscious recreation of the form and style of 1950s cinema, and specifically Sirkian melodrama, certainly qualifies it as a paradigmatic postmodern nostalgia film. But it also shows why indulging in visual spectacle and obsolete, non-representational media codes (at the expense of explicitly addressing a history of purportedly 'significant' events) does not preclude a critical and meaningful exploration of the past and the present or grant insight into the means by which we access and come to understand history. In fact, *Far From Heaven* does more than simply reveal how both tendencies might coexist. The very same visual elements that signify and elicit nostalgia are also complicit in the film's penetrating critique of how racism, homophobia and patriarchal oppressions permeate the fabric of everyday life, structuring the relationships between 'ordinary' people in postwar and present-day America. Visual spectacles fashioned by vibrant colour palettes, elaborate set designs and extravagant dresses are not set in opposition to a narrative critique of the 1950s, the

Fifties, or nostalgia itself. Their role in the film is far more complex and one that acknowledges the postwar discourses in which they were implicated and how, during the 1950s, they could very well have been mobilized to challenge their authorized role in the expression of conspicuous consumption.

Far From Heaven also demonstrates how activating the nostalgia mode as a critical tool does not prohibit its constituent elements from eliciting nostalgic sentiment or any other kind of deeply felt emotional response including empathy for characters or frustration at injustice. Critical distance does not necessarily go hand in hand with emotional distance, a point eloquently made by Richard Dyer who admits to deriving a kind of analytical pleasure from Haynes's sophisticated cinephelia while, at times, being unable to see the screen through his tears (2007: 174). The film has the potential to generate affect in a number of ways which ultimately depend on the subject position and experiences of the spectator. Its technicolor aesthetic may evoke nostalgia for a period or genre of Hollywood film. It may prompt longing for the kind of intense emotional investment we imagine the ideal spectator to have had in Sirk's melodramatic worlds. It may incite yearning for the kind of meaningful spectatorial experience during which we feel unreservedly for (and with) the characters on screen, the kind we ascribe to earlier cinema audiences who we assume enjoyed direct and unproblematic identification with protagonists whose values, attitudes and experiences mirrored their own.[14] Certainly recent ethnographic studies into the history of reception have revealed the deep investment many generations have had in cinema theatres, stars and individual films or, at the very least, the intensity of their nostalgic memories of cinemagoing. Of course this does not mean that all responded with equal passion nor that these kinds of experiences are no longer possible.

Far From Heaven is not nostalgic for the Fifties or 1950s in the way *American Graffiti*, *Forrest Gump* or countless coming-of-age dramas are. It is nostalgic for what Sirkian cinema accomplished during the 1950s, how it managed to move audiences, to offer both visual and analytical pleasures at the same time as it launched a stinging critique of postwar life.[15] As such, it manages to rescue not only nostalgia, but Fifties nostalgia as something that can be divorced from its conservative uses. It locates in the Fifties (and the 1950s) moments of subversion that, however subtle and personal, are courageous in light of the social contexts in which they are performed. Sirk's subversion of the Production Code—much like Cathy's expressions of desire through dress, Frank's decision to finally embrace his homosexuality or the confidence with which Raymond moves through the still-segregated spaces of Hartford—is an individual act of resistance but one with far-reaching social significance. These kinds of acts and the courage they require are the objects of *Far From Heaven*'s nostalgia. They are also what end up providing more insight into the past than the injections of 'official' history against which they are juxtaposed. And given the persistence of the present enabled by the film's self-reflexive devices, the histories told visually through costume and colour encourage us to evaluate our contemporary moment and films against Haynes's Hartford. *Far From Heaven* does not mobilize the Fifties to show how far we have come, to tell us not to worry for Cathy or Frank because the 1960s are just around the corner. On the contrary, its deeply unhappy ending betrays a pessimistic view of the present and the United States' current neo-conservative culture in which social conventions, pressures and prejudices continue to marginalize and oppress on the basis of race, gender and sexuality. Cathy, Raymond and Frank may be trapped in a hermetically sealed fictional realm. But it seems we might just be trapped there with them.

Notes

1. Once again, comments made by the filmmakers have been obtained from special features on the DVD release.
2. 'Technicolor aesthetic' as a type of deliberate archaism is the subject of the following chapter and will be discussed at greater length there. Briefly defined, it describes the look achieved by contemporary films that visually replicate the colour schemes associated with Technicolor processes used in Hollywood since the 1920s.
3. They also point outward or laterally to the persistence of the New Look in contemporary fashion, advertising and film and thus the nostalgia economy.
4. See for example Bruzzi (1997), Berry (2000), Street (2001), Cook (1996), Pidduck (2004), Moseley (2005), Gaines and Herzog (1990).
5. It also might evoke *The Color Purple* by Alice Walker or speak to the significance of purple as a feminist colour historically. See J. Goldman for a discussion of how purple came to signify a feminine subjectivity (1998: 177). My thanks to Bridget Elliott for bringing this to my attention.
6. Frank is employed as an executive for a television manufacturer called Magnatech.
7. For an extended discussion of this and other visual mediations as well as aural mediations see Joyrich (2004).
8. However, the New Look itself was not entirely new. Cawthorne explains that it 'harked back to the styles of the *Belle Époque*, the secure and comfortable period before the First World War when Dior had grown up.' (1996: 109). Turim explains that the New Look silhouette had not only been seen during the period of Dior's youth (the late nineteenth century),

but also well before that in the courts of Louis XV in the eighteenth century (1990: 215). However, to the young women of Europe and America who had become accustomed to the rather comfortable uniforms and trousers that their wartime careers required, the look was certainly different and for all intents and purposes, 'new'.

9. This colour palette—inspired by Edward Hopper's 1942 painting 'Nighthawks'—mirrors that of the gay bar patronized by Frank earlier in the film and thus unites these two spaces, both of which are marginalized by Hartford's white suburban class.

10. Another key strategy to alert audiences to *Far From Heaven*'s status as a film involves several actions which are represented in real time but should have, for the sake of realism, involved elliptical editing. On one occasion Cathy passes Sybil a plate of food which she asks to be wrapped up for her to take to Frank. Almost as soon as she lets go of the plate, Sybil hands her back a sealed Tupperware container. Likewise, barely a second elapses between hearing Cathy's doorbell ring and seeing the flash of Mrs Leacock's camera. These moments are overtly unreal and impossible, staged and artificial.

11. At times the film's characterization of Sybil and Raymond as cinematic constructions, based on *Imitation of Life* and Sidney Poitier films respectively, seem too subtle, and thus reinforce rather than deconstruct Hollywood's roles for and stereotyping of African-American actors. What *Far From Heaven* does not always manage to do is reveal the persistence of racist tendencies in purportedly anti-racist films of the 1960s and 1970s. Perhaps the most potent critiques of past and present day racism are effected through self-consciously cinematic moments that encourage spectators to see Dennis Haysbert and Viola Davis as actors and as African-American individuals who have been asked to inhabit Haynes's racist Hartford. Especially heart-wrenching is thinking about how Haynes would have had to explain to twelve year old Jordan Puryear (Sarah) that she would be the victim of a violent hate crime—especially since such crimes are not a thing of the past but a brutal reality in present day America.

12. The absence of mauve in her ensemble is explained by her surprise (and subsequent embarrassment for being surprised) that Raymond too has attended this event.

13. Incidentally, the stage direction called for Picasso's 1937 painting 'Weeping Woman', a work that mirrors the colour palette for this scene. The blue of the central area of the composition is precisely the shade on the walls of the gallery and the deeper blue, red and yellow are a match to the colours of light streaming in through the windows. Unfortunately, Picasso never made the final cut and instead we catch glimpses of the red and orange abstract composition that enchanted Cathy.

14. This is a point that will be pursued at greater length in the next chapter.

15. Perhaps Haynes is even somewhat nostalgic for how the 1950s brand of dogmatic conservatism offered critics like Sirk clear-cut channels for rebellion and transgression. My thanks to the anonymous reader who suggested this.

Chapter 6

The Aviator: Deliberate Archaism, Technicolor Aesthetics and Style as Substance

However dissimilar *Far From Heaven* and *Sin City* may seem, both exhibit features central to contemporary understandings of the nostalgia film. They draw on the cultural significance of key props, replicate the look of past media forms and invest (wholesale or in part) in nostalgia's dominant object—the Fifties. Both films demonstrate how such an investment has the potential to initiate critical readings that engage history rather than efface it and explore the kinds of relationships that exist between the present and the past in its mythic and mediated forms. While the Fifties remains dominant in the nostalgia economy of the twenty-first century, other decade- and event-related constructs have also grown in number and popularity. Accordingly, in this final chapter I would like to move away from the Fifties and focus on *The Aviator*, a film which announces its setting as the 1920s to the 1940s yet makes use of the visual strategies inaugurated through cinematic recreations of the Fifties. Specifically, it makes use of a strategy that defines the contemporary nostalgia film from its 1930s and 1940s antecedents: the practice of deliberate archaism and, in this instance, the use of what I am calling a 'technicolor aesthetic'.[1] In recreating Technicolor's interwar palettes, *The Aviator* thus demands that we expand our conception of Technicolor itself. It forces us to acknowledge that the cinematographic look generated in postwar Hollywood studios—that generating contemporary nostalgia culture and visual perceptions of the Fifties—is but one of many. Even more importantly, the film suggests that each of these looks is implicated in, and thus grants access to, discourses and debates that shaped cinema history.

Technicolor Aesthetics

A 'technicolor aesthetic' is a *type* of deliberate archaism and thus one of the key defining features of the nostalgia film. Deliberate archaism, as we recall from chapter 3, describes the practice of creating new-old films which mine the memories of media forms and strive to recreate not only the look and feel of the period in question but also the appearance of art from that distant time (Le Sueur 1977: 193–94). Though similar to pastiche, the two terms are not synonymous. Deliberate archaism is best understood as a form of pastiche that involves self-conscious simulations as well as reinterpretations of past visual styles. As Richard Dyer (2007) rightly points out, pastiche almost always involves a dialectic of present and past. However, it is also well-suited to describing imitations of one media form by another (e.g., films and advertisements that pastiche video games with which they are contemporaneous). Moreover, deliberate archaism describes an exclusively visual practice whereas pastiche in film extends its reach to character types, generic conventions, dialogue and so forth.

Given the unquantifiable range of visual styles at a filmmaker's disposal, the store of templates with the capacity to source deliberately archaic practices is virtually limitless. Consider the stylistic shifts between different artistic periods, movements and even schools. Consider, too, how slight changes in nineteenth- and twentieth-century technologies of representation could effect dramatic shifts in the look of images. Technological processes specific to photography, film, television and print have given us a remarkably varied array of black-and-white and colour palettes. Any one or combination of these palettes can be exploited by cultural producers aiming to manufacture visual pastness. So why combine 'technicolor' and 'aesthetic' to describe one kind of deliberately archaic look? To answer this I will discuss the relevance of each in turn.

'Technicolor' has become a brand eponym rather than the brand name attached to a registered colour process and corporation (e.g., Technicolor, Inc.). It has evolved into a generic descriptor with the ability to call to mind a vibrant palette of bright and slightly artificial-looking colours. It is also used to describe, perhaps unfairly, the look of Hollywood films that actually employed other colour processes such as Kodak's Eastman Color. Although Technicolor, Inc. produced a broad range of colour palettes starting early in the twentieth century, its three-strip process associated with films like *Gentlemen Prefer Blondes* tends to stand out in cultural memory. This is the look favoured for calendars, postcards, packaging and advertising seeking to appeal to both nostalgic and ironic sensibilities.

I want to adopt the term 'technicolor' primarily for its association in the popular imagination with postwar Hollywood spectacle. But I also want it to function as an umbrella term that admits under its rubric the specific colour schemes generated by the various Technicolor processes. This will accommodate the growing variety of past cinematic looks currently being revived in contemporary film and acknowledge the increasing sophistication with which audiences call on their historical knowledge of cinema during the viewing experience. This brings me to the other reason for employing the term. Despite its many uses across popular visual media and in the nostalgia economy, Technicolor remains grounded in its cinematic past. We are aware of its origins, its 'cinematicness' and perhaps even its connection to specific genres. Technicolor appeared during the early and mid twentieth century almost exclusively in musicals, fantasies and melodramas and thus remains attached to the type of diegetic realties constructed by these films.

The other term, 'aesthetic', is perhaps the more charged of the two and may conjure up the 'disinterestedness' or 'purposiveness without purpose' of Kantian fame. My use of it here draws less on its classical application in the philosophy of art (or aesthetics proper) than it does on its colloquial understanding as a look, visual style or way of describing the quality and texture of an image. Having said that, I do want to preserve something of its etymological roots, specifically its relation to feeling and emotion. In other words, while 'technicolor aesthetic' may describe a particular look, it also admits the potential for this look to evoke an affective response. As such, it shares with Dyer's account of pastiche the quality of being both 'cerebrally observed' and 'felt' (2007: 133).

Films that make use of a technicolor aesthetic, or another kind of deliberately archaic look, are easy targets for the charge of 'all style, no substance'. *Sky Captain and the World of Tomorrow* and *The Good German* were both lambasted by reviewers for intertextual indulgences that most spectators would fail to 'get' and for offering viewers little in the way of story, drama or character development. Perhaps these critics are right (especially in the case of the former). But while these films might fail some audiences—as entertainment created to serve a variety of pleasures—they remain fascinating cultural objects through which to think about how our present moment envisions and mediates the past and the kinds of access to history that certain visual constructions enable. Here, I want to focus on *The Aviator* (2004), directed by Martin Scorsese, in order to examine how style might indeed lead to substance.

The Aviator and the Filmmaker

The Aviator has received a fair bit of criticism in the popular press but of a somewhat less vitriolic nature than that directed at *Sky Captain and the World of Tomorrow*. And like *The Good German* it has also been faulted for appealing only to film buffs and film historians because it invests more in recreating the look of Hollywood cinema of the 1920s and 1930s than it does in telling us about Howard Hughes or history. However, its use of a technicolor aesthetic does more than secure its place as a nostalgia film or betray Scorsese's own nostalgia for the work of his predecessors. It is mobilized in complex and sophisticated ways that grant access to film history and, specifically, the uses and effects of colour in Hollywood cinema of the interwar years. But at the same time that *The Aviator* reveals how non-representational aesthetic codes might offer both affective and conceptual insight into the history of colour cinema it also encourages us to weigh this history against that represented through archival footage and thus against a purportedly more 'official' history. The film's technicolor aesthetic also accomplishes something else. As Dyer says of pastiche, it allows us to experience that which is being imitated (Dyer 2007: 60). By doing so, *The Aviator* provides us with an opportunity to become Slavoj Žižek's 'mythical naïve spectator', an enviable if not wholly utopian position, but one that is also potentially alarming.

The Aviator attempts to salvage the reputation of American billionaire Howard Hughes by advocating his 'genius' in the fields of aviation and filmmaking and celebrating his pioneering contributions to both industries from the late 1920s through to the mid 1940s (Figure 6.1). The debilitating effects of Hughes' Obsessive Compulsive Disorder loom large throughout this biopic, foregrounded, at times, to provide insight into how its symptoms impacted his daily life. And while the film makes an effort to deconstruct thoughtfully the stereotypes associated with Hughes and his illness, ones well-entrenched in the popular consciousness (thanks to *The Simpsons*),[2] it does little to counter the stereotype that some kind of 'madness' is a necessary precondition for genius and artistic creativity. To enable audience identification and empathy, the film also effaces the disturbing extent of Hughes' racism, anti-communism and capitalistic ruthlessness as well as his sexual predation of young women, preferring instead to commemorate his heroic achievements as an American entrepreneur.

Figure 6.1 Leonardo DiCaprio in *The Aviator* (2004). Warner Bros/The Kobal Collection.

Narratively, the film follows most of the conventions of the biopic. Scorsese and his team isolated and dramatized what they felt were personally and historically significant moments in Hughes' life from his late teens to his early forties. Visually, however, the film departs in certain respects from the ways in which this genre tends to signify the periods it recreates. On the one hand, it succeeds in crafting a convincing surface realism through materially and digitally manufactured props (e.g., airplanes, furniture, personal grooming items) and places (e.g., Grauman's Chinese Theater, The Cocoanut Grove, Hughes' mansion). It makes use of archival photographs and films, Hollywood movies and promotional material as well as print advertising and fan publications as the basis for costume, hair and makeup design. Archival photographs also provide the blueprint for a digitally created 1947 skyline, *The Front Page* (1931) serves as the model for the pace and rhythm of the dialogue and images of the 1939 World's Fair and William Cameron Menzies' *The Shape of Things to Come* (1936) inspire the futuristic look of certain props and shots. According to the production designers, much time, effort and research went into getting the look 'right'.[3] In other words, they took great pains to mobilize a set of recognizable visual cues capable of convincing spectators of the authenticity of the 1920s, 1930s and 1940s on offer—of the film's historical verisimilitude. On the other hand, the film indulges in a kind of self-conscious deliberate archaism. It replicates the look of two-strip Technicolor for the first half of the film and then, close to the time three-strip was actually introduced to Hollywood in the 1930s, shifts to this particular colour palette for the remainder.[4]

From Rembrandt to Phantom of the Opera: Digitizing Archaisms

The Miramax and Warner Bros. logos may foretell the coming of two-strip Technicolor, but the film does not plunge directly into this particular aesthetic until the second scene. Instead, it opens with a very different kind of deliberately archaic look, one rooted in art history rather than film history. It is a look informed by seventeenth-century Dutch and Flemish painting and, though no less a mediation of reality than two-strip Technicolor, appears more real in light of what follows. The opening shot shows a seven- or eight-year-old Howard standing naked in a tub of water, outlined by light from an unseen source and visually overwhelmed by the surrounding darkness. A scattering of soft yellowish lights gradually appears, emanating from candles, the fireplace, floor lamps and a low-hung chandelier that decorate the cavernous interior of the Hughes' living room. They describe the multiple planes and thus the depth of the space but fail to penetrate the darkness, in a way that recalls Rembrandt's 'Philosopher in Mediation' (1632) or Gerrit Dou's 'Astronomer by Candlelight' (1665). Rembrandt's palette of deep, rich browns and hazy, glowing yellows is echoed in the look of this scene in which Hughes' mother bathes him and, according to the film, contaminates him with her own obsession with germs.

Hughes was born in 1905 and thus we can surmise that this scene takes place around 1912 or 1913, nearly two decades after the first exhibition of a motion picture. One might expect that, in keeping with the visual logic of *The Aviator*, Scorsese would have appropriated one of the many cinematic looks developed at this time. However, crafting a palette reminiscent of seventeenth-century northern European art serves a purpose. The dark brown tones and warm yellow light that define it are at the furthest visual remove from the vivid hues generated by the two-strip process. As a result, two-strip seems even more unrealistic than it already does and, more importantly, even more cinematic. This cinematic quality is narratively reinforced by its introduction through a cut from the dark oppressive interior of Hughes' living room to the bright, vast expanse of the California desert airstrip and set location for Hughes' epic, *Hell's Angels* (1930). In a self-reflexive manoeuvre indicating the start of the film's cinematic consciousness, a close-up of a clapboard announces 'scene 147B, take 5'. Authenticating cinch marks pass through the frame as the camera loader stands in front of one of the many First World War biplanes being readied for a *Hell's Angels* combat sequence. That we are about to watch a film (and a life played out on film and defined by a profound investment in film) is further confirmed by the startling appearance of vibrant, preternatural reds (based in magenta), cyan and dusty, peachy beiges. It seems entirely artificial, especially when expanses of blue grass or blue foliage fill the frame. It is a look specific to the cinema and thus evocative of this media form alone. Whereas what might be described as a 1950s technicolor aesthetic (whether it is Technicolor proper or Eastman Color is beside the point) appeared in film, advertising and comics of the period and since across the spectrum of visual culture, the look of two-strip remains exclusively cinematic.

The two-strip Technicolor created for *The Aviator* is one of many two-strip looks. From the advent of two-strip in the 1920s through to the introduction of three-strip in the mid 1930s, the look of this dye-transfer process varied widely from studio to studio and even from one batch of films to the next.[5] Scorsese cites this particular era of filmmaking and the different forms of colour it produced as formative for his own practice (Scorsese in Goldman 2005: 14).

These colours and colour schemes are almost palpable to him and come to mind whenever his thoughts turn to 'Old Hollywood'. They are firmly imprinted on his consciousness and form the basis of 'sense memories' of having watched films from this 'great period' as a child. These comments betray a deeply felt personal nostalgia for the pioneering efforts of 1920s and 1930s Hollywood, a nostalgia likely intensified by Technicolor's decision to permanently decommission its dye-transfer processes in 2002 (Goldman 2005: 14–15).[6] This combination of a long-standing nostalgia for Hollywood's experimental period and the end of celluloid Technicolor is probably what motivated (if not necessitated) Scorsese's move to digital filmmaking.

To recreate the look of two- and three-strip Technicolor that so enamoured Scorsese, Robert Legato (the visual effects supervisor) turned to digital technology as well as to colour scientists at Technicolor, Inc. He found three-strip reasonably easy to emulate with the use of Adobe After Effects and Photoshop CS. Two-strip, on the other hand, proved to be a greater challenge and required the help of Dick Goldberg, a retired dye-transfer expert who had collaborated with Technicolor pioneers Herbert and Natalie Kalmus (Goldman 2004: 7). Together they discovered that what worked in the 1920s to correct some of the unnatural results achieved by mixing cyan and magenta also worked digitally: small amounts of yellow had to be added to each of the two layers of colour (Goldman 2004: 7). Scorsese was instantly taken with the degree of control digital filmmaking offered and was attracted to the experimental possibilities contained in this new technology. This permitted him to feel an affinity with his forebears by offering contemporary audiences the kind of colourful spectacles that so astonished him as a child. However, I doubt this is the only reason *The Aviator*'s Technicolor ended up being of the digital variety.

While *The Aviator* faithfully recreates the hues that defined the particular brand of two-strip seen in the spectacular 'Bal Masque' sequence of the 1925/29 version of *The Phantom of the Opera*, unsurprisingly, the two films look substantially different. The clarity, sharpness, tint and tonal variations achieved digitally renders *The Aviator* more visually seductive (for the contemporary blockbuster audience) than its celluloid antecedents, films characterized by less nuanced colour, starker tonal contrasts and a grainier texture. Cinematic experiments with colour and colour processes during the 1920s, 1930s and 1940s may have produced some brilliant results. But I suspect that a truly faithful recreation of the film aesthetics from that period would have been rejected outright by Miramax or Warner Bros. executives and especially if an 'idealized' or perfected version was technologically possible. The two-strip look of *The Phantom of the Opera* may be nostalgically potent to Scorsese and certain facets of the filmgoing audience. However, its place in memory is far more magical than its ability to enchant the key 18–34 (or increasingly 16–22) demographic enamoured with Leonardo DiCaprio and accustomed to sleek, crisp images.

Scorsese's nostalgically inspired homage to 'Old Hollywood' through a digitally adulterated technicolor aesthetic may certainly seem a personal indulgence in visual style. Indeed it may even seem jarringly disconnected from the subject at hand—Howard Hughes. However, as we shall see in the discussion that follows, Scorsese's deliberately archaic practices yield visually and conceptually rich engagements with cinema history and the cinematic potential of colour. Arguably, the film's visual pastness is less an effacement of history (as Jameson might say) than its story of Howard Hughes. What follows is a close visual analysis of select scenes and, especially, *The Aviator*'s separation of its two- and three-strip halves with an archival interface in order to reveal the critical potential contained in its use of a technicolor aesthetic.

Introducing (the uses of) Two-Strip

Two-strip Technicolor is used throughout the first half of the film, slipping in and out of consciousness as a distinctly cinematic strategy in the service of spectacle, narrative and emotion. In short, it catalogues the very literal uses and assumed effects of colour on the diegesis and spectator of early Hollywood cinema. For example, dramatic and fast-paced exchanges between characters shot in close-up leave little room to admit the flashes of preternatural reds and aqua blues that might disturb the surface of the image and detract from the content of the dialogue. Certain settings, like the California desert, are well-served by the limited palette and especially by the quality of the dusty beiges it allows. Some sequences are even designed to foreground colour and the clash of red and cyan. Hughes' world-record-breaking flight starts on a dusty beige desert airstrip and ends with a crash landing in a lush beet field. As the plane slices through the vegetation, deep red beet juice sprays the blue foliage and fuselage. In this instance the stark juxtaposition of saturated red and blue heightens the dramatic impact of the crash; both colour and event serve the interests of spectacle.

Two-strip (and later three-strip) is also used to visually spectacular effect in scenes set in the Cocoanut Grove, a famed Hollywood nightclub frequented by the stars and revisited by Hughes several times throughout the course of the film. Turquoise neon lettering and red neon palm trees float on screen like an inter-title as the camera cranes over the packed dance floor. The interior is lavish, an indulgence in Art Deco luxury featuring extravagant floral arrangements, richly patterned wallpaper, life-sized palm trees, lush fringed drapery, cigarette girls in Egyptian dress and showgirls on swings trailing iridescent streamers above the crowd. Several long shots and gliding crane shots attempt to take in the full effect of the space, as does a key establishing shot from Hughes' point of view. At these moments the full potential of two-strip colour is realized from punctuating flashes of pure saturated red to vibrant turquoise as well as everything possible in between. The seemingly limited two-strip palette belies a richness and intensity of expression well-suited to the glamour and opulence embodied in the Cocoanut Grove experience *and* Hollywood cinema of the 1920s.

The final two scenes rendered in two-strip Technicolor also seem to experiment with the expressive potential of its hues. Whereas the penultimate scene, set in Katharine Hepburn's (Cate Blanchett) bedroom, mobilizes the full spectrum of peachy beiges on variously textured surfaces to romantic effect, the final two-strip scene, set in Hepburn's bathroom, features cyan and its preternatural red counterpart in its purest forms. The stark contrasts achieved by juxtaposing clearly defined solid areas of cyan, red, black and white visually reinforces the dramatic intensity of the lengthy conversation that takes place here between Hepburn and Hughes. Hepburn's blouse is deep red patterned with small black and white abstract forms, the walls and Hughes dress shirt are white, countertops are black, the tiles alternate between cyan and black and sections of decorative wallpaper are red, cyan and white. A lampshade and a few towels provide some of the only hints of beige in this space. Thus, the final scene functions as a testament to the source and essence of the two-strip look, providing one last glimpse of its foundational colours in their purest form before abandoning them for a very different aesthetic.

In these ways, *The Aviator*'s deliberate archaism engages with history (rather than evacuates it) by performing a kind of preservation work that approximates the look of specific technological processes and, more importantly, the significance of colour in early cinema. Scorsese has for a long time been involved in efforts to conserve and make available to contemporary audiences early—and rapidly deteriorating—films. In the painstaking process of digitally replicating the specific type of two-strip on display in *The Aviator*, Robert Legato and his Technicolor advisors actually managed to develop software coded with a methodology to emulate other vintage looks (Goldman 2005: 26). Perhaps our access to early-twentieth-century films will come to depend as much on our ability to restore celluloid as it does on our capacity to not just digitally transfer, but also digitally recreate aspects of these works.

Yet acts of historical preservation are necessarily motivated by presuppositions about what is worth saving. Such acts also reveal much about the present concerns and desires that shape archives and historical collections, editing out from time to time what no longer forms a necessary part of our conception of the past. In performing this kind of work, Scorsese too has plagued *The Aviator*—as a biography and engagement with film history—with the very same problems that affect virtually any historical text. Why privilege the two-strip look of *The Phantom of the Opera* Bal Masque sequence and not the Handschiegl Process[7] used in the remainder of this film or in Hughes' own *Hell's Angels*? Might Handschiegl seem too stylized for a contemporary audience? Experiments with two-colour processes (whether additive or subtractive) were often deemed failures (Higgins 2000: 363). Was *The Phantom of the Opera*'s use of colour a success? If so, why? Did Scorsese's use of this particular look stem from its impact on him personally rather than its contributions to film technology and significance in film history? Did *The Phantom of the Opera*'s palette translate better digitally or was it easier to access than other early two-strip examples? Might its recognizability to a contemporary audience ensure the kind of intertextual delight that a more obscure work of early cinema would be less likely to deliver? Was the colour palette of the Bal Masque sequence selected for preservation because, like a transformative historical event, it is extraordinary rather than ordinary?

Despite these questions, *The Aviator*'s preservation of early Technicolor palettes does important historical work. It performs the mundane but necessary task of reminding contemporary audiences of the presence of colour in 1920s and 1930s film. This audience includes some of my own students who assume that film before 1950 was black and white and that *The Wizard of Oz* (1939) was colourized only later for their benefit. More importantly, by mimicking *how* colour was used *The Aviator* also engages with the expressive potential it was thought to contain and its relationship to narrative events.

The Archival Interface: Documentary, Fiction and the Mediation of History

Three-strip Technicolor is not unveiled immediately following the final two-strip scene. A short black-and-white sequence functions as an interface between the two colour registers, one well worth considering for what it contributes to the film's engagement with mediation and the history of early colour cinema. This black-and-white sequence is comprised of documentary footage celebrating Hughes' successful 1938 solo circumnavigation of the globe in a record four days (Figure 6.2). Over the course of thirty seconds, fourteen cuts offer a rapid-fire succession of images capturing his flight, reporters positioning themselves along the runway and crowds assembling to welcome him home. Though cobbled together from actual newsreel footage of the event, this montage has been digitally altered to allow Leonardo DiCaprio to appear in place of Howard Hughes. Film of DiCaprio miming Hughes' disembarkation, his gestures and waves to the crowd during a New York City tickertape parade have been seamlessly grafted into the original footage.

The digital insertion of an actor into extant documentary footage was first accomplished by the special-effects technicians working on *Forrest Gump*. This technological innovation allowed the eponymous 'everyman' to interact with presidents and participate in the historic desegregation of a Little Rock high school. But it did so not without controversy. On the one hand, the intentional blurring of the lines between fact and fiction prompted charges of historical inaccuracy and the deliberate suppression of historical truth. The seamlessness of the effect led critics to worry that audiences might be convinced of the authenticity of the footage and come to believe that Forrest Gump did indeed meet JFK or pick up the textbook dropped by one of the young black women entering the exclusively white Little Rock school for the first time. Recent scholarly work on the film is more optimistic and puts faith in the intellectual capacity of audiences to recognize the technological tricks on display. On the other hand, although the film's overt conservative bias is almost always readily acknowledged, some critics, like Vivian Sobchack, have shifted their focus to consider how it uses history and engages with mediated views of the past. Sobchack describes *Forrest Gump* as a 'historically conscious' document, one that contends with the late-twentieth-century's fascination with history (including this era's desire to admit both 'trivial' and 'significant' events into historical canons) and with spectators who see themselves as self-consciously historical subjects (Sobchack 1996: 2–3).

Figure 6.2 Howard Hughes in the New York tickertape parade, July 15, 1938. Keystone/Hulton Archive/Getty Images.

For Robert Burgoyne, *Forrest Gump*'s digital manipulations literalize the concept of 'prosthetic memory'. Borrowing Alison Landsberg's definition of the term as a kind of publicly circulating memory experienced through technologies of representation, Burgoyne argues that *Forrest Gump* offers insight into how the cinema, as an apparatus of cultural memory, transforms history into memory. In other words, films can translate significant historical events into personal memories that are deeply felt and formative to the identities of individuals separated temporally and/or geographically from the original event. He also suggests that the controversies generated by films about history like *Forrest Gump*, 'point to the idea that film has somehow claimed the mantle of authenticity and meaningfulness with relation to the past—not necessarily of accuracy or fidelity to the record, but of meaningfulness, understood in terms of emotional and affective truth' (Burgoyne 1999). Burgoyne explains that 'this suturing the spectator, through identification with Forrest Gump, into an actual historical scene collapses the distinction between the personal and the historical and foregrounds the multiple and complicated relations between individual and collective memory' (1999).

While *Forrest Gump* sutures the spectator into the past, rendering history affectively and conceptually meaningful as personal memory, *The Aviator* uses this grafting technology to a slightly different effect. *The Aviator* too (through identification with its protagonist) holds the potential to place us in history, to insert us into the midst of celebrations marking an aviation milestone. It makes accessible on an affective level the extraordinary events and achievements that defined Hughes' life, enabling identification with, if not the specific event, then at least with the sentiments and significance attached to personal triumph. Hughes' achievement is thus understood in terms of its emotional and affective truth—what breaking this particular aviation record meant to Hughes personally and the nation collectively. More than this, it might well appeal to a desire to see oneself through the adoring eyes of the public, as part of an archival record and thus as part of history. Inserting us, through Hughes, into historical footage is tantamount to inserting us into history itself.

But identification is rarely an uncomplicated affair. The various subject positions inhabited by spectators as well as the degree to which an individual is willing to invest in the filmic reality represented may militate against any kind of direct or unproblematic identification with the protagonist. As a star construct 'Leonardo DiCaprio' necessarily brings to Hughes traces of his past roles. His performance as a well-known public personality may also, and especially in this instance, remind audiences of the oft-heard criticism that DiCaprio looks too young for the roles he has been chosen to play. As with Tom Hanks in *Forrest Gump*, part of the pleasure in seeing DiCaprio assume Hughes' place in the tickertape parade may stem from recognizing this sequence as a digital sleight of hand, acknowledging and enjoying the actor's performance as a performance or perhaps even critically contemplating the film's layering of different moments in time and its blurring of fact and fiction.

The difference between *Forrest Gump* and *The Aviator*'s use of this digital graft lies in its relationship to the other ways in which 'history' enters the film and the extent to which this relationship reveals the mediated nature of history itself. In *Forrest Gump*, the digitized footage appears black and white on television sets and colourized when part of the diegesis. Gump shaking hands with presidents may fascinate and arrest narrative continuity, but every attempt has been made to seamlessly integrate these sequences into the logic of the film. In *The Aviator*, DiCaprio's digital graft is only one of many visually distinct injections of 'real' history through the incorporation or simulation of extant footage. Convention dictates that we ought to read newsreel footage as documentary evidence and allow its 'authenticity' to inflect our consumption of the information it contains. This is confirmed not only visually through its black and white and slightly grainy quality, but also aurally through the rhythm and timbre of the announcer's narration that dates this segment, if not to the late 1930s, then at least to that general time. However its authenticity is also challenged by overt digital manipulation, rendering this clip neither fact nor fiction but a confluence of both. *The Aviator* seems less concerned with exploring (or challenging) the truth value of documentary record than it does with the potential for digitally manufactured deliberate archaic regimes to enable their own kind of access to history. In this film both are equally adept at engaging the past, both are equally mediated, manipulated and malleable and both belong to a set of representational practices of which no one is privileged as more authentic or valid than another.

For example, the integration of clips from landmark films including *The Jazz Singer* (1927) and Hughes' own *Hell's Angels* and *The Outlaw* (1943), encourages our recognition of them as cinematic milestones but also an awareness that our access to them, like our access to Howard Hughes and to history itself, is always mediated, yet not necessarily any less meaningful or historically significant as a result (Figure 6.3). *Hell's Angels* is seen in several formats throughout the course of *The Aviator*: on screens in public theatres and private screening rooms, as a film that occupies the entire frame, as newsreel footage documenting the filming of aerial manoeuvres, as digitally recreated scenes, and through intensely coloured filters used to signify the depths of Hughes' psychosis. Access to this film is thus mediated and self-consciously so in ways that visually transform its look with each iteration. No one 'view' of the film emerges as the privileged view. Instead *Hell's Angel*'s exists within *The Aviator* as a significant cultural text, accessed then, as now, in a variety of formats and contexts, each with the capacity to generate its own set of meanings. It is represented as a crafted object under critical scrutiny by industry professionals, a landmark film screened for past audiences. At the same time, its full-screen appearances make it seem contemporary for present audiences, a newsworthy event showcasing both aviation and the cinema as expressions of modernity, a part of Hughes' everyday lived reality and the product of a personal obsession. It exists on cinema screens, in personal and collective memory, in black and white, digital two-strip Technicolor and in its original Multi- and Handschiegl Color. Films, like significant events or achievements, are themselves history and as such are encountered, envisioned and consumed in a variety of ways.

Unveiling (the History of) Three-Strip

Almost as intriguing as the shifts from Technicolor to Handschiegl or from documentary to cinematic fiction are the ways in which transitions between visually distinct segments are effected, further alerting us to how representational practices mediate what they portray. Some of these transitions are sudden, punctuated by abrupt cuts between shots. Others are subtle and involve smooth and gradual shifts in colour. The use of documentary footage celebrating Hughes' 1938 flight as an interface between two-strip and three-strip Technicolor makes use of both. For instance, the transition from two-strip to newsreel is sharp and jarring, rendering explicit the film's replacement of colour with monochrome and the end of the two-strip palette. The introduction of the three-strip look is gradual, on an almost colour-by-colour basis and starting with the infusion of a limited array of colour into a black and white image of the top of the Chrysler building. Although the sharpness of this image confirms that it is not part of the newsreel footage, the bright blue sky surrounding this gleaming silver structure barely hints at the palette shift that, by this point, has already happened. The next shot confirms this change through the introduction of green in Juan Trippe's (Alec Baldwin)

Figure 6.3 Leonardo DiCaprio and Matt Ross watch Jane Russell on the screen in *The Aviator* (2004). Warner Bros/The Kobal Collection.

office. Green has not been added randomly here simply to demonstrate the expanded palette now at the film's disposal. It is used self-reflexively to signal the end to cyan's dominance and its past uses to describe that which ought to have been green. In this scene green is used liberally and to describe that which ought to be blue: the oceans on the vast panoramic map decorating the walls of Trippe's lavish Deco interior. The introduction of green in this way signifies more than just the appearance of a new colour. It speaks to the cultural significance of colour and its conventionalized uses. And by subverting expectations generated through its past uses, the film not only foregrounds colour's expressive potential but also speaks to its capacity to generate meaning.

The introduction of yellow in the next scene is no less dramatic and no less an engagement with the history of colour in the cinema. An establishing shot of throngs of fans and reporters lining the red carpet at the entrance of the Pantages Theater showcases the new shades of reds (venetian, burgundy, scarlet, etc.) made possible with three-strip Technicolor. The scene then cuts to an 'American shot' of Hepburn and Hughes, barely recognizable under the glare of spotlights and the flash of camera bulbs. After a few moments Hepburn's assistant removes her cape from her shoulders to reveal her (dried?) mustard yellow silk gown. It is an odd colour for an evening gown and distinct from the jewel-toned costumes worn by other celebrities attending this movie premiere. It effectively confirms Hepburn's individuality and reluctance to conform to Hollywood's norms. But it also, quite crucially, introduces into *The Aviator* a colour noticeably absent in the first half of the film. The continual barrage of flashes directed at Hepburn, now in a medium shot as she makes her way toward the entrance of the theatre, maintains focus on both the star and this startling new hue. Once inside the foyer the full spectrum of pinks and purples also becomes apparent. Women wearing vibrant, solid-coloured dresses cross the background and foreground in a parade of aubergine, fuchsia, salmon, and carnation.

That this sequence celebrates the revelation of yellow and ultimately the full palette of three-strip Technicolor is confirmed by the choice of film screened at the premiere attended by Hepburn and Hughes. Posters outside the Pantages identify the film as George Cukor's *The Women* (1939). Starring Norma Shearer, Joan Crawford and Rosalind Russell, this black-and-white comedy classic boasts a nearly six-minute Technicolor fashion show intended to put colour, as much as Adrian's extravagant sartorial creations, on display. Introduced as a 'glimpse of the future', this fashion show is pure spectacle in every sense, employing highly stylized sets, sharply dressed monkeys as props and outrageous beach, leisure and evening wear including a cape decorated with a bejewelled prosthetic hand. It also employs a self-reflexive mise en abyme effect by staging a fashion show within a fashion show, thereby consciously asserting the theatricality and fantastical nature of this scene. The use of colour seems fully justified here for the entire sequence sits quite comfortably *outside* the logic of the filmic reality produced in *The Women*. As spectacle it disrupts the narrative flow. But as a moment designed for visual pleasure and indulgence, this is precisely what it seems it should be doing. And this is also what happens in the foyer of the Pantages Theater. Here too the narrative is constantly interrupted by splashes of vibrant colours that cross diegetic space and compete for attention. (In a somewhat indirect way this actually serves the narrative events which are focused first on Hepburn's competition with Hughes for media attention and then on Hughes' competition for Hepburn's attention.) Like the fashion show staged in *The Women*, *The Aviator*'s premiere featuring *The Women* splits the audience's attention between narrative events and visual spectacle. In this instance, visual pleasure has the potential to yield a kind of conceptual or analytical pleasure, one derived from recognizing this scene's cinematic antecedents and from thinking through what colour can accomplish.

As seen in the examples throughout this chapter, *The Aviator* uses colour to draw attention to itself as spectacle, to heighten the intensity of dramatic events, to underscore the emotional lens through which characters view the world and to appeal to the cultural connotations typically ascribed to them. The film's use of colour for these ends is, for the most part, obvious and uncomplicated. It recalls cinema's early uses of colour in the service of fantasy as well as the debates generated in response to the dictates set forth by Natalie Kalmus, head of the Color Advisory Service and consultant on virtually every major studio Technicolor production from the 1930s to the 1950s (Higgins 1999: 65). Advancements in colour technology were often put on display to 'flaunt colour as a novel element' as in *La Cucaracha* (1934), Technicolor's three-strip 'prototype film' designed to test the full range of effects made possible by different uses and combinations of colours (Higgins 2000: 361). However, this is precisely what Kalmus argued against. She lobbied for the restrained use of colour and its subservience to narrative and drama. Yet however much her influence can be seen in the subdued colours that characterize the majority of early three-strip films (Higgins 1999: 56), use of colour remained, for the most part, literal and over-determined.

Though *The Aviator*'s use of colour is rarely restrained (and when it is, is ostensibly so, through the almost complete evacuation of red and cyan from certain scenes), it often directly supports narrative and drama. In fact it sometimes calls attention to itself as doing precisely that. During the two-strip half of the film, the blue of DiCaprio's eyes intensifies at times, usually to signify the increasing intensity of his passion for aviation. This literal correlation between colour and narrative is almost impossible to ignore, announcing itself as a cinematographic strategy. The film's self-consciousness in representing the different and sometimes conflicting uses and assumptions about the role of colour brings to the screen the various positions assumed in debates about the uses and effects of colour in the first half of the twentieth century. In short, *The Aviator* demonstrates how style can generate substance by visually articulating the discourses about colour cinema that circulated during the periods it represents. In doing so, it also weighs in on contemporary debates, for the early concerns about colour's potential to distract from the narrative or indulge only visual spectacle are echoed in some of the charges currently being levelled against digital cinema. But for Scorsese, who cut his teeth on digital filmmaking with *The Aviator*, this highlights an important parallel between the 1920s/1930s and the present: the arrival of a new cinematic technology with the potential to usher in a 'great period' of experimentation.

Digital Spectacle and the Resurrection of the Mythic Spectator

The digital technology at Scorsese's disposal permitted him to clean up and correct two- and three-strip looks. In the end, they are but versions of the original and thus lack a degree of historical verisimilitude. But where they fall short in delivering a kind of visual truth, they make up for this by delivering the kind of meaningfulness in terms of affect described by Burgoyne. For as much as *The Aviator* preserves something of the aesthetics of early film, it also manages to recreate the spectatorial experience and excitement of witnessing, for the first time, a stunning visual innovation. That is, *The Aviator*'s brand of two-strip aims to look as stunning to a contemporary audience as *The Phantom of the Opera*'s Bal Masque sequence did to 1920s cinemagoers. By doing so, it seems to try to erase the division that typifies the spectatorial experience of nostalgia films as theorized by Slavoj Žižek.

Žižek argues (specifically with American film noir of the 1940s and the neo-noirs of recent decades) that our consumption of these genres results in a split experience involving both fascination and ironic distance. He suggests that what fascinates us about noir is the gaze of the 'hypothetical mythic spectator from the '40s who was supposedly able to identify immediately with the universe of noir ... the mythic "naïve" spectator, the one who was "still able to take it seriously" ... the one who "believes in it" for us, in place of us' (1991: 112). However, because we are no longer able to identify with the worlds created, we tend to maintain an 'ironic distance toward its diegetic reality' (1991: 112). Žižek contends that this is what happens when we watch film noir and what happens in its 'purest form' during our experience of neo-noirs (1991: 112).

The Aviator's self-reflexive strategies designed to foreground colour and its once overt and literal cinematic uses certainly allows for an ironic distance as do the multiple and mediated representations of films like *Hell's Angels* or *The Outlaw*. However, integrating clips from these early classics evokes more than a fascination with the original gaze of the hypothetical mythic spectator. These clips, along with the film's self-reflexive deliberate archaism, encourage us to *become* this mythic naïve spectator. *The Aviator* seems to promise that our reward for doing so, for taking seriously and investing without doubt or cynicism in the diegetic reality created, is the kind of intensely satisfying spectatorial experience possible only for this mythic naïve viewer. In short, *The Aviator* both engages conceptually with cinema history *and* seeks to provide for the cynical, over-stimulated, 'seen-it-all-already' contemporary audience the kind of visual and emotional spectacle that Scorsese believed moved interwar audiences and that remains a potent object of his own nostalgia.

This, of course, has its dangers and, specifically, ones shared with both prosthetic memory and nostalgia itself. While neither is inherently good or bad, harmless or insidious, they can be used for a variety of different ends. While Landsberg sees prosthetic memory as the 'basis for mediated collective identification and for the production of public spheres around memory that might manage collective crises, or crises of the nation' (Landsberg 1996), the capacity for technologies of representation to supply (and, in the process, construct) memories can certainly serve reactionary and propagandistic agendas.[8] The very same can be said for nostalgia. The same can also be said for a film like *The Aviator*, which encourages a deep and wholesale investment in the magic of cinema while it reframes Hughes' ruthlessly capitalistic practices as a kind of spirited entrepreneurship, his sexual predation as flirtatiousness and all but evacuates in its entirety his virulent racism.

The Aviator thus reverses the dialectic between narrative and visual spectacle that, for Higson and Dika, give nostalgia films their critical potential. In *The Aviator* it is the technicolor aesthetic on its own as well as in conjunction with other self-consciously mediated moments that opens up history (and cinema history) for analysis and reflection, and not, crucially, the narrative or narrative strategies. It is the source of the film's activation and engagement with nostalgia as well as its identification as a nostalgia film. And most importantly, *The Aviator*'s use of a two- and three-strip technicolor aesthetic enables meaningful explorations of the uses and effects of cinematic colour, the affective potential and truths of the cinema, and history itself as something always, inevitably and variously mediated.

Notes

1. I first used this term in a study of *Swingers, The Truman Show* (1998) and *Pleasantville* (1998), (Sprengler 2001).
2. The episode entitled '$pringfield (Or, How I Learned to Stop Worrying and Love Legalized Gambling)' charts Mr Burns' (the town's ruthless billionaire) transformation into a kind of Howard Hughes complete with long fingernails and tissue boxes on his feet. He even forces his assistant to accompany him on the inaugural flight of his wooden 'Spruce Moose'.
3. This information was obtained from commentary included on the DVD release of the film.
4. 'Strip' is a bit of a misnomer, for most colour processes did not employ multiple strips to achieve their effects. In fact two-strip went through several incarnations or 'processes' as they were called. One involved recording on two rolls of black-and-white film, one of which was sensitized for teal/green and the other for red. The two strips were composited and colours were added during a dye-transfer process when prints were made (see www.technicolor.com). Scorsese's two-strip closely resembles Process 2 (as seen in *The Phantom of the Opera*, 1925/29), but also resembles Multicolor which was used in Hughes own *Hell's Angels* (1930). The difference between Process 2 and Multicolor lies in the quality of the blue/green. Whereas Process 2 is closer to the green register, Multicolor is closer to the blue. Three-strip Technicolor (or Process 4) involved three colours in its dye transfer process: cyan, magenta and yellow. For a technological history of Technicolor processes see Higgins (2000).
5. Three-strip technology became available in 1932 and the first feature-length film to employ it was *Becky Sharp*, released in 1935.
6. I suspect that this decision rendered the technicolor aesthetic as much an object of nostalgia as it is a tool used to signify or evoke nostalgia.

7. The Handschiegl Color Process, developed by Max Handschiegl, was similar to Technicolor processes but involved hand-colouring as part of its first step.
8. See Braun and Ellis's marketing study on the ability of autobiographical referencing to evoke nostalgia and convince consumers they had experiences they never did nor ever could have. In one experiment, viewing adverts using images of children shaking hands with Mickey Mouse increased the confidence of the spectator that they too had shaken hands with Mickey Mouse. The researches found the same result for an impossible event: shaking hands with Bugs Bunny (a non-Disney character) at a Disney resort (2002: 1–23).

Conclusion

The Good German and the Good of Nostalgia

I want to conclude this exploration of nostalgia and the cinema with one more example, one that not only permits us to revisit the visual strategies identified in the preceding pages as central to the nostalgia film, but also renders explicit the ways in which these strategies effect potent critiques of history and the present. Several fit the bill and, after some deliberation, I opted to enlist *The Good German* in this effort. Set in 1945 in Berlin—and filmed as though it were made in 1945—it involves an American reporter embroiled in a doomed romance, a murder mystery and a covert operation to evacuate Nazi scientists out of Germany. However—and this is my main reason for selecting this film—it also deals with one of the most pressing, contemporary issues in American politics, namely, the war in Iraq.

The Good German makes use of nearly every strategy central to the contemporary American nostalgia film. It employs props in the service of surface realism, including the 1937 Rolls Phantom 3 owned by Field Marshall Montgomery, a 1936 Chrysler Airflow limousine driven during the Potsdam conference and countless antique props flown in from Germany including telephones, light switches, toilets, stoves and street signs.[1] Costumes too were carefully researched and designed to reflect the desperate poverty of postwar Berlin and worn in ways that spoke to the sartorial practices and survival strategies adopted by women at this time. Headscarves were used to hide unwashed hair and bulky coats were worn to appear unattractive in an environment where rape was commonplace.[2] The film is also deliberately archaic in its recreation of the black-and-white look and expressionistic feel of 1940s film noir (Figure 7.1). Its score is distinctly cinematic and its actors appear displaced in time. Peter Travers observed that although 'Soderbergh couldn't bring Humphrey Bogart and Ingrid Bergman back from the dead … he did the next best thing' (2006: 134). That is, he and casting director

Figure 7.1 George Clooney and Cate Blanchett in *The Good German* (2006). Warner Bros/Virtual/The Kobal Collection/Melinda Sue Gordon.

Debbie Zane (period) cast George Clooney as Jake, Cate Blanchett as Lena and Tobey Maguire as Tully. The film also opens with a montage sequence that establishes the time and place by using archival footage of Berlin in ruins intercut with close-ups of both soldiers and ordinary people.

Perhaps unsurprisingly, these strategies have invited criticism. J. Hoberman titled his review for *The Good German* 'Nostalgia Trip' with the subheading 'Steven Soderbergh tries, and largely fails, to make 'em like they used to' (2006: 91). Todd McCarthy's review expresses a similar sentiment, also making use of the language of nostalgia: 'Steven Soderbergh tries to make one like they used to and comes up short with *The Good German*' (2006: 55). The film 'comes up short' in these and other critics' estimations because it simply is not as 'good' as *Casablanca* or *The Third Man* (1949) and because of its investment in visual style and visual pastness at the expense of narrative logic, dramatic tension and character development.

There is, however, one lone voice that not only offers a reasonably positive review of the film, but also suggests that its nostalgia mode may facilitate an engagement with our contemporary moment. Graham Fuller observes that *The Good German* 'uses black and white nostalgia to illuminate present realities' and, specifically, that its 1940s Hollywood noir style might 'offer a distanced perspective on the 21st century's new world order' including 'Bush era democratisation' (2007: 58). Though Fuller does not explain precisely how the film accomplishes this, his review is significant as it speaks to the shift in conceptions of nostalgia and the value of the nostalgia film. More than this, it locates part of the film's critical potential in its visual dimensions. I would like to explore what Fuller did not (or rather could not in the context of a short film review) in order to suggest how and to what end *The Good German* makes use of the nostalgia mode. As a film that takes its deliberate archaism even farther than *Far From Heaven*, I also want to examine what this kind of nostalgia film can accomplish. In other words, I want to use *The Good German* as a springboard to offer some concluding and speculative thoughts on what nostalgia is good for.

Soderbergh himself has offered detailed accounts of how the film was staged, lit, shot, edited, scored and acted as a Hollywood film would have been in the 1940s. Filming was confined to a Hollywood backlot and local sites, uncoated 1940s lenses were used, many scenes were shot with one camera, boom mikes captured dialogue, swipe cuts were employed and the acting was deliberately theatrical. The actors themselves had to 'feel like they could have been under contract in 1945'. Thomas Newman (son of famed Hollywood composer Alfred Newman) crafted a score reminiscent of 1940s film noir that was used to punctuate dramatic moments and in a way that called attention to itself. Even the tricks and cheats used by 1940s filmmakers to redress sets were put into practice here. But what evoked critics' ire as much as Soderbergh's blanket deliberate archaism were his sometimes overt references to the films that sourced the look and narrative of *The Good German*, most notably his restaging of *Casablanca*'s final scene and Cate Blanchett's nearly parodic synthesis of Marlene Dietrich, Greta Garbo and Ingrid Bergman. Equally intertextual—though somewhat less reviled—was Soderbergh's use of Billy Wilder and William Wyler's 1945 archival footage of Berlin.

The Good German's wholesale deliberate archaism and filmic references have invited comparisons from critics (Bradshaw 2007) and even Soderbergh himself with *Far From Heaven*. In fact, this comparison extends beyond both films' resurrection of mid-twentieth-century Hollywood genres and visual styles. Like Todd Haynes, Soderbergh wanted to make the kind of film that he imagines filmmakers would have made had they not been restricted by the Production Code. For Haynes, this meant openly engaging with issues involving race, gender and sexuality while for Soderbergh, it meant staging a relatively explicit sex scene and inserting an ample number of 'fucks' into the dialogue. By doing so, Soderbergh hoped to blend a past style with a contemporary perspective. On the face of it, *The Good German* certainly seems to lack the sophistication and nuance that rendered *Far From Heaven* a stinging critique of bourgeois America's racism, sexism and homophobia. Sex and profanity may remind audiences of the presence of the present, but its particular uses do little to engage with sexuality, gender or the way in which multiple forms of expression were (and are) circumscribed by social and cinematic convention. However, there are moments during which *The Good German* involves its contemporaneity and visual pastness in intricate plays of fact and fiction and past and present to facilitate political critique. While *Far From Heaven* set its sights on postwar and contemporary cultural politics, *The Good German* sets its sights on postwar and contemporary geopolitics.

The first and perhaps most effective scene to launch this critique involves Tully chauffeuring Jake from the airport to his temporary residence. It also happens to be a scene singled out and faulted by reviewers for its awkwardness. This awkwardness is attributed to the extended length of the scene, Clooney and Maguire's performances, and the fact that the speed at which their vehicle moves appears to be out of sync with the rate at which the documentary back projection scrolls by outside the car (McCarthy 2006: 55). McCarthy suggests that right from the start, this 'puts the viewer at arm's length' (2006: 55). Indeed it does. But whether or not this critical distanciation was intended by Soderbergh, it manages to foreground aspects of the scene that enable us to filter what follows through a contemporary (political) lens and thus to compare America's actions in postwar Berlin with its actions in present-day Iraq. In the process, the film also questions the extent to which domestic prosperity came to postwar America at the expense of justice.

The first exchange between Jake and Tully introduces us to their characters. Jake is an American reporter sent to cover the Potsdam peace conference. Tully is an American army driver assigned to ferry Jake around Berlin. While this information serves the narrative, the dialogue, acting and visual and narrative strategies designed to inject 'reality' into the fiction serve political critique. Jake identifies his employer as *The New Republic*—an actual journal established in 1914. Until the mid twentieth century—and thus during the time Jake is supposedly employed by the publication—it espoused politically liberal and socially progressive opinion. Since then it has shifted gradually to the right, assuming a neoliberal stance on economic and foreign policy matters. As such, *The New Republic* helps to articulate the political position from which the film speaks, something borne out by how it evaluates the corrupt practices of both the Russians and Americans in postwar Berlin.

Dropping the name of *The New Republic* is not the only strategy employed in this scene to establish the political perspective of the film. This is also accomplished by Clooney himself, an actor who willingly articulates his ideological stance in interviews and through his own films, most notably *Good Night and Good Luck*.[3] But what brings Clooney's politics rather than Jake's imagined politics into the fray is Clooney's performance in this sequence. Here, Clooney plays himself or rather the kind of person we imagine him to be from his star persona. He is confident, aloof and a bit of a joker. His comment to Tully that Franz Bettmann (a fictional Nazi scientist) 'aimed one of his Roman candles about a hundred feet away from me [and] broke all my martini glasses' evokes his conscious association with the Lounge Fifties and Rat Pack lifestyle. However, Clooney's investment in journalistic integrity and progressive politics are articulated through his explanation of his attire. He says to Tully that his uniform—standard military garb with 'war correspondent' emblazoned on its jacket—is 'the army's idea of a joke'. Jake is essentially an embedded reporter of the kind currently stationed in Iraq. He is keenly aware of the pressures on him and that his refusal to comply with the army's requests makes him a potential target.

Whereas this performance cues us to see George Clooney as George Clooney, Tobey Maguire's performance channels Bud from *Pleasantville*. Tully is the do-good, all-American, small-town boy who longs to return home in time for the harvest dance, praises his mom's apple pie and boasts about his girlfriend's first-place ribbon for her rhubarb pie and second-place ribbon for her gourds. Initially and in the presence of the military brass, Tully is friendly, helpful and even somewhat generous, giving Jake a bottle of scotch as a housewarming gift. He seems well-intentioned, if a bit naïve, not having heard of *The New Republic* or Franz Bettmann and admitting to Jake that he wishes he too could write. It is not until Tully's voiceover starts that we learn about his true nature. While he might be politically ignorant and illiterate, he is a cunning racketeer who takes advantage of Berlin's black market. He is a sociopath with little respect for human life and enthuses that the war was the best thing that ever happened to him. War made him rich and money, he says, 'allows you to be who you truly are'. Later, when Tully suggests that 'it doesn't seem like the American way just to lock up a person for something they didn't have anything to do with'—a comment clearly intended to evoke Guantanamo Bay—we know he does not really mean this. In many ways, while Tully's innocent act is the United States personified and envisioned through its own political rhetoric (young, enthusiastic, well-intentioned, moral, and courageous), Tully's true self is the United States as envisioned by its critics (opportunistic, corrupt, hypocritical, ignorant and ruthless).[4]

Dialogue and costume help to foreground present geopolitical realities in this staged postwar past. However, a very 'real' past remains present throughout this scene in the form of a back projection documenting the war time destruction of Berlin. In a continuation of the introductory montage sequence (itself confirmed as 'real' by antiquated typescript announcing the place, date and the impending arrival of Truman, Churchill and Stalin for the Potsdam conference), archival footage of the bombed ruins provide the backdrop to Jake and Tully's conversation. In comparison with the fiction, this footage is starker, brighter and grainier, retaining the marks and traces that identify its documentary realism.[5] As such it testifies to very real destruction caused by conflict in an age where death and battles are sanitized and footage censored to accord with the Pentagon's closely regulated image of war. These visually distinctive oppositions between fact and fiction, past and present serve to remind viewers of the contemporary political lens that *The Good German* offers, one adept at exposing parallels between American involvement in each of the two conflicts. But while the past serves to indict the present, the present also helps to illuminate the myths of the past and specifically the 'good war' myth emphasizing American altruism during and after the Second World War.

The Good German's narrative tells of the battle between the Americans and Russians to locate and kidnap Nazi scientists to employ in their respective space programs. Both sides are willing to overlook the atrocities committed by these individuals, to whitewash their pasts and illegally evacuate them from Berlin. Franz Bettmann and Emile Brandt are fictional scientists, but they are included along with Werner von Braun in what Jake describes as the 'Kraut brain trust, the guys who build the V-2s'. The film suggests that America's Cold War supremacy was achieved at the expense of justice.[6] It also attempts to expose the hypocrisy of the political rhetoric espoused at the time, one that resonates loudly today. For example, an elaborate crystal chandelier fades into a wide shot of a rubble-strewn street. Poverty and wealth are juxtaposed for dramatic effect. That this wealth is enjoyed by American officers and bureaucrats is confirmed as the camera tilts down to capture a lavish party and Colonel Muller explaining how to identify top quality champagne. Shortly thereafter we hear this segment of Truman's Potsdam speech:

> We are here today to raise the flag of victory over the capital of our greatest adversary. Let's not forget that we are fighting for peace and for the welfare of mankind. There's not one piece of territory or one thing of a monetary nature that we want out of this war. We want peace and prosperity for the world as a whole. If we can put this tremendous machine of ours, which has made this victory possible, to work for peace, we can look forward to the greatest age in the history of mankind.

By this point in the film (and at the point at which I write this) Truman's words are nothing but deeply ironic. Domestic prosperity became possible precisely because of the United State's involvement in the Second World War. Populuxe is intricately tied to the spoils of war and not just because its flashy and colourful products rolled off the very same assembly lines that once produced military hardware. Peace is far less profitable than war and not at all the desired state of affairs for those invested in the Military Industrial Complex. The

Cold War followed close on the heels of the Second World War and spawned many of its own bloody and prolonged conflicts. The American army continues to maintain a presence in Germany,[7] using its bases as launching pads for theatres east. The massive military installations already erected in Iraq suggest a similar strategic plan that, while not involving claims to land, does involve maintaining a presence in order to further various economic and strategic interests in the region.

In this way *The Good German* operates allegorically, a point Soderbergh tentatively admits in an interview posted on the film's official website. (He acknowledges that it offers parallels with today but quickly switches topics to say that it is a timeless story with enduring contemporary relevance.) It is set in both a real and cinematic past, blending fictional with archival footage. And by rendering the fiction explicitly so and distinctively cinematic through intertextual references and pastiches of iconic filmic moments the archival footage seems, at certain points, somehow more 'real' by comparison.[8] These juxtapositions of fact and fiction and past and present imbue the film's documentary moments with an urgency that lends weight and force to the film's allusions to present-day politics and especially the physical, emotional and moral implications of war.

The Good German's capacity to illuminate these specific present realities is interesting in light of a point made earlier and articulated through Soderbergh's structuring question: 'What if filmmakers working in Hollywood in 1945 had the same creative freedom we have today?' On the one hand, his ostensible answer is that sex and profanity—as much realities of 1940s life as they are of twenty-first century life—would have been woven into the fabric of the film. But here, as noted above, they do not constitute explorations of sexuality or expression. Instead they operate in ways that suggest the immorality and corruption of American (and other) officials stationed in postwar Berlin. Sex is depicted on only two occasions: Tully penetrating an anonymous prostitute (perhaps Lena?) from behind as he expounds in voiceover the delights of postwar Berlin, and Lena being raped by a Russian soldier whom she manages to shoot in the head. 'Fuck' is really the only profanity of note. Though hardly remarkable when it passes Jake's lips, it is uttered often and with maniacal force by Tully. This presents a picture of American soldiers as well as officers and bureaucrats markedly at odds with those offered by (most) postwar films as well as oft-rehearsed histories of liberation and kindness.[9]

On the other hand, one might respond to Soderbergh's question with another: How much creative freedom do filmmakers working today for major studios like Warner Bros. actually enjoy? These studios are themselves beholden to interests of various kinds: economic, social and political. They also have the Classification and Ratings Administration (CARA)—operated by Motion Picture Association of America (MPAA) and the National Association of Theater Owners (NATO)—to consider. CARA is the film ratings body which recent publications (as well as Kirby Dick's 2006 documentary *This Film is Not Yet Rated*) have revealed as disturbingly secretive and inconsistent in their practices (Sandler 2001; Leone 2002; West and West 2006). CARA's actions have even prompted Sandler to suggest that 'the Production Code has risen from the ashes' (2001: 87).[10] Under these pressures and in the United States' current neo-conservative climate—one often compared to postwar McCarthyism—creative freedom is indeed a concern. Filmmakers working independently may practice their craft unimpeded assuming their financers care little about what they produce. But forces at work in marketing, distribution and exhibition can severely limit a film's exposure and prevent it from being seen by more than a handful of people. One wonders how much pressure Soderbergh would have faced (from Warner Bros. and its investors) had he intended his film to explicitly address America's involvement and practices in Iraq and Afghanistan.[11] What kinds of obstacles might he have met for presenting disturbing portraits of American soldiers and military officials at a time of war? One that recounts the very real incidence of torture, rape and murder coming to light in the news media: Abu Ghraib, Guantanamo Bay, the Haditha, Hamdaniya and Mahmoudiya incidents as well as many other violations of the Geneva convention. Consider the initial efforts to suppress and then delay the television broadcast of images from Abu Ghraib and the continued suppression of even the mention of extant videos depicting the sodomy of male and female prisoners at this same institution (Hersh 2007).

Allegory is a powerful rhetorical tool with the potential to provide as much critical insight as straightforward representations of a subject. It is also often a necessary tool in repressive social and political climates. In the case of *The Good German*, allegorical moments are supported rather than foiled by the film's overt intertextuality and nostalgia mode. References to classic films and deliberate archaism are important strategies that contribute in multiple ways to the film's critical consciousness. On one level, they make possible the interplay of fact and fiction, past and present, that permits contemporary geopolitical issues to surface. On another level, they provide a cloak of pastness and visual spectacle under which the film plays out its indictments of corruption and hypocrisy. *The Good German* takes advantage of the perception that visual pastness and cinematic allusion lack substance and depth. Its style is its alibi, distancing the film from the present and reality but all the while providing cover for its engagement with present realities.

Admittedly *The Good German* illustrates only one of the ways in which the visual dimensions of the nostalgia film offers insight into the past, the present and the relationship between the two. *Sin City*, *Far From Heaven* and *The Aviator* represent additional ways that not only encourage or facilitate critical readings, but speak to the myriad uses, manifestations and possibilities of the nostalgia mode. These and other films released in recent years are testaments to the complexity with which nostalgia functions as well as the extent to which its cinematic expressions rely on visual strategies *as well as* music and narrative. They also reveal the extent to which nostalgia has shifted from a tool employed in the service of conservative ideology to a tool used in the service of critiques of reactionary politics. From Reagan's Fifties to *Far From Heaven*'s Fifties to other constructs modelled on this dominant object and in accord with nostalgia's dominant strain, the nostalgia mode—either aligned with or divorced from the nostalgia mood—has become integral to the generation of meaning, the stimulation of critique and the enjoyment of analytical pleasure.

The films discussed here explore the limits of deliberate archaism and surface realism. In the process, they reveal the depths of pastness and what the nostalgia mode might accomplish and enable. They are experimental in many respects, investigating the ways in which past worlds and aesthetics can be rendered either digitally or by resurrecting obsolete tools and methods. That nostalgia films should employ both forward- and backward-looking strategies seems rather fitting and something, I suspect, we will continue to see in the years to come. *Sin City, Far From Heaven, The Aviator* and *The Good German* are part of a cycle of nostalgia films that has far from exhausted itself, a cycle with enduring and contemporary relevance. These films reflect more than a lingering and protracted fin-de-millénnium nostalgia. They register a continuing if not increasing fascination with history and one that extends beyond the facts, events and people documented to have shaped the past. This fascination envelops the representational practices and visual languages that might yield their own specific kinds of access to (and knowledge of) the past, including histories typically denigrated and marginalized. It also envelops the way these representational practices provide insight into how periods and cultures imag(in)ed themselves, how they cast their myths into enduring visual and thus visible forms. As such, these films acknowledge the politics of representation and how the ideologies resurrected through images can be subject to analysis, evaluation and deconstruction. Far from depthless, these films are valuable cultural objects with the potential to source critical engagements with the past and testify to the nature and limits of our present historical consciousness.

Notes

1. All information about *The Good German*'s visual and technological strategies as well as comments by Soderbergh and his crew are (unless otherwise noted) from interviews and commentary posted on the film's official website: www.thegoodgerman.warnerbros.com.
2. Costume designer Louise Frogley also explains that she had to spend time teaching young actors how to properly wear trousers and hats.
3. In an interview with Ali Jafaar in *Sight and Sound*, Clooney admits: 'I'm an old leftie [and] I make no apologies for it' (Fuller 2006) However, given his perspective on certain issues, he is more liberal than left and thus prone like many Americans to envision the political spectrum as one shifted further to the right than Europeans.
4. Tully's performance could, of course, also be read as an indictment of George W. Bush—ignorant but cunning with his country folk performance.
5. The difference between the black and white of the archival footage and the black and white of the film has a lot to do with the fact that Soderbergh shot on colour stock and pulled the black and white out later. Additionally, little attempt seems to have been made to synchronize visually the two black and white aesthetics. This is a strategy also employed in *Down With Love* which used back projections originally seen in the Doris Day–Rock Hudson comedies it pastiches.
6. Complicity with the Nazis is also partially suggested through the choice of Germanic surnames given to American characters in the film: Geismer, Breimer, Muller, Teitel and Schaeffer.
7. There are currently over fifty different types of American military installations in Germany. Several of these are set to close in the next few years (US Department of Defense, www.defenselink.mil. Accessed 7 July 2007).
8. Newman's score is especially central in this regard for it is at its most cinematic and most hyperbolic during segments featuring archival footage. In these instances, the noticeable disconnect between fact and fiction draws attention to the status of each.

9. These histories tend to foreground iconic moments and images including, most notably, German children excitedly receiving candy and chocolate from American soldiers. However, this image has replaced other more poignant ones that speak to the complexities of social relations at war time. Oral histories tell of African-American soldiers (ones who were not afforded the same rights as their white counterparts at the time) who actively sought out bread and other staples—necessities—to give to those very same children and their families.
10. Sandler explains that the current ratings system 'alerts the industry to what could be considered "harmless entertainment" for those adults most likely to attack Hollywood's products as antithetical to appropriate American values. Today, the American Family Association, the Religious Right, and government officials are some of the most influential crusaders against "improper" Hollywood entertainment' (2001: 70).
11. Films explicitly critical of recent American activities in the Middle East have difficulty finding distributors or exhibitors. Consider, for example, the media blackout on Jamie Doran's *Afghan Massacre* (2002) about US personnel's complicity in war crimes.

Filmography

A Passage to India, 1985, EMI Films/HBO, David Lean.
A Place in the Sun, 1951, Paramount Pictures, George Stevens.
Absolute Beginners, 1986, Goldcrest Films International/Palace Pictures/Virgin, Julien Temple.
Adam Had Four Sons, 1941, Columbia Pictures, Gregory Ratoff.
Afghan Massacre, 2003, Altantic Celtic Films, Jamie Doran.
Alfie, 1966, Lewis Gilbert/Sheldrake, Lewis Gilbert.
Alfie, 2004, Paramount Pictures/Patalex, Charles Shyer.
All About Eve, 1950, Twentieth Century Fox, Joseph L. Mankiewicz.
All That Heaven Allows, 1955, Universal International Pictures, Douglas Sirk.
All the King's Men, 2006, Columbia Pictures/Phoenix/AKM, Steven Zaillian.
American Graffiti, 1973, Lucas Film/The Coppola Company/Universal Pictures, George Lucas.
An American in Paris, 1951, Loew's/MGM, Vincente Minnelli.
Angel, 1999–2004, Mutant Enemy/Kuzui/Sandollar/Twentieth Century Fox, The WB Television Network.
Another Country, 1984, Castlezone/Eastern Counties Newspaper/Goldcrest Films/NFFC/Virgin, Marek Kanievska.
Austin Powers, 1997, Capella International/New Line Cinema/Eric's Boy/KC Medien/Moving Pictures, Jay Roach.
Back Street, 1941, Universal Pictures, Robert Stevenson.
Back to the Future, 1985, Amblin Entertainment/Universal, Robert Zemeckis.
Badlands, 1973, Badlands/Pressman-Williams, Terrence Malik.
Bastard Out of Carolina, 1996, Showtime Networks, Anjelica Huston.
Becky Sharp, 1935, Pioneer Pictures, Rouben Mamoulian.
Blast From the Past, 1999, Forge/Midnight Sun/New Line Cinema, Hugh Wilson.
Body Heat, 1981, The Ladd Company, Lawrence Kasden.
Casablanca, 1942, Warner Bros., Michael Curtiz.

Casino Royale, 1967, Columbia Pictures/Famous Artists, Val Guest, Ken Hughes, John Huston, Joseph McGrath, Robert Parrish.

Chariots of Fire, 1981, Enigma Productions/Goldcrest Films/Warner Bros., Hugh Hudson.

Cheers for Miss Bishop, 1941, Richard A. Roland Productions, Tay Garnett.

Chinatown, 1974, Long Road/Paramount/Penthouse, Roman Polanski.

Christine, 1983, Columbia Pictures/Delphi Premier Productions/Polar Films, John Carpenter.

Cinema Paradiso, 1988, Christaldfilm/Les Film Ariane/Radiotelevisione Italiana/TF1Films Productions, Giuseppe Tornatore.

Citizen Cohn, 1992, Breakheart Films/Spring Creek Productions/Viacom Productions, Frank Pearson.

Citizen Kane, 1941, Mercury Productions/RKO Radio Pictures, Orson Welles.

Cold War, 1998, CNN/Jeremy Isaacs Productions, Tessa Coombs.

Detour, 1945, Producers Releasing Corporation, Edgar G. Ulmer.

Down With Love, 2003, Epsilon Motion Pictures/Fox 2000/Jinks-Cohen Co./Mediastream Dritte Film/Regency Enterprises, Peyton Reed.

Edward Scissorhands, 1990, Twentieth Century Fox, Tim Burton.

Far From Heaven, 2002, Clear Blue Sky Productions/Section Eight/Killer Films/John Wells/TF1 International/USA Films/Vulcan Productions, Todd Haynes.

Father Knows Best, 1954–1960, Rodney-Young Productions/Screen Gem Productions, ABC/CBS/NBC.

Father Knows Best: Home for Christmas, 1977, Columbia Pictures, Norman Abbott.

Father of the Bride, 1950, MGM, Vincente Minnelli.

Fellow Traveller, 1989, BBC/HBO, Philip Saville.

Forrest Gump, 1994, Paramount Pictures, Robert Zemeckis.

Gentlemen Prefer Blondes, 1953, Twentieth Century Fox, Howard Hawks.

Going All the Way, 1997, Lakeshore Entertainment/Polygram Filmed Entertainment, Mark Pellington.

Gone With the Wind, 1939, Selznick International Picture/MGM, Victor Flemming.

Good Night and Good Luck, 2005, Warner Independent Pictures/2929 Productions/Participant Productions/Davis-Films/Redbus Pictures/Tohokushinsha Film Corp/Section Eight/Good Night Good Luck/Metropolitan, George Clooney.

Grease, 1978, Paramount Pictures, Randal Kleiser.
Guilty by Suspicion, 1991, Canal+/Warner Bros., Irwin Winkler.
Happy Days, 1974–1984, Paramount/Henderson/Miller-Milkis, ABC.
Hearts in Atlantis, 2001, Castle Rock Entertainment/NVP/Village Roadshow, Scott Hicks.
Hell's Angels, 1930, The Caddo Company, Howard Hughes.
Hollywoodland, 2006, Back Lot Pictures/Focus Features/Miramax Films, Allen Coulter.
How Green Was My Valley, 1941, Twentieth Century Fox, John Ford.
I Wonder Who's Kissing Her Now, 1947, Twentieth Century Fox, Lloyd Bacon.
Imitation of Life, 1959, Universal International Pictures, Douglas Sirk.
Inventing the Abbotts, 1997, Fox 2000 Pictures/Imagine Entertainment/Twentieth Century Fox, Pat O'Connor.
June Bride, 1948, Warner Bros., Bretaigne Windust.
King Arthur, 2004, Touchstone Pictures/Jerry Bruckheimer Films/Green Hills Productions/World 2000 Entertainment, Antoine Fuqua.
Kiss Me Deadly, 1955, Parklane Pictures, Robert Aldrich.
L.A. Confidential, 1997, Monarchy Enterprises/Regency Enterprises/Warner Bros., Curtis Hanson.
La Cucaracha, 1934, Pioneer Pictures, Lloyd Corrigan.
Last Exit to Brooklyn, 1989, Allied Filmmakers/Bavaria Film/Neue Constantin Film, Uli Edel.
Laverne and Shirley, 1976–1983, Miller-Milkis/Henderson Pictures/Paramount, ABC.
Leatherheads, 2008, Casey Silver Productions/Smoke House, George Clooney.
Leave it to Beaver, 1977–1963, Gomalco Productions/Kayro Vue Productions/Revue Studios, ABC/CBS.
Let the Good Times Roll, 1973, Cinema Associates/Metromedia Producers, Robert Abel, Sidney Levin.
Lost Horizon, 1937, Columbia Pictures, Frank Capra.
*M*A*S*H*, 1972–1983, Twentieth Century Fox Television, CBS.
Magnificent Obsession, 1954, Universal International Pictures, Douglas Sirk.
Maytime, 1937, MGM, Robert Z. Leonard.
Meet Me in St. Louis, 1959, MGM/Talent Associates, George Schaeffer.
My Three Sons, 1960–1972, Don Fedderson Productions/Greg-Don Inc./MCA Television, ABC/CBS.

O Brother Where Art Thou, 2000, Touchstone Pictures/Universal Pictures/Studio Canal/Working Title Film/Mike Zoss Productions, Joel Coen, Ethan Coen.
Ocean's Eleven, 2001, Jerry Weintraub Productions/Warner Bros./Section Eight/Village Roadshow Pictures/WV Films, Steven Soderbergh.
Ocean's Thirteen, 2007, Jerry Weintraub Productions/Warner Bros./Section Eight/Village Roadshow Pictures/WV Films, Steven Soderbergh.
Ocean's Twelve, 2004, Jerry Weintraub Productions/Warner Bros./Section Eight/Village Roadshow Pictures/WV Films, Steven Soderbergh.
Our Dancing Daughters, 1928, Cosmopolitan/MGM, Harry Beaumont.
Pearl Harbor, 2001, Touchstone Pictures/Jerry Bruckheimer Films, Michael Bay.
Pleasantville, 1998, New Line Cinema/Larger Than Life Productions, Gary Ross.
Quantum Leap, 1989–1993, Belasarius Productions/Universal TV, NBC.
Rebel Without a Cause, 1955, Warner Bros., Nicholas Ray.
Roman Holiday, 1953, Paramount Pictures, William Wyler.
Room With a View, 1985, Goldcrest/NFFC/Curzon/Film Four International/Merchant Ivory Productions, James Ivory.
Silk Hat Kid, 1935, Fox Film Corporation, H. Bruce Humberstone.
Sin City, 2005, Frank Miller, Dimension Films/Troublemaker Studios, Robert Rodriguez.
Sky Captain and the World of Tomorrow, 2004, Brooklyn Films/Riff Raff Films/Blue Flower Productions/Filmauro/Natural Nylon Entertainment, Kerry Conran.
Smiling Through, 1941, Loew's/MGM, Frank Borzage.
Stand by Me, 1986, Act III/Columbia Pictures/The Body, Rob Reiner.
Star Wars, 1977, Lucasfilm/Twentieth Century Fox, George Lucas.
Starship Troopers, 1997, Big Bug Pictures/Touchstone Pictures/Tristar Pictures, Paul Verhoeven.
Swingers, 1996, Independent Pictures/The Alfred Shay Company, Doug Liman.
Terminator, 1984, Helmdale Film/Cinema 84/Euro Film Funding/Pacific Western, James Cameron.

Terminator 2, 1991, Canal+/Carolco Pictures/Lightstorm Entertainment/ Pacific Entertainment/T2 Productions, James Cameron.
The Adventures of Ozzie and Harriet, 1952–1966, Stage Five/Volcano, ABC.
The Adventures of Robin Hood, 1938, Willian Keighley, Warner Bros., Michael Curtiz.
The Aldrich Family, 1949–1953, NBC, NBC.
The Aviator, 2004, Forward Pass/Appian Way/IMF/IEG/Warner Bros./Village/Miramax, Martin Scorsese.
The Big Sleep, 1946, Warner Bros., Howard Hawks.
The Black Dahlia, 2006, Millennium Films/Nu Image Films/Signature Films/Art Linson Productions/Davis Films/Equity Pictures, Brian DePalma.
The Brady Bunch, 1968–1974, Paramount/Redwood/ABC.
The Donna Reed Show, 1958–1966, Screen Gems/Todon, ABC.
The Front Page, 1931, The Caddo Company, Lewis Milestone.
The Good German, 2006, Sunset Gower Studios/Warner Bros./Section Eight/Virtual Studios, Steven Soderberg.
The Green Mile, 1999, Castle Rock Pictures/Darkwoods Productions/Warner Bros., Frank Darabont.
The Interpreter, 2005, Working Title Film/Misher Films/Mirage Entertainment/Studio Canal, Sidney Pollack.
The Jazz Singer, 1927, Warner Bros., Alan Crosland.
The Last Picture Show, 1971, BBS Productions/Columbia Pictures, Peter Bogdonavich.
The Long Day Closes, 1992, BFI/Channel Four Films, Terence Davies.
The Lord of the Rings Trilogy, 2001, 2002, 2003, New Line Films/Wingnut Films, Peter Jackson.
The Maltese Falcon, 1941, Warner Bros., John Huston.
The Man in the Gray Flannel Suit, 1956, Twentieth Century Fox, Nannally Johnson.
The Outlaw, 1941, Howard Hughes Productions, Howard Hughes.
The Phanton of the Opera, 1925/29, Universal Pictures, Rupert Julian.
The Reflecting Skin, 1990, Bialystock & Bloom Limited/BBC/British Screen Productions/Fugitive Features/National Film Trustees/Ontario Film Development Corporation/Téléfilm Canada/Zenith Entertainment Ltd., Philip Ridley.
The Sea Hawk, 1940, Warner Bros., Michael Curtiz.
Schindler's List, 1993, Amblin Entertainment, Steven Spielberg.

The Shape of Things to Come, 1936, London Film Productions, William Cameron Menzies.
The Simpsons, 1989-, Twentieth Century Fox/Gracie Films/Film Roman Productions, Fox Network.
The Singing Detective, 2003, Haft Entertainment/Icon Entertainment International, Keith Gordon.
The Strawberry Blonde, 1941, Warner Bros., Raoul Walsh.
The Talented Mr. Ripley, 1999, Mirage Enterprises/Miramax Films/Paramount Pictures/Timnick Films, Anthony Minghella.
The Wizard of Oz, 1939, MGM/Loew's International, Victor Fleming.
The Women, 1939, MGM, George Cukor.
To Have and Have Not, 1944, Warner Bros., Howard Hawks.
To Mary, With Love, 1936, Twentieth Century Fox, John Cromwell.
Two Lane Black Top, 1971, Michael McLaughlin Productions, Universal Pictures, Monte Hellman.
Where the Truth Lies, 2005, Serendipity Point Films/Ego Film Arts/First Choice Films/Movie Central Network/TMN/Téléfilm Canada, Atom Egoyan.
White Jazz, 2008, Cherry Road Films/Smoke House, Joe Carnahan.
Written on the Wind, 1956, Universal Pictures International, Douglas Sirk.

References

'Auction Frenzy over Hepburn Dress'. 2006. BBC News, 5 December. Retrieved 12 February 2007 from www.news.bbc.co.uk/2/hi/ entertainment/6209658.stm

'From the '60s to the '70s: Dissent and Discovery'. 1969. *Time*, 19 December, 22–28.

'The Nifty Fifties'. 1972. *Life*, 16 June, 38–50.

Adams, M. 1933. 'Four Decades of Fashion's Pageant', *The New York Times*, 22 October, SM12.

Baker, R. 1973. 'The Nostalgia Affair', *The New York Times*, 14 August, 33.

Barnes, C. 1972. '*Grease*: 1959 as Nostalgia', *The New York Times*, 15 February, 27.

Barnwell, J. 2004. *Production Design: Architects of the Screen*. London: Wallflower.

Barnouw, E. 1982. *Tube of Plenty: The Evolution of American Television*. New York: Oxford University Press.

Barthes, R. 1972. *Mythologies*, trans. A. Lavers. New York: Hill and Wang.

—— 1977. *Image, Music, Text*, trans. S. Heath. New York: Hill and Wang.

Bassin, D. 1994. 'Maternal Subjectivity in the Culture of Nostalgia: Mourning and Memory', in D. Bassin, M. Honey and M. Kaplan (eds), *Representations of Motherhood*. New Haven: Yale University Press, pp. 162–73.

Berry, S. 2000. *Screen Style: Fashion and Femininity in 1930s Hollywood*. Minneapolis: University of Minnesota Press.

Birkerts, S. 1989. 'The Nostalgia Disease', *Tikkun* 4(2): 20–22; 117–18.

Boym, S. 2001. *The Future of Nostalgia*. New York: Basic Books.

Bradshaw, P. 2005. 'Sin City', *The Guardian*, 3 June. Retrieved 14 March 2007 from www.guardian.co.uk/News_Story/Critic_Review/ Guardian_Film_of_the_week/0,,1497709,00.html

—— 2007. 'The Good German', *The Guardian*, 9 March. Retrieved 11 July 2007 from www.guardian.co.uk/News_Story/Critic_Review/ Guardian_review/0,,2029252,00.html

Brady, T. 1941. 'Stars of Silent Screen Still Active. With Few Exceptions They Appear Unnoticed as Bit Players in Many Films', *The New York Times*, 4 May, X5.

Brandt, A. 1978. 'A Short Natural History of Nostalgia', *Atlantic Monthly* 242 (December): 58–65.

Braun, K.A. and R. Ellis. 2002. 'Make My Memory: How Advertising Can Change our Memories of the Past', *Psychology and Marketing* 19(1): 1–23.

Bruzzi, S. 1997. *Undressing Cinema: Clothing and Identity in the Movies*. London: Routledge.

Buckley, T. 1974. 'Those Were The Days, Those Good Old Ones', *The New York Times*, 14 April, 165.

Burgoyne, R. 1999. 'Prosthetic memory/traumatic memory: *Forrest Gump*', *Screening the Past*, 16 April. Retrieved 29 May 2000 from www.latrobe.edu.au/www/screeningthepast/firstrelease/fr0499/ rbfr6a.htm

Carroll, M.T. 2000. *Popular Modernity in America: Experience, Technology, Mythohistory*. New York: State University of New York Press.

Casey, E. 1977. 'Imagining and Remembering', *Review of Metaphysics* 31 (December): 187–209.

—— 1987. 'The World of Nostalgia', *Man and World: An International Philosophical Review* 20(4): 361–84.

Cashman, R. 2006. 'Critical Nostalgia and Material Culture in Northern Ireland', *Journal of American Folklore* 119(472): 137–60.

Cawthorne, N. 1996. *The New Look: The Dior Revolution*. Edison, New Jersey: The Wellfleet Press.

Chocano, C. 2005. 'Sin City', *The Los Angeles Times*, 1 April. Retrieved 14 March 2007 from www.calendarlive.com/movies/chocano/cl-et-sincity1apr01,0,4258832.story

Cook, P. 1996. *Fashioning the Nation: Costume and Identity in British Cinema*. London: British Film Institute Publishing.

—— 2005. *Screening the Past: Memory and Nostalgia in Cinema*. London: Routledge.

Crowther, B. 1941a. 'Annual Message; Mr. Hays's Report Speaks a Word for the "Therapeutic Value" of Entertainment', *The New York Times*, 6 April, X5.

—— 1941b. 'The Screen. James Cagney in a Nostalgic Comedy of the 1890s, "Strawberry Blonde" at the Strand', *The New York Times*, 22 February, 11.

Davis, F. 1979. *Yearning for Yesterday: A Sociology of Nostalgia*. New York: The Free Press.

DeFalco, A. 2004. 'A Double-Edged Longing: Nostalgia, Melodrama, and Todd Haynes's *Far From Heaven*', *Iowa Journal of Cultural Studies* 5(Spring): 26–40.
Dickinson, G. 1997. 'Memories for Sale: Nostalgia and the Construction of Identity in Old Pasedena', *The Quarterly Journal of Speech* 83(1): 1–27.
Dika, V. 2003. *Recycled Culture in Contemporary Art and Film: The Uses of Nostalgia*. Cambridge: Cambridge University Press.
Doane, J. and D. Hodges (eds). 1987. *Nostalgia and Sexual Difference: The Resistance to Contemporary Feminism*. New York: Methuen.
Dyer, R. 2007. *Pastiche*. London: Routledge.
Felski, R. 1995. *The Gender of Modernity*. Cambridge, MA: Harvard University Press.
Finch Kelly, F. 1932. 'A Touch of Homesickness for an Old America', *The New York Times*, 23 October, BR4.
Flinn, C. 1992. *Strains of Utopia: Gender, Nostalgia and Hollywood Film Music*. New Jersey: Princeton University Press.
Fodor, N. 1950. 'Varieties of Nostalgia', *Psychoanalytic Review* 37: 25–38.
Forty, A. 1986. *Objects of Desire: Design and Society Since 1750*. London: Thames and Hudson.
Frazer, J.M. and T.C. Frazer. 1993. '*Father Knows Best* and *The Cosby Show*: Nostalgia and the Sitcom Tradition', *Journal of Popular Culture* 27(3): 163–72.
French, P. 2005. 'Looks Good, Feels Bad', *The Observer*, 5 June. Retrieved 14 March from www.film.guardian.co.ukwww.guardian.co.uk/News_Story/Critic_ Review/Observer_Film_of_the week/0,,1499404,html
Fritzman, J.M. 1993. 'The Future of Nostalgia and the Time of the Sublime', *Clio* 23(2): 167–89.
Fuller, G. 2007. 'The Good German', *Sight and Sound* 17(3): 58, 60.
Gaines, J. and C. Herzog (eds). 1990. *Fabrications: Costume and the Female Body*. London: Routledge.
Galt Crowell, S. 1999. 'Spectral History: Narrative, Nostalgia, and the Time of the I', *Research in Phenomenology* 29: 83–104.
Gibbs, J. 2002. *Mise-en-scène: Film Style and Interpretation*. London: Wallflower.
Gill, P. 1999. 'Technostalgia: Making the Future Past Perfect', *Camera Obscura* 40–41: 163–80.
Goldman, J. 1998. *The Feminist Aesthetics of Virginia Woolf*. Cambridge: Cambridge University Press.

Goldman, M. 2004. 'Film: Seeking Vintage Color', *Millimeter* 32(12): 7.
—— 2005. 'Scorsese's Color Homage: Director Enters Digital Realm to Craft The Aviator's Vintage, Dye-Transfer Palette', *Millimeter* 33(1): 14–18, 20, 22, 24, 26.
Gould, J. 1959. 'TV: Slice of Americana. Two-Hour 'Meet Me in St. Louis' Offers Nostalgic Excursion on Channel 2', *The New York Times*, 27 April, 49.
Graham, A. 1984. 'History, Nostalgia, and the Criminality of Popular Culture', *The Georgia Review* 38(2): 348–80.
Grainge, P. 2002. *Monochrome Memories: Nostalgia and Style in Retro America*. Westport: Praeger.
Green Harris, R. 1938. 'Art and Stiff Frivolity. Being a Footnote to French Psychology, Social Significance and Outings', *The New York Times*, 25 September, 164.
Greene, G. 1991. 'Feminist Fiction and the Uses of Memory', *Signs* 16(2): 290–321.
Hall, S.G. 1904. *Adolescence: Its Psychology and Its Relations to Physiology, Anthropology, Sociology, Sex, Crime, Religion, and Education*. New York: D. Appleton and Co.
Hanes, E.L. 1941. *The Minds and Nerves of Soldiers*. Pasedena: The Login Press.
Harari, J. 1989. 'Nostalgia and Critical Theory', in T.M. Kavanagh (ed.), *The Limits of Theory*. Stanford: Stanford University Press, pp. 168–93.
Hart, J.G. 1973. 'Toward a Phenomenology of Nostalgia', *Man and World: An International Philosophical Review* 6(4): 397–420.
Hebdige, D. 1988. *Hiding in the Light*. London: Routledge.
Herron, J. 1993. 'Homer Simpson's Eyes and the Culture of Late Nostalgia', *Representations* 43(Summer): 1–26.
Hersh, S. 2007. 'The General's Report', *The New Yorker*, 25 June. Retrieved 14 July 2007 from www.newyorker.com/reporting/2007/06/25/070625fa_fact_hersh
Hewison, R. 1996. *Culture and Consensus: England, Art and Politics Since 1940*. London: Methuen.
Higgins, S. 1999. 'Technology and Aesthetics: Technicolor Cinematography and Design in the Late 1930s', *Film History* 11(1): 55–76.
—— 2000. 'Demonstrating Three-Color Technicolor: Early Three-Colour Aesthetics and Design', *Film History* 12(4): 358–83.
Higson, A. 1993. 'Re-presenting the National Past: Nostalgia and Pastiche in the Heritage Film', in L. Friedman (ed.), *British Cinema and Thatcherism*. London: UCL Press, pp. 109–29.

Hine, T. 1986. *Populuxe*. New York: MFJ Books.
Hoberman, J. 2006. 'Nostalgia Trip', *Village Voice* 51(50): 91.
Hodges, F.B. 1944. 'Sheer Nostalgia Strikes. Sound of Tin Horn Awakens Memories of Rag-Bag Days', *The New York Times*, 22 July, 14.
Hofer, J. 1934. 'Medical Dissertation on Nostalgia', trans. C.K. Anspach. *Bulletin of the History of Medicine* 2: 376–91.
Holbrook, M. 1993. 'On the New Nostalgia: "These Foolish Things" and Echoes of the Dear Departed Past', in R. Brown and R. Ambrosetti (eds), *Continuities in Popular Culture*. Bowling Green: Bowling Green State University, pp. 74–120.
Huffer, L. 1998. *Maternal Pasts, Feminist Futures: Nostalgia, Ethics and the Question of Difference*. Stanford: Stanford University Press.
Hutcheon, L. 1989. *The Politics of Postmodernism*. London: Routledge.
Jackson, S.W. 1986. *Melancholia and Depression: From Hippocratic to Modern Times*. New Haven: Yale University Press.
Jacobus, M. 1987. 'Freud's Mnemonic: Women, Screen Memories, and Feminist Nostalgia', *Michigan Quarterly Review* 26(1): 117–39.
Jameson, F. 1991. *Postmodernism, Or the Cultural Logic of Late Capitalism*. Durham: Duke University Press.
Jewell, E.A. 1930. 'A Fine Native Showing. Big Exhibition in Washington Reveals Contemporary American Art at Its Best', *The New York Times*, 7 December, 135.
Joyrich, L. 2004. 'Written on the Screen: Mediation and Immersion in *Far From Heaven*', *Camera Obscura* 19(3): 186–219.
Kaplan, H.A. 1987. 'The Psychopathology of Nostalgia', *Psychoanalytic Review* 74(4): 463–86
Kramer, H. 1973. 'A Nostalgia for the Fifties?' *The New York Times*, 4 February, 127.
Krämer, Peter. 1996. 'The Lure of the Big Picture: Film, Television and Hollywood', in J. Hill and M. McLoone (eds), *Big Picture, Small Screen: The Relations Between Film and Television*. Luton: University of Luton Press, pp. 9–46.
Kuhn, A. 2002. *An Everyday Magic: Cinema and Cultural Memory*. London: I.B. Tauris & Co. Ltd.
Landsberg, A. 1996. 'Prosthetic Memory: The Logics and Politics of Memory in Modern American Culture', Ph.D. dissertation. Chicago: University of Chicago.
Laurence, W.L. 1933. 'Patriotism Viewed as Mild Nostalgia', *The New York Times*, 8 September, 15.

Leibman, N. 1995. *Living Room Lectures: The Fifties Family in Film and Television*. Austin: University of Texas Press.

Leone, R. 2002. 'Contemplating Ratings: An Examination of What the MPAA Considers "Too Far for R" and Why', *Journal of Communication* 52(4): 938–54.

Le Sueur, M. 1977. 'Theory Number Five: Anatomy of Nostalgia Films: Heritage and Methods', *Journal of Popular Film* 6(2): 187–97.

Lewallen, C.M. and S. Seid. 2004. *Ant Farm: 1968–1978*. Berkeley: University of California Press.

Long, T. 1942. 'Bragging By Yanks Laid to Nostalgia. British Canteen Girls Advised on How to Listen to U.S. Soldiers They Serve', *The New York Times*, 28 December, 16.

Lowenthal, D. 1985. *The Past is a Foreign Country*. Cambridge: Cambridge University Press.

Lury, K. 2000. 'Here and Then: Space, Place and Nostalgia in British Youth Cinema of the 1990s', in R. Murphy (ed.), *British Cinema of the '90s*. London: British Film Institute Publishing, pp. 100–108.

Marcus, D. 2004. *Happy Days and Wonder Years: The Fifties and the Sixties in Contemporary Cultural Politics*. New Brunswick, New Jersey: Rutgers University Press.

Marling, K.A. 1994. *As Seen On TV: The Visual Culture of Everyday Life in the 1950s*. Cambridge, MA: Harvard University Press.

Martin, A. 1954. 'Nostalgia', *American Journal of Psychoanalysis* 14: 93–104.

Massey, A. 2000. *Hollywood Beyond the Screen: Design and Material Culture*. Oxford: Berg.

McCann, W. 1943. 'Nostalgia: A Descriptive and Comparative Study', *Journal of Genetic Psychology* 62: 97–104.

McCarthy, T. 2006. 'The Good German', *Variety* 405(3): 55–56.

McClure, J.W. 1963. *Advertising Today Yesterday Tomorrow: An Omnibus of Advertising Prepared by Printer's Ink in its 75th Year of Publication*. New York: McGraw Hill.

McDermott, S. 2002. 'Memory, Nostalgia, and Gender in *A Thousand Acres*', *Signs* 28(1): 389–407.

Miller, M.L. 1956. *Nostalgia: A Psychoanalytic Study of Marcel Proust*. Boston: Houghton Mifflin.

Moran, J. 2002. 'Childhood and Nostalgia in Contemporary Culture', *European Journal of Cultural Studies* 5(2): 155–73.

Mosely, R. (ed). 2005. *Fashioning Film Stars: Dress, Culture, Identity*. London: British Film Institute Publishing.

Moseley, R. 2002. *Growing Up with Audrey Hepburn: Text, Audience, Resonance*. Manchester: Manchester University Press.

Mulvey, L. 1996. *Fetishism and Curiosity*. Bloomington: University of Indiana Press.

Nevins, A. 1936. 'War—and the Death of a World', *Wall Street Journal*, 30 July, SM1.

O'Hare McCormick, A. 1947. 'Abroad. 'Nostalgia for a Time That is Past', *The New York Times*, 7 May, C26.

Pickering, J. and S. Kehde (eds). 1997. *Narratives of Nostalgia, Gender and Nationalism*. New York: New York University Press.

Pidduck. J. 2004. *Contemporary Costume Film: Space, Place and the Past*. London: British Film Institute Publishing.

Pope, V. 1940. 'New Styles Give Nostalgic Motif. Spirit of Yesterday and the Sophistication of Today Are Combined in Gown Show', *The New York Times*, 4 October, 27.

Powrie, P. 2007. 'French Neo-noir to Hyper-noir', in A. Spicer (ed.), *European Film Noir*. Manchester: Manchester University Press, pp. 55–83.

Purdy, A. 2002. 'Unearthing the Past: The Archaeology of Bog Bodies in Glob, Atwood, Hébert and Drabble', *Textual Practice* 16(3): 443–58.

Radstone, S. 1993. 'Remembering Medea: The Uses of Nostalgia', *Critical Inquiry* 35(3): 54–63.

Robertson, R. 1990. 'After Nostalgia? Wilful Nostalgia and the Phases of Globalization', in B.S. Turner (ed.), *Theories of Modernity and Postmodernity*. London: Sage, pp. 45–61.

Roth, M. 1991. 'The Time of Nostalgia: Medicine, History, and Normality in 19th Century France', *History and Memory* 3(1): 5–29.

Ruml, B. 1946. 'Some Notes on Nostalgia', *Saturday Review of Literature* 22 June: 7–9.

Samuel, R. 1994. *Theatres of Memory*. London: Verso.

Sandler, K.S. 2001. 'The Naked Truth: *Showgirls* and the Fate of the X/NC-17 Rating', *Cinema Journal* 40(3): 69–94.

Schrag, C.O. 1992. *The Resources of Rationality: A Response to the Postmodern Challenge*. Bloomington: Indiana University Press.

Schumach, M. 1948. 'Nickel Nostalgia', *The New York Times*, 30 May, SM36.

Sennwald, A. 1935. 'The Screen. At the Globe', *The New York Times*, 7 August, 22.

Shaw, C. and M. Chase. 1989. 'The Dimensions of Nostalgia', in C. Shaw and M. Chase (eds), *The Imagined Past: History and Nostalgia*. Manchester: Manchester University Press, pp. 1–17.

Shumway, D.R. 1999. 'Rock 'n' Roll Sound Tracks and the Production of Nostalgia', *Cinema Journal* 38(2): 36–51.
Sloane, L. 1970. 'Nostalgia for Extinct Pop Culture Creates Industry', *The New York Times*, 22 March, 171.
Sobchack, V. 1996. 'Introduction: History Happens', in V. Sobchack (ed.), *The Persistence of History: Cinema, Television and the Modern Event*. London: Routledge, pp. 1–14.
Spigel, L. 1995. 'From the Dark Ages to the Golden Age: Women's Memories and Television Reruns', *Screen* 36(1): 16–33.
Sprengler, C. 2001. 'Imag(in)ing the Past: Roles for the '50s in '90s Film', *Film & History* (2000 Annual CD-ROM): n.pag.
Stark, S.D. 1997. *Glued to the Set: The 60s Television Shows and the Events That Made Us Who We Are Today*. New York: Free Press.
Starobinski, J. 1966. 'The Idea of Nostalgia', *Diogenes* 34: 81–103.
Stewart, K. 1992. 'Nostalgia: A Polemic', in G. Marcus (ed.), *Rereading Cultural Anthropology*. Durham: Duke University Press, pp. 252–66.
Stewart, S. 1993. *On Longing: Narratives of the Miniature, the Gigantic, the Souvenir, the Collection*. Durham: Duke University Press.
St. John, J. 1971. 'The Nostalgia Backlash', *The New York Times*, 7 April, 43.
Street, S. 2001. *Costume and Cinema: Dress Codes in Popular Film*. London: Wallflower.
Tannock, S. 1995. 'Nostalgia Critique', *Cultural Studies* 9(3): 453–64.
Tashiro, C.S. 1998. *Pretty Pictures: Production Design and the History Film*. Austin: University of Texas Press.
Taylor, E. 1989. *Prime-Time Families: Television Culture in Postwar America*. Los Angeles: University of California Press.
Tester, K. 1993. *The Life and Times of Postmodernity*. London: Routledge.
Travers, P. 2006. 'Good German', *Rolling Stone*, 14 December, 134.
Turim, M. 1990. 'Designing Women: The Emergence of the New Sweetheart Line', in J. Gaines and C. Herzog (eds), *Fabrications: Costume and the Female Body*. London: Routledge, pp. 212–27.
Turner, B.S. 1987. 'A Note on Nostalgia', *Theory, Culture and Society* 4(1): 147–56.
Unger, L.S., D.M. McConocha and J.A. Faier. 1991. 'The Use of Nostalgia in Television Advertising: A Content Analysis', *Journalism Quarterly* 68(3): 345–53.

Van Gelder, R. 1933. 'The Night Club in Retrospect', *The New York Times*, 12 November, BR5.
West, J.M. and D. West. 2006. 'MPAA Ratings, Black Holes and My Film: An Interview with Kirby Dick', *Cineaste* 32(1): 14–21.
Wilson, J. 1999. 'Nostalgic Narratives: An Exploration of Black Nostalgia for the 1950s', *Narrative Inquiry* 9(2): 303–25.
_____ 2005. *Nostalgia: Sanctuary of Meaning*. Lewisburg: Bucknell University Press.
Wilson, P.W. 1933. 'Victorian Days That Beckon Us. A Picture of That Bygone Age of Frills and Furbelows Toward Which, With Strange Nostalgia, We Turn Our Eyes from the Contemplation of Our Own', *The New York Times*, 30 April, SM10.
Wollen, T. 1991. 'Over Our Shoulders: Nostalgic Screen Fictions for the 1980s', in J. Corner and S. Harvey (eds), *Enterprise and Heritage: Crosscurrents of National Culture*. London: Routledge, pp. 178–93.
Wood, L. 1935. 'High Court Uneasy in its New Home. Nostalgia Grips Veterans as They Strive to Settle in Their Superb Quarters', *The New York Times*, 13 October, E11.
Wood, M. 1974. 'Nostalgia or Never: You Can't Go Home Again', *New Society* 7 Nov.: 343–46.
Žižek, S. 1991. *Looking Awry: An Introduction to Jacques Lacan through Popular Culture*. Cambridge, MA: The MIT Press.
Zwingmann, C.A.A. 1959. '"Heimweh" or "Nostalgic Reaction": A Conceptual Analysis and Interpretation of a Medico-Psychological Phenomenon', Ph.D. dissertation. California: Stanford University.

Index

1890s. *See* Nineties (nostalgic construct)
1950s (historical period), 39–41, 47–49, 64n1. *See also* Fifties (nostalgic construct); Populuxe Fifties
1960s (historical period), 28–31, 45–46, 102
1970s (historical period), 30–31, 39–40
   economic conditions and, 47–48
   nostalgia for the Fifties/1950s, 6, 43, 46–49, 90n2, 102–3

abstract art. *See* modern art; painting, abstract
accessories. *See* clothing and accessories
access to history and the past, 59, 64, 135, 141. *See also* history; past, the
   in *The Aviator*, 142, 152–53
   in *Far From Heaven*, 118, 121–22, 135, 139
   in *The Good German*, 171–72
   nostalgia films and, 172–73
actors and actresses
   Bacall, Lauren, 91n4
   Blanchett, Cate, 81, 164–66
   Bogart, Humphrey, 69–70, 91n4
   Clooney, George, 81–82, 164–69, 173n3
   DiCaprio, Leonardo, 150–53
   Gugino, Carla, 80
   Hepburn, Audrey, 70–71
   Hepburn, Katharine, 148, 156
   Maguire, Tobey, 81, 165–68
   Moore, Julianne, 80, 117
   Murphy, Brittany, 107
   Reagan, Ronald, 62
Adams, Mildred, 27
Adventures of Ozzie and Harriet, The, 50, 52, 58–59
advertising, 51, 54, 56–58. *See also* marketing; television advertising
   cars, 56–57, 112, 119

nostalgia and, 40, 66n19
allegory in film, 169–71
American Dream, the, 40, 48–49
   consumerism and, 60
   impossibility of, 102
American Graffiti, 99–102, 114n8
animals, nostalgia and, 20
Ant Farm (artist collective), 93–94
archaism. *See* deliberate archaism
Arnold, Thomas, 13
art and art criticism, 23. *See also* Ant Farm (artist collective); Miró, Joan; modern art; painting, abstract
Art Deco, 69–70
artefacts, 49, 58–59, 66n17
aural effects, 24, 76. *See also* montages; music; visual attributes and effects (strategies)
autobiographical referencing, 161n8
automobile industry
   advertising and marketing, 56–57, 112, 119. *See also* cars
   planned obsolescence and, 57, 94
   television and, 54–57
Aviator, The, 7–8, 139, 142–60
   access to history and the past, 142, 152–53
   deliberate archaism, 140, 144, 148, 159
   use of colour, 142–58. *See also* technicolor aesthetic

Bacall, Lauren, 91n4
Barthes, Roland, 5
benefits/value of nostalgia, 32–33, 36nn21–23, 165, 172. *See also* recuperation of nostalgia
Berlin (city), 163, 165–68, 170
biopics, 144
Blanchett, Cate, 81, 164–66
Blast from the Past, 79
B-noir films. *See* film noir
Bogart, Humphrey, 69–70, 91n4
Boissier de Sauvages, Françoise, 13

Boym, Svetlana, 13, 15, 60, 68
Bruzzi, Stella, 123, 126
Buckley, Tom, 31
Burgoyne, Robert, 152

Cadillac Ranch installation, 93–94
Cadillacs
　1959 model, 111–13
　tail fins and, 93–94
capitalism, 48–49. *See also* consumerism
　television and, 49
　vision of, 113
cars
　advertising, 56–57, 112, 119
　Cadillacs, 93–94, 111–13
　colour(s) and, 102, 110–12, 115n17
　cultural significance, 99–102, 109–10, 113, 115n17
　as embodiment of femininity or masculinity, 57, 110
　as props, 102–4, 109–11
　transformative power, 100, 102–3
　women and, 109–10, 119–20
Casablanca, 166
Casey, Edward, 11
casting, film, 80–83. *See also* period casting (film)
Chase, Malcolm, 17
childhood and childhood home, 16, 29, 48, 74–75
Christine, 102–4, 114n9
cinema. *See* films and *see under* individual film titles
cinema (theatres), 71–72, 91n7
Civil Rights Movement, 46, 102. *See also* racism
Civil War, 18, 35n5, 85
Clooney, George, 81–82, 164–69, 173n3
clothing and accessories, 70–71, 124, 126–30. *See also* costumes; fashion in film
　New Look design, 123, 125–29, 137n3, 137n8
　Sweetheart Line, 128–29
Cocoanut Grove (nightclub), 148
Cold War, 47, 49–50, 94, 169–70
colourization of film, 106, 144–50, 160n4, 173n5. *See also* technicolor aesthetic
　Handschiegl process, 161n7
　Technicolor, 140, 144–49, 154, 156–57

colour(s)
　cars and, 102, 110–12, 115n17
　cultural significance, 94, 112, 132–34, 137n5, 138n9
　use/role of, 121, 124, 142, 156–57, 160
comic books and comics, 105–8, 112
commodity culture, 41–43, 49, 64
conservatism, 45–46, 136–37. *See also* reactionary politics; regression/regressive aspects
　British, 89
　nostalgia and, 22, 29, 32, 62–63, 84
　nostalgia films and, 150, 171–72
conspicuous consumption, 49–50, 52, 60–62, 93–95. *See also* capitalism; consumerism
consumerism, 49–50, 66n18. *See also* capitalism; conspicuous consumption
　celebration of, 54–57
　costumes and, 128–30
　nostalgia and, 34, 58, 60–62, 66n19
　patriotism and, 52, 95
　role of desire, 64, 112
　symbolic meanings and, 64
Cook, Pam, 121
costumes, 7–8. *See also* clothing and accessories; fashion in film; props, film; surface realism
　consumerism and, 128–30
　cultural significance, 126–29
　in *Far From Heaven*, 8, 122–33, 137n3, 137n8
　Fifties (nostalgic construct) and, 128
　social aspects, 122–26
counterculture, British, 99–102
creativity. *See* freedom of expression
crime and corruption, 79, 110, 138n11, 174n11
　corporate, 60
　postwar Berlin, 167–68, 170
　postwar urban United States, 113
Crowther, Bosley, 24

Davis, Fred, 21, 35n6, 35n7
DeFalco, Amelia, 121
deliberate archaism, 89, 121. *See also* strategies, aesthetic; visual pastness
　in *The Aviator*, 140, 144, 148, 159
　in *The Good German*, 165–66, 171–72
Del Mar racetrack, 91n4
depiction of women's lives, 65n12
　television commercials and, 56–57

designers and design, 97–98. *See also* obsolescence, planned; production designers
  Art Deco, 69–70
  Dior, Christian, 128
  New Look design, 123, 125–29, 137n3, 137n8
  Sweetheart Line, 128–29
desire, manufacturing, 64. *See also* conspicuous consumption; consumerism
DiCaprio, Leonardo, 150–53
digital film technology, 146, 152–53, 158
digital video discs (DVDs), 5
Dika, Vera, 7, 68, 88–89
Dior, Christian, 128
directors, film. *See* film directors
distribution of films, 171, 174n11
domestic comedies, 50–51
Donna Reed Show, The, 50, 65n16
dresses. *See* costumes
DVDs (digital video discs), 5
Dyer, Richard, 122, 136, 140–42

economic conditions, 60–61. *See also* capitalism; conspicuous consumption; consumerism; prosperity
  1950s (historical period), 47–49
  1970s (historical period), 47–48
Eisenhower, Dwight D., 47, 52
epistemophilia, 5, 9n4
experience. *See also* object and experience; time and space
  commodification of, 61
  of history, 64, 118
  nostalgia and, 59. *See also* object and experience: nostalgia and
  spectatorship, 141–42, 159, 161n8

families, 16, 45, 50. *See also* childhood and childhood home; domestic comedies
fans and fan clubs, 5, 70, 72
Far From Heaven, 7–8, 117–37, 138n10, 166
  colour(s) and, 123–24, 132–35
  nostalgia and, 135–37
  props and costumes and, 119, 122–33
  Sirkian cinema and, 117–18, 135–36

fashion in film. *See also* clothing and accessories; costumes
  colour and, 123–24, 132–33, 156–57
  history and, 125
  restorative nostalgia and, 70–71
Father Knows Best, 50, 65n16
feminism and femininity. *See also* Women's Movement
  car as embodiment of, 57, 110
  clothing and accessories and, 124, 126–30
  constructs of, 70–71, 86, 119–20, 137n5
  nostalgia and, 32, 36n18
femme fatale stereotypes, 107–8
Fifties (nostalgic construct), 6, 34, 39–64, 64n1, 65n4, 79–80, 88–90. *See also* 1950s (historical period)
  celebration of, 43
  critique of/resistance to, 136–37
  films and, 90n2, 100–104
  lounge lifestyle, 41–42
  mass-media and, 62
  music, 44–45, 100
  mythological aspects, 62
  nostalgia of 1970s for, 6, 43, 46–49, 90n2, 102–3
  Populuxe. *See* Populuxe Fifties
  props as signifiers and, 97
  television and, 45, 49
film casting. *See* casting, film
film colourization, 106, 144–50, 160n4, 173n5. *See also under* colourization of film
film criticism, 7, 68, 83–89
film directors
  Haynes, Todd, 117–18, 166
  Lucas, George, 100
  Miller, Frank, 105–6
  Rodriguez, Robert, 105–7
  Scorsese, Martin, 142, 145–49, 158–59
  Sirk, Douglas, 117–18, 136
  Soderbergh, Steven, 165–67, 170–71
film distribution. *See* distribution of films
film history. *See* history of film
film industry, 91n4
  nostalgia and, 25
  regulation of, 49, 171, 174n10. *See also* freedom of expression; Production Code (film industry)

film noir, 42, 105–8, 114n11, 114n14, 159
  1940s, 80, 165–66
  neo-noir, 159
films. *See also* film industry; film titles; Hollywood; nostalgia films; *under* individual film titles
  allegorical aspects, 169–71
  attending, 72. *See also* cinema (physical structures)
  classification of, 171, 174n10. *See also* Production Code (film industry)
  history and, 168. *See also* access to history and the past; history of film nostalgia and, 71–72, 91n8. *See also* nostalgia
  political aspects, 165–69, 173n3. *See also* political aspects of nostalgia
  preservation of, 149
  Web sites, 72, 173n1
films, nostalgia. *See* nostalgia films
film titles
  American Graffiti, 99–102, 114n8
  The Aviator, 7–8, 139, 142–60
  Blast from the Past, 79
  Casablanca, 166
  Christine, 102–4, 114n9
  Far From Heaven, 7–8, 117–37, 138n10, 166
  Forrest Gump, 150, 152
  Going All the Way, 78
  The Good German, 163–73
  Hearts in Atlantis, 74–75
  Hell's Angels, 154
  L.A. Confidential, 79–80
  The Reflecting Skin, 104–5
  Sin City, 7, 95, 105–13
  The Strawberry Blonde, 24–26
  The Women, 156–57
fixation, nostalgia and, 16, 35n4
flashbacks, 74–76, 86. *See also* intertextuality
flea markets, 58–59
Flinn, Carol, 77
Forrest Gump, 150, 152
Forty, Adrian, 97
freedom of expression, 118, 136–37, 170–71, 174n11. *See also* film industry: regulation of
Freud, Sigmund, 16, 35n3
Fuller, Graham, 165

Gay Rights Movement, 46, 102

gender, 107–8, 112, 118–19, 131–32, 166
geopolitics, 165–69. *See also* political aspects of nostalgia
Gibbs, John, 96
Gill, Pat, 75
Going All the Way, 78
Good German, The, 163–73
  allegorical aspects, 169–71
  deliberate archaism, 165–66, 171–72
  visual attributes and effects (strategies), 165
Grainge, Paul, 7, 64, 88, 90
Gugino, Carla, 80

Handschiegl colour process, 161n7
Haynes, Todd, 117–18, 166
Hays, Will, 24
Hearts in Atlantis, 74–75
Hebdige, Dick, 97–99
Hell's Angels, 145, 154
Hepburn, Audrey, 70–71
Hepburn, Katharine, 148, 156
Hewison, Robert, 89
Higson, Andrew, 89
Hine, Thomas, 42
historical consciousness, 4
history
  access to, 118, 131, 135, 168. *See also* access to history and the past
  experience of, 64, 118
  mediation of, 153
  nostalgia and, 87–90, 95, 114n2, 121–22
history of film, 8, 117–18, 135–36, 142, 165–66
Hoberman, J., 165
Hofer, Johannes, 11–13, 18–19
Hollywood, 73, 78. *See also* film industry; films
  design and, 128
  nostalgia and, 84, 117–19, 165–66
  studios. *See* film industry
home decorating, 69–70
homesickness. *See* nostalgia
Huffer, Lynne, 13
Hughes, Howard, 142, 144–45, 150, 152, 159–60
Hutcheon, Linda, 2, 68, 87
interior decorating and design. *See* home decorating
intertextuality, 121–22, 170–71. *See also* flashbacks

Iraq War, 2003-, 163, 167–68, 170
irony, 87

Jameson, Fredric, 7, 68, 83, 87–88
Joyner, Steve, 108
Joyrich, Lynne, 121

Kalmus, Natalie, 146, 157
Kramer, Hilton, 45–46
Krämer, Peter, 49
Kuhn, Annette, 72

L.A. Confidential, 79–80
Landsberg, Alison, 152, 159
Leave It to Beaver, 50, 65n16
Legato, Robert, 146, 149
Leibman, Nina, 50–51
Le Sueur, Marc, 7, 83–86
literature and literary criticism, 22, 28, 31–32, 86–87
Livingston, E. Arthur, 31
longing. *See* nostalgia
loss, feelings of. *See* nostalgia
Lounge Fifties, 41–42
Lucas, George, 100

Maguire, Tobey, 81, 165–68
Marcus, Daniel, 62
marketing. *See also* advertising
  automobile industry and, 56–57, 112, 119
  nostalgia and, 36n21, 70
  Populuxe, 60
  strategies, 94
Marling, Karal Ann, 57–58, 128
masculinity, 70, 91n4, 102, 110
mass media, 30, 33–34, 36n16, 41, 62
materialism. *See* consumerism
McCarthy, Todd, 165
meaning, inscribing, 97–99, 102, 113, 119. *See also* popular culture
medical aspects of nostalgia, 3, 13–14, 18–19, 21
memorabilia, 29
memory/memories, 72, 159. *See also* flashbacks; past, the
  commodification of, 61
  history and, 121, 152
  individual and collective, 152
  traces, 74
militarism, 170. *See also* wars
military implications of nostalgia, 13, 19–21, 34n2
Miller, Frank, 105–6

Miró, Joan, 133–35
Misery Index, 47
mnemotopes, 74
modern art, 132–35. *See also* painting, abstract
montages
  aural, 76
  opening sequences, 78–80, 165
Moore, Julianne, 80, 117
Moseley, Rachael, 70–71
motion picture industry. *See* film industry
movie industry. *See* film industry
movie palaces. *See* cinema (theatres)
movies. *See* films
Mulvey, Laura, 9n4
Murphy, Brittany, 107
music, 166, 173n8. *See also* aural effects
  Fifties (nostalgic construct) and, 44–45
  nostalgia and, 23–24, 35n8, 76–78, 100

narrative structures and narratives, 16, 50–51, 72–74, 88–90
neo-noir films. *See* film noir
Nevins, Allan, 21–22
New Look design, 123, 125–29, 137n3, 137n8
New Republic, The, 167
Nineties (nostalgic construct), 25–26
nostalgia, 1–8, 11–12, 28–31, 161n8. *See also under* compound entries for nostalgia
  advertising and. *See* advertising
  art criticism and, 23
  artefacts and, 49, 58–59
  aural effects and, 24, 76
  autobiographical referencing and, 161n8
  benefits/value of, 32–33, 36nn21–23, 165, 172. *See also* recuperation of nostalgia
  conservatism and, 22, 62, 71
  consumerism and, 34, 58, 60–62, 66n19
  critique of, 31
  experience. *See* object and experience
  family and childhood and, 16. *See also* childhood and childhood home
  feminism and femininity and, 32, 36n18

fixation and, 35n4
history and, 2–3, 15, 84, 87–90, 95, 114n2, 121–22
literary criticism and literature and, 22, 28, 31–32, 86–87
marketing and. *See* marketing
media and, 30, 33–34, 36n16, 41
medical aspects of, 3, 13–14, 18–19, 21
military implications and, 13, 19–21, 34n2. See also *Good German, The*
music and, 23, 35n8, 76–78, 100
objects. *See* object and experience; objects; props, film
patriotism and, 14, 20
political aspects, 5, 14–15, 22, 30, 59, 62
popular culture and, 2–4, 6, 28–30, 64, 69–72. *See also under* popular culture
progressives and, 62
psychoanalysis and, 16–17
psychology and, 30–31
reactionary aspects, 32, 36n18
recuperation of. *See* recuperation of nostalgia
regression and. *See* regression/regressive aspects
scholarship and, 17, 31, 36n17, 68
social and sociological aspects, 15, 17, 36n17
television and, 28, 43. *See also* television programmes
theatre and, 23
time and space and, 16, 21–23, 76
visual attributes and effects (strategies), 24–27, 33–34, 43, 49, 89–90, 134–35
nostalgia, history of, 3, 6, 39–64
Europe (1688–c.1900), 11–17
United States (1900–50), 17–28, 35n10
United States (post–1950), 28–34
United States (pre–1900), 18, 35n5
nostalgia, melancholic, 84–85
nostalgia, reflective, 68, 71–72
nostalgia, restorative, 68–71, 84, 91n4
clothing and accessories and, 70–71
fashion in film and, 70–71
home decorating and, 69–70
nostalgia films, 3, 6–7, 67–68, 83–90, 121, 158–60

access to history and the past, 172–73
aesthetic strategies, 140–42, 144–48, 172
The Aviator, 139–60
conservative/reactionary aspects and, 150, 172. *See also* conservatism; reactionary politics; regression/regressive aspects
cultural significance, 173
Far From Heaven, 117–37
The Good German, 163–73
history and, 87–88
Sin City, 93–113
value of, 165, 172–73. *See also* benefits/value of nostalgia; recuperation of nostalgia
nostalgia mode, 88, 106, 172
The Good German, 165
support for allegory, 171
nostalgia poems, 35n12

object and experience, 36n19, 62–63, 84
conflating, 6, 32–34, 62
nostalgia and, 2, 91n7, 172
separating, 6, 36n19, 63
objects. *See also* object and experience; props, film
accumulating meaning/cultural significance, 95–113, 119
canonical, 48, 58–60
design of, 97–98
obsolescence, planned, 49, 52, 56–57, 94–95
Oedipal narrative. *See* narrative structures and narratives
Ozzie and Harriet. See *Adventures of Ozzie and Harriet, The*

painting, abstract, 45–46. *See also* modern art
parody, 87
past, the. *See also* access to history and the past; history; memory/memories
access to, 59, 64, 135, 141
falsification of, 32
invention of, 31
revisiting, 74–76
pastiche, 87, 121–22, 140–42, 170
patriotism
consumerism and, 52, 95
nostalgia and, 14, 20

period casting (film), 80–83, 165
period details and verisimilitude. *See* strategies, aesthetic
political aspects of nostalgia, 5, 14–15, 22, 30, 59, 62. *See also* films: political aspects; geopolitics
politics. *See* political aspects of nostalgia
popular culture, 2–4, 6, 28–30, 48, 64, 69–72
  cars and, 99–102, 109–11, 113, 115n17
  costumes and, 126–29
  objects and props and, 94–113, 119
Populuxe, 111, 169. *See also* Populuxe Fifties
  consumerism and, 43
  marketing of, 60
Populuxe Fifties, 42–43. *See also* Populuxe
  anxiety and, 42, 112
  artefacts, 49
  nostalgia for, 60–62
  props and, 94–96
  visual imagery, 78
Production Code (film industry), 118, 136–37, 166, 171. *See also* film industry: regulation of
production designers, 96, 114n5
props, film, 64, 114n4. *See also* colour(s); costumes; objects
  canonical, 58–60
  cars, 102–4, 109–11
  cultural significance, 95–113, 119
  Far From Heaven and, 119
  Fifties (nostalgic construct) and, 97
  Populuxe Fifties and, 94–96
  scholarship, 7, 95–99
  Sin City and, 105–13
  surface realism and, 89, 163
  tail fins (on cars), 93–97
  the Vespa, 98–99
prosperity, 47–50, 94–95. *See also* conspicuous consumption; consumerism; economic conditions
  postwar, 102, 112–13
  price of, 167–69
psychoanalysis, 16–17
psychology, 30–31
pulp novels, 105–7, 112
Purdy, Anthony, 74
Puritan ethic, 52, 54

racism, 118–19, 131–32, 138n11, 166. *See also* Civil Rights Movement
reactionary politics, 2. *See also* conservatism; regression/regressive aspects
  critique of, 172
  nostalgia and, 32, 36n18
Reagan, Ronald, 62
recuperation of nostalgia, 2–3, 7, 33, 36n22, 68, 86. *See also* benefits/value of nostalgia; nostalgia films: value of
Reflecting Skin, The, 104–5
regression/regressive aspects, 16, 35n4, 40, 43, 63, 71. *See also* conservatism; reactionary politics
reminiscences. *See* flashbacks; memory/memories; nostalgia, reflective; past, the
retro performativity, 71
Rodriguez, Robert, 105–7
Roe vs. Wade, 46

Scheuchzer, J.J., 13
scholarship
  nostalgia, 12, 17, 31, 36n17, 68
  prop, 7, 95–99
Scorsese, Martin, 142, 145–49, 158–59
sexuality, 107, 112, 118–19
  in *Far From Heaven*, 124–25, 131–32, 135–37
  in *The Good German*, 166, 170
  in *Sin City*, 107–8
Shaw, Christopher, 17
Shumway, David, 76
Sin City, 7, 95, 105–13
  femme fatale stereotypes and, 107
  Fifties (nostalgic construct) and, 112
  nostalgia films and, 105–6
  props, 107–13
  role of cars, 108–9, 112–13
  sexuality and, 107–8
  visual attributes and effects, 106–7
Sirk, Douglas, 117–18, 136
sitcoms. *See* domestic comedies
Sobchack, Vivian, 150
social aspects of consumption, 61. *See also* conspicuous consumption; consumerism
social institutions, 46
sociology and social aspects of nostalgia, 15, 17, 36n17

Soderbergh, Steven, 165–67, 170–71
soldiers, nostalgia and. *See* military implications of nostalgia
sound effects. *See* aural effects
space and time. *See* time and space
space programme, 94
spectatorship, 5, 141–42, 159, 161n8
Stewart, Susan, 61
St. John, Jeffrey, 29–30
strategies, aesthetic, 7, 83–86, 90. *See also* visual pastness
  in *The Aviator*, 139–42, 144–48
  cinematographic, 158
  deliberate archaism, 89, 121, 140, 165–66
  in *Far From Heaven*, 118, 135
  in *The Good German*, 171
  irony, 87
  limits of, 172
  parody, 87
  pastiche, 87, 121–22, 140–42, 170
  period details and verisimilitude, 85, 144
  surface realism, 85, 89, 118, 163, 172
Strathairn, David, 80–81
Strawberry Blonde, The, 24–26, 35n9
Street, Sarah, 126
surface realism, 85, 89, 118, 163, 172
Sweetheart Line, 128–29

tail fins (on cars), 93–94, 119
  as embodiment of masculinity, 102
  nostalgia and, 99–102
  as prop with cultural significance, 95–97
  as signifier of the fifties, 102–5
  use to critique nostalgia, 104–5
Tashiro, Charles, 96
Taylor, Ella, 50
Technicolor
  three-strip, 140, 144–47, 154, 156–57
  two-strip, 144–49
technicolor aesthetic, 8, 137n2, 139–42, 144–47, 160
television, 41, 49–56. *See also* television programmes
  automobile industry and, 54–55
  consumer capitalism and, 49
  domestic comedies and, 50, 56–57, 65n11

  influence of sponsors, 51–52
  nostalgia and, 28, 43
  portrayal of the fifties, 45, 49
  programming, 51–52, 65n16
  regulation of, 49
  representational narratives, 50–51
  television advertising, 51–52, 58, 65n13
  television commercials. *See* television advertising; television: domestic comedies and
television programmes
  The Adventures of Ozzie and Harriet, 50, 52, 58–59
  The Donna Reed Show, 50, 65n16
  Father Knows Best, 50, 65n16
  Leave It to Beaver, 50, 65n16
theatre, evocation of nostalgia, 23
Thomasville (furniture manufacturer), 69–70
thrillers, 114n11
time and space, 15–16, 21–23, 34, 76
Turim, Maureen, 128–29
TV dinners, 57–58

Vespa, the, 98–101
Victorian Era, 27
Vietnam War, 47, 65n9, 76–77
visual attributes and effects (strategies), 89–90, 134–35, 165
  analyses, 4
  elements of, 96
  nostalgia and, 24–27, 33–34, 43, 49
visual pastness, 2–4, 7, 27, 122, 126. *See also* deliberate archaism
voice-overs, 75–76, 168, 170

wars, 170. *See also* Cold War; Iraq War, 2003–; Vietnam War
  filmic portrayal, 76–77, 163–73
  social relations and, 174n9
Web sites. *See under* films: Web sites
Wilson, P. W., 27
Women, The, 156–57.
Women's Movement, 46, 102. *See also* feminism and femininity

yearning. *See* nostalgia

Žižek, Slavoj, 142, 158–59

www.ingramcontent.com/pod-product-compliance
Ingram Content Group UK Ltd.
Pitfield, Milton Keynes, MK11 3LW, UK
UKHW021833140426
5217IPUK00021B/1429